# KASHMIR CRISIS

UGC RESEARCH PROJECT

**Research Team**

1. **Prof. Ali Mohammad**
   Principal Investigator

2. **Dr. S.W.A. Ashraf**
   Co-Principal Investigator

3. **Dr. Abdul Bari Naik**
   Research Associate

4. Research Assistance
   1. **Abdulla Khan**
   2. **Bushra Iqrar**

---

**About the Authors**

**Prof. Ali Mohammad** at present is working as an 'Eminent Professor' under UGC scheme in the Department of Geography, Aligarh Muslim University Aligarh. He is author of many books on Kashmir as well as 15 other volumes on India. He is the member of various academic bodies both at national and international level.

**Dr. S.W.A. Ashraf** is working as an Associate Professor in the Department of Geography, Aligarh Muslim University. He has published many books on rural health and diseases and large number of research articles in national and international journals.

# KASHMIR CRISIS

## Resource Mobilization and Prospects of Peace

ALI MOHAMMAD

S.W.A. ASHRAF

**CONCEPT PUBLISHING COMPANY PVT. LTD.**

**NEW DELHI-110059**

Research Project sponsored by U.G.C., New Delhi.



**ISBN-13 : 978-93-5125-052-4**

First Published 2014

*Published and Printed by*

Concept Since 1974

**Concept Publishing Company Pvt. Ltd.**
A/15-16, Commercial Block, Mohan Garden
New Delhi-110059 (India)
*T*: 25351460, 25351794, *F*: 091-11-25357109
E: publishing@conceptpub.com, W: www.conceptpub.com
**Editorial Office:** H-13, Bali Nagar, New Delhi-110 015, India.

Cataloging in Publication Data—*Courtesy:* D.K. Agencies (P) Ltd. <docinfo@dkagencies.com>

**Mohammad, Ali, 1946-**
Kashmir crisis : resource mobilization and prospects of peace / Ali Mohammad, S.W.A. Ashraf.
p. cm.
Includes bibliographical references (p. ) and index.
ISBN 9789351250524

1. Economic development—India—Kashmir, Vale of. 2. Peace-building—Economic aspects—India—Kashmir, Vale of. 3. Manpower policy—India—Kashmir, Vale of. 4. Social planning—India—Kashmir, Vale of. 5. Kashmir, Vale of (India).—Politics and government. I. Ashraf, S. Waseem A., 1952-, joint author. II. Title.

DDC 338.9546 23

# Preface

The book is an outcome of a major research project from UGC. The basic objective of the present work is to analyse the resource mobilization of J & K State and generate the employment opportunities as well to develop the economic sectors for peace and prosperity. All the sectors of economy and all the sections of the society have been discussed at great length. The problems and prospects of peace through the development of economic sectors have been the major focus of this work.

The most important sectors identified are agricultural and horticultural which still occupies about 60 per cent of the total working force. The scope of economic development is enormous by developing the horticultural sector through agro-based industries. There are many high valued crops if managed properly can contribute in economic development. The water is another source not well developed. The characteristics of scarcity in plenty is the level of water use in all the sectors such as hydro electricity, irrigation, urban and industrial water and potable water. The scope of development is enormous to absorb the unemployed people. The sector of tourism was the backbone of the economy in Kashmir but after 1979 it is not developing rather converted into the major unemployment sector where enormous opportunities of employment exist. The forest lands are highly economic and it is characterized most economic because of its classified species available along with large number of medicinal plants. The employment opportunities have been traced more as compared to other Himalayan States of India. Other sectors of economy have also been analysed for the mobilization of resources and employment.

The author wishes to express thanks to the University Grants Commission of India for major financial assistance for extensive fieldwork in this mountainous region. I am also thankful to people of Kashmir for a peaceful environment to conduct the fieldwork. The author is thankful to the highly educated persons working in colleges and universities because most of them were either my colleagues and students at P.G. level and Ph.D. under my guidance. Prof. Mohiuddin Mir and Dr. Abdul Raufshah working in the centre of Central Asian studies in Kashmir University. The author is also grateful to Dr. Abdul Bari Naik (Research Associate under this scheme) worked very honestly without him to complete the work was not possible.

Finally, I am greatly indebted to Prof. V. Manhas, Prof. of Geography in Jammu University for the survey of the refugee camps located in Jammu. Also grateful to Dr. R.P. Sharma. Department of Geography, Jammu University. I am also thankful to all my colleagues of the Department of Geography, Aligarh Muslim University, Aligarh.

The entire responsibility for the views and opinion as also for any error of analysis and omission in the book which may appear is, of course, solely that of the Principal Investigator (Prof. Ali Mohammad).

**Ali Mohammad**
**Department of Geography**
AMU, Aligarh

# Contents

# List of Tables

# List of Figures

# List of Figures

# 1
# Introduction

## Study Area

Kashmir is the name of a Himalayan valley situated about 5,000 feet above sea level. 80 miles in length from North West to South East and 40 miles in width, carved by river Jehlum, the *Vatista* of the *Rigveda*, pronounced as "*Vyath* in Kashmiri," is the largest valley of its kind in the world. The *Vyath* rises from Verinag springs on the foot of the Panchal range that surrounds this valley; flows north through the capital city of Srinagar and Wular lake and then enters the mountains through a gorge resembling the mouth of a boar called "Varaha" in Sanskrit near the town named "*Varaha Molla*" now called Baramula on the northern tip of the valley. The valleys of the Liddar, the Sindh and a number of smaller streams that flow into the Jehlum add to the size and beauty of this celebrated valley. According to tradition recorded in a number of Sanskrit texts and chronicles of Kashmir this valley was once a vast lake. It was converted into an alluvial plain when Kashyap, a great "Rishi," made an opening into the surrounding mountains near Baramula. As a result the water of the lake was drained out and the submerged land became a habitable valley. It then came to be known as "*Kashyap Marga*" the abode of Kashyap from which the name Kashmir is derived. Geomorphological evidence has confirmed that the valley was originally a vast lake.

Kashmir crisis is a political issue. The Kashmir crisis originated after the British withdrew from the Indian subcontinent in 1947. When India and Pakistan were partitioned, the ruler of the princely state of Kashmir was given the right to decide on whether to merge with either Pakistan or India or remain independent with certain reservations. After a few months of dilemma, Maharaja Hari Singh, the Hindu ruler of a predominantly

Muslim state, decided to sign an Instrument of Accession to the Indian Union in October 1947. This enraged the Pakistani leaders. They attacked Jammu & Kashmir as they felt that all areas of India with Muslim majority should be under their control. Pakistani troops overran most of the state and the Maharaja took refuge in India. India, wanting to confirm the act of accession and defend its territory, sent troops to Kashmir. But by then Pakistan had captured a considerable chunk of the region. This gave rise to a localized warfare that continued through 1948, with Pakistan retaining control of a large area of the state, but India keeping a larger part. The Indian Prime Minister Jawaharlal Nehru soon declared a unilateral ceasefire and called for a plebiscite. India filed a complaint with the UN Security Council, which established the United Nations Commission for India and Pakistan (UNCIP). Pakistan was accused of invading the region, and was asked to withdraw its forces from Jammu & Kashmir. The UNCIP also passed a resolution stating: "The question of accession of the state of Jammu & Kashmir to India or Pakistan will be decided through the democratic method of free and impartial plebiscite." However, this could not take place because Pakistan did not comply with the UN resolution and refused to withdraw from the state. The international community failed to play a decisive role in the matter saying that Jammu & Kashmir is a "disputed territory". In 1949, with the intervention of the United Nations, India and Pakistan defined a ceasefire line ("Line of Control") that divided in the two countries. This left Kashmir a divided and disturbed territory. In September 1951, elections were held in the Indian Jammu & Kashmir, and National Conference under the leadership of Sheikh Abdullah came to power, with the inauguration of the Constituent Assembly of the State of Jammu & Kashmir. The ceasefire reaffirmed the notion that a referendum should ultimately determine the status of Kashmir and approved the existing ceasefire line until such referendum should occur. Five years passed without a referendum, and in 1954 the Constituent Assembly of Jammu and Kashmir ratified the accession to India. The legal authority of the Constituent Assembly and the ratification of the accession remained questionable, in August 1965, the conflict resumed in Kashmir. The second Indo-Pak war was fought in three weeks and again ended in UN-facilitated ceasefire. In signing the Tashkent Agreement, in 1965, both parties agreed to return to the *status quo* ceasefire line negotiated previously, and pledged to refrain from the use of force to resolve the dispute. The resolution of the 1971 war, which was not directly related to the Kashmir question, produced an accord that nevertheless addressed the issue.

The Shimla Accord emphasized the need for peaceful means of dispute resolution, and it stressed the use of bilateral dialogue and working groups for all future conflicts between the two states. Furthermore, the two countries agreed that the current Kashmir ceasefire line, which was renamed the 'Line of Control', would be respected by both sides "without prejudice to the recognized positions of either side." In 1974 the Kashmir state government reached an accord with the Indian Government, which affirmed its status as "a constituent Unit of the Union of India". Pakistan rejected the accord. After a decade of relative quiet, the militant movement in the Kashmir Valley began in 1987 as many questioned the validity of the recent assembly elections. With the end of the war with the Soviets in Afghanistan in 1989 many of the *Mujahideen* came to Pakistan, bringing Islamist extremism to what had begun as a secular/nationalist militant movement. India detonated its first nuclear device in 1974 in Rajasthan, near the Pakistani border, thus establishing India as a nuclear power and adding a new, dangerous dimension to Indo-Pak relations. Pakistan also began testing its first surface to surface missiles, and by 1992 Pakistan claimed to have nuclear capabilities. Since then, India-Pakistan relations have included the possibility of nuclear escalation. In 1998, India detonated five more nuclear devices in Rajasthan. Pakistan responded by itself detonating six devices in Baluchistan. Pakistan also test launched its first medium-range ballistic missile (900-mile range). Pakistan has made clear that it will employ a necessary first-use approach to the use of nuclear weapons. The United Nations expressed concern with the parties' strategies on nuclear warfare, and the G-8 threatened numerous economic sanctions. The year of 1997 marked fifty years of independence for the two Countries. It also marked fifty years of conflict over Kashmir's status. With that in mind, India and Pakistan redoubled diplomatic efforts in search of a solution to the dispute over Kashmir. Though the talks began with a positive outlook, they quickly halted, with the parties agreeing to continue the dialogue at a later time. Dialogue between India and Pakistan resumed in 1999. Indian Prime Minister Atal Bihari Vajpayee and Pakistani Prime Minister Nawaz Sharif signed the Lahore Accord in February 1999. The Accord again reaffirmed the parties' desires to settle the dispute over Jammu and Kashmir. However, the Accord held only until May of the same year. An Indian patrol spotted intruders across the Line of Control. The Indian military began air raids in the region, and in response Pakistan began shelling the Kargil region. International pressure brought an end to the struggle but not before displacing some 30,000 people on both sides of the Line of Control. Shortly after Kargil, a coup led by General Pervez Musharraf toppled the Sharif government. Although, the Pakistani Supreme Court granted legitimacy to Musharraf's rule for three years, the international community expressed their disapproval of Musharraf's ascension until 2001. The year 2001 proved tumultuous in the world and in India-Pakistan relations. In May, India ended a ceasefire against Kashmiri militants, while also asking for dialogue. Musharraf and Vajpayee met at Agra in July for a three-day summit, but failed to produce any agreement on Kashmir. The events of September 11, 2001 improved the bargaining power of Pakistan as it became a key ally of the United States in the subsequent War on Terror.

In October and December 2000, tensions increased as twin bombings of the Kashmiri Assembly and the Indian Parliament killed fifty people. Troops were amassed by both sides along the Line of Control, leading to minor skirmishes. In January 2002, Musharraf called for talks between the countries. Dialogue was not, however, forthcoming. Rather, 2002 was marked by tensions on both sides of the Line of Control. Nuclear tensions continued between New Delhi and Islamabad and then increased in the early months of the year, which was reinforced by an active exchange of accusations in the media. The October election in Indian-held Kashmir further strained relations. It is argued that over 500 deaths resulted from clashes between Kashmiri protestors to the elections and Indian security forces. A heightened level of tension between India and Pakistan continued through the early months of 2003.

The year began with each nation expelling the other's diplomats. In Srinagar on April 18, 2003, however, Prime Minister Vajpayee made his own overture to Musharraf. By May, India agreed to reestablish diplomatic ties with Islamabad, and by October, some bus and rail ties were resumed between the two countries. India also made an important concession, by agreeing to open a line of dialogue with the All Parties Hurriyat Conference. Talks with Kashmiri groups have previously been denied outright. On November 26 a ceasefire offered by Pakistan to India went into effect in Kashmiri territory. The year 2004 began with renewed dialogue between Musharraf and Vajpayee at a summit meeting of South Asian nations. Recent strikes at Musharraf by militant groups may be the catalyst for an aggressive approach by Pakistanis to curb the activities of militants, generating momentum to the long-delayed status talks with India.

The optimism has in part been fuelled by the fact that the January 5 Islamabad declaration identified the willingness of the parties to negotiate a peaceful settlement of all bilateral issues. As the brief historical overview indicates, the Kashmir negotiations will involve discussions of final status, demilitarization and decommissioning, and humanitarian issues.

The parties will unlikely be able to discuss final status without simultaneous talks regarding demilitarization. For example, the UN Security Council resolution supported a plebiscite but only after a total troop withdrawal.

Negotiations of humanitarian issues are necessary because all sides of the dispute cite humanitarian concerns as a basis for their positions on final status and decommissioning and demilitarization. Thus, it is likely that negotiations of all three issues will be ongoing throughout the negotiation simulation.

## Political Divisions of Jammu & Kashmir

In the year 1947 the State of Jammu and Kashmir was invaded by Pakistan. India and Pakistan fought for more than a year when cease fire was agreed upon on lst of January, 1949 and the fighting stopped. A ceasefire line of demarcation gave 79788 sq. kms. of area of the state of Jammu and Kashmir to Pakistan.

The district of Poonch lost 52 per cent of its area to Pakistan. The district of Muzaffarabad lost some area in tehsil Muzaffarabad, Uri and Karnah. The whole of Gilgit district, Asotre district and Mirpore district also went to Pakistan. The whole of Askardu tehsil and a part of tehsil Kargil went to Pakistan. Invasion of China in 1962 also made the State to suffer a loss of its area. In 1971 Pakistan once again made unlawful possession of Chhamb, Deva, Chakla and Manawar. The State of Jammu Kashmir, therefore, suffered serious splitting in area and population. Only four districts—Udhampur, Jammu, Kathua and Anantnag—suffered no change; other districts suffered loss in area, either wholly or partially to Pakistan. Re-organization was necessary; therefore, new districts like Pulwama, Doda, Rajouri and Poonch were created.

The state of Jammu and Kashmir is divided into fourteen districts. The districts are the administrative units of the state and have been further subdivided into blocks and tehsils that facilitate the government in the administration of the district. The state has 119 blocks and 59 tehsils. The districts of Jammu and Kashmir comprise 54 towns, 3 municipalities, 281 uninhabited villages and the 6477 inhabited villages.

***Anantnag*:** Covering an area of 3934 square kilometres, the district of Anantnag is situated 55 kilometres to the south east of the district of

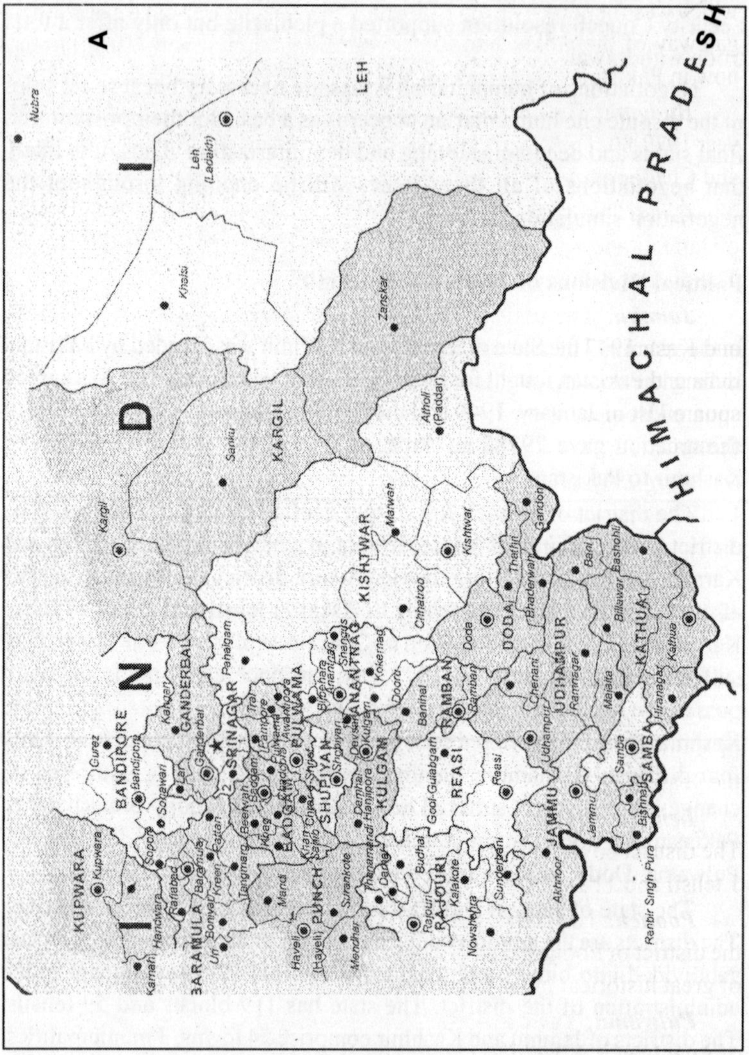
I N D I A
HIMACHAL PRADESH
KUPWARA
BARAMULA
BANDIPORE
GANDERBAL
SRINAGAR
PULWAMA
SHUPIYAN
KULGAM
ANANTNAG
KISHTWAR
DODA
RAMBAN
REASI
UDHAMPUR
KATHUA
SAMBA
JAMMU
RAJOURI
PUNCH
KARGIL
LEH

Srinagar. With a vast area of fertile land, the district is also known as the "Granary of the Kashmir Valley".

***Baramulla***: The headquarters of the district is the city of Baramulla, which was founded by Raja Bhimsina. The district was once a prominent gateway of the valley into the cities of Rawalpindi and Muzaffarabad now in Pakistan.

***Budgam:*** The district was formed from the district of Srinagar in the year 1979-80. The district is divided into three tehsils of Budgam, Beerwah and Chadoora.

***Doda:*** The district of Doda is one of the largest districts of the State of Jammu and Kashmir covering an area of 11,691 square kilometres. The district is divided into seven tehsils.

***Jammu:*** The district is the winter capital of the State of Jammu and Kashmir. The administrative offices shift from Srinagar to Jammu during the months of November to April. Covering an area of 3097 square kilometres, the district is one of the most populated districts of the state.

***Kargil:*** The rocky district of Kargil was created out of the district of Ladakh in the year 1979. The district is situated in the heart of the Kashmir Valley at a distance of 205 kilometres from Srinagar.

***Kathua:*** The district of Kathua is situated in the south-eastern end of the State of Jammu and Kashmir. The total area of 2651 square kilometres is divided into the four tehsils of Kathua, Billawar, Basholi and Hiranagar.

***Kupwara***: At a distance of 90 kilometres from Srinagar lies the district of Kupwara. The district was created out of the district of Baramulla in the year 1979.

***Leh***: The district of Leh and Kargil are a part of the region of Ladakh. The district covers an area of 44,000 square kilometres. The district has 1 tehsil and 112 villages

***Poonch:*** The smallest district of the State of Jammu and Kashmir is the district of Poonch. The district comprises three tehsils. This district is of great historical importance to the state.

***Pulwama:*** The district of Pulwama was created out of the district of Anantnag. Of the total geographical area of 1398 square kilometres, 1011 square kilometres are occupied by the forest areas. The district is reputed for the saffron cultivation and the growth of Ambree apples.

***Rajouri:*** The district of Rajouri shares its borders with the Mirpur area of Pakistan occupied Kashmir. The district was earlier a part of the district of Poonch. It covers an area of 2630 square kilometres.

***Srinagar***: The district of Srinagar is centrally located in the valley of Kashmir and is flanked by five districts on all sides. The district is the summer capital of the state and is the commercial hub of Jammu and Kashmir.

***Udhampur:*** The district has its headquarters in the city of Udhampur. It is one of the largest districts of the state. The district is subdivided into 5 tehsils and 12 community blocks.

Some of the other Jammu and Kashmir districts are Samba, Reasi, Kishtwar, Ganderbal, Kulgam, Ramban, Shopian and Bandipore. The State of Jammu and Kashmir is an integral part of the Indian Union. The President of the Indian Union appoints the Governor. The Governor orders the leader of the major political party in the State Legislature, which consists of the Legislative Assembly and the Legislative Council, to form the Ministry to run the Government.

The Government thus formed, by the elected representatives of the people functions with the Opposition in the Legislature. The judiciary is separate from the executive. The judges of the High Court are appointed by the President of the Indian Union. Since 1990, the state is under Presidential rule due to militancy. The Governor runs the administration with the help of Advisers appointed by the Centre. In addition to the State's own Constitution, the Constitution of India applies to the State of Jammu and Kashmir like the rest of the country but with a special status under Article 370. It guarantees equal rights for all irrespective of caste, creed, colour and religion. As already stated above each province is divided into various districts, which are administered by Deputy Commissioners, and each district is divided into Tehsils, which are under Tehsildars and each Tehsil is further sub-divided into Niabats, which are under Naib Tehsildars. There is one Divisional Commissioner who is the provincial head.

## Major Divisions of Jammu & Kashmir

Jammu and Kashmir consists of three divisions: Jammu, Kashmir Valley and Ladakh, and is further divided into 22 districts. The Siachen Glacier, although under Indian military control, does not lie under the administration of the State of Jammu and Kashmir.

Kishtwar, Ramban, Reasi, Samba, Bandipora, Ganderbal, Kulgam and Shopian are newly formed districts.

| *Jammu region* | *Kashmir region* | *Ladakh region* |
|---|---|---|
| Kathua District | Anantnag District | Kargil District |
| Jammu District | Kulgam District | Leh District |
| Samba District | Pulwama District | Kishtwar Distric |
| Udhampur District | Shopian District | Kupwara District |
| Reasi District | Budgam District | |
| Rajouri District | Srinagar District | |
| Poonch District | Ganderbal District | |
| Doda District | Bandipora District | |
| Ramban District | Baramulla District | |

**Structure of the Study**

In addition to this introductory chapter, this study will be completed within six chapters. Chapter one is based on the area to be studied, treated as an introductory. Chapter two will provide the key historical background, facts and the emergence crisis during different periods. Besides this with the subsequent development of a two-nation theory that led to Indian independence and the birth of Pakistan on the basis of religion in 1947. Gradually, this discussion will flow into the post-1947 period. This assessment will help in understanding the basis of Kashmir Crisis and the remedial measures to control on the crisis and how to bring peace prospects in Central Asia in general and particularly in Kashmir Valley—the disputed region of whole Central Asia.

Going back to the Mughal period is important, during that period the Kashmir was connected to Central Asia and remaining other countries by several passes which enhance in the development of trade.

This trade brought socio-economic development of the region on one hand and engaged the people with economic activities on other hand leads to emergence of peace in said period.

This enquiry is important, as the current identity-politics debates in India, as mentioned before, are claiming that different types of injustice done by the State Government or Central Government with the people is the main cause of Kashmir Crisis.

Besides this, chapter two also includes different accords, meetings as well as agreements and the impact of these on the peace prospects of region in general and Kashmir valley in particular.

The thrust of chapter three will be on Human Resource Development and an assessment of amenities, facilities and comparative study assessment with other states of India. This chapter will first discuss the strategic oversight and how various amenities and facilities vary with neighbouring states of India.

Chapter four will examine the Economic Resource Development in relation to economic development and characteristics of population with regard to different economic activities. In this chapter again comparative study has been done with other states of India in relation to population, education level, schooling, colleges and universities, along with the economic activities such as Horticulture, Tourism, etc. in Jammu & Kashmir.

Chapter fifth deals with the strategic aspects of the rise of Kashmir insurgency in 1989 and how the military exercises of India and Pakistan affected it. In order to see the bigger picture, strategic cultures of India and Pakistan will also be discussed. Finally, this chapter will look at the 1989-2009 political situation and their impact on the Kashmir issue. This chapter will also explore whether the region will remain disputed area and what are the measures to control the crisis and bring the peace prospects in general and for bringing the socio-economic development in particular. On the whole, this chapter will examine the evidence and generalizations to provide alternative explanations for the thrust areas: Kashmir crisis, peace prospects and Kashmir dispute conflict. Finally, to find out the major findings and implications of the India-Pakistan conflict over Kashmir and suggest recommendations for long-term peace in the region.

## Statement of the Problem and Research Questions

A nation torn apart and the people lose their life is how we now know Kashmir. So much different from the land that was once famous for its pristine beauty and peace, the valley that lies in the lap of the gigantic Himalayas is now saddled with troubled political relationships, sensitive bilateral ties, memories of the Indo-Pak wars and strained histories.

The basic need for development of the region is decency in life—free of terrorism, chaos and other problems related with, so that our generations will live in peace and prosperity.

With the increase of knowledge in every field such as economic, political and social development, only development is not and social and economic injustices are also recorded through various methods of knowledge the society became aware. If injustices in economic development are realized a decent society can never be seen. There are various regions; Kashmir is not alone in the grip of problem, like Eastern East India and Naxal Zones of eastern part of India. So the present study recorded all these above mentioned records.

The Kashmir conflict is one of the most staggering conflicts in international politics, and its persistence involving two nuclear powers is well known. Even after four wars, a decisive resolution to the conflict appears unlikely — the medley of treaties, agreements, and declarations notwithstanding. Though the parties involved in the conflict have their own perspectives regarding the cause and course of conflict, almost all agree (at least in declarations and statements) that the region is in dire need of peace as well as substantial economic development. Indeed, a several decades of violence is on verge of ending without any positive achievement for the people. Due to the ongoing peace process, however, the atmosphere appears conducive for the launch of sustainable development initiatives in the conflict-ridden state. After all, this is the era of "sunrise" and "peace through economic reconstruction and the State of Jammu and Kashmir has an opportunity it would be well advised to take advantage of. In spite of a decisive war between India and Pakistan in 1971, relations between India and Pakistan did not improve.

The background situation kept on changing with the ever evolving thinking, response and actions of political leadership, both in India and Pakistan— especially the role of political leaders. The Kashmir dispute has existed since 1947, but local peace in Kashmir was never a matter of concern until 1989.

This leads us to a question of whether Kashmir is the cause of the India Pakistan conflict or if it is a symptom of this conflict. Researchers like Robert G. Wirsing (2008) are convinced—as mentioned before— that Kashmir is not the reason for the India-Pakistan conflict. As such, there is a need to understand this phenomenon with different views taking into consideration.

Not to mention, some researchers have also examined the Kashmir dispute from a realist and revisionist perspective. Discussing from a realist point of view, Frey (2007) is unable to pinpoint if Indian nuclear tests were actually a reaction to the growing power of China.

Frey also mentions the Indian nuclear tests were a strategic loss in relation to Pakistan, as India would never be able to win a nuclear war with Pakistan. Meanwhile, Mitra looks at India-Pakistan relations to all intents and purposes as a Hindu-Muslim conflict emphasizing democratization when he constructs his case against the standard "structural realist" perception of India. The costs of the conflict have been increasingly unbearable for all involved. According to the official estimates, some 40,000 lives have been lost since the onset of insurgency in 1989, though other estimates put the toll much higher. Large-scale displacement from different parts of the state is an integral part of the Kashmir conflict (Shekhawat, 2006, ch. 3). An estimated one million people have been displaced in the state due to militancy as well as security forces inhuman acts. Even mass rural migration took place due to innocent killing by security persons.

Besides this whole village were burnt as well as the killing of innocent people like in Chattisinghpora in March 2000. Other humanitarian costs include negative impact on women and other vulnerable groups and a noticeable increase in the psychiatric problems of the victims (Medicins Sans Frontiers, 2006). For instance, the number of patients visiting hospitals in Srinagar for psychiatric diseases in 2003-2006 amounted to a staggering 45,000. The conflict has also cost the Indian government heavily in terms of the deployment of security forces as well as other financial responsibilities. The economic cost of the conflict cannot be confined to a particular sector of industry or investment prospects. It has affected the important sources of livelihood of local people such as tourism, horticulture and handicrafts industries. Besides exacting extensive damage to the infrastructure of the region, the violent conflict has discouraged private investment, pushing the economy towards stagnation.

The downward trend of economy has been acutely felt since late 1980s when militancy gained momentum. It is a vicious circle in which violence has led to underdevelopment and *vice versa*, and in this gruesome scenario it is the common people of the region who suffer the most.

There is also an urgent need to renew the indigenous industries as well as explore the new areas. The prospects of intra-Kashmir trade, which can bring economic prosperity to the region by trade in commodities produced on both sides, has remained unexplored so far.

## Purpose and Significance of the Study

The goal of this study is to find out the Prospects of Peace which directly related with the socio-economic development of the Valley, firstly and brought the peace prospects for the nation as a whole. Secondly, is there any relation with the development of militancy and crisis in Kashmir Valley in relation to economic injustices? The region is having high potential of resources and also the content of natural resources are very high but the region is not developed or developing at par with another neighbouring states of India. Kashmir Valley is having an important position in Central Asia, so there is urgent need for development of peace in the region. Besides this within the larger territories of India and Pakistan it is having an important position. The peace efforts in the last 60 years have not been able to extract India and Pakistan out of the Kashmir dispute. But the origin of dispute is having a long history. However, there is a need to examine the period before 1947 to understand the conflict in a proper manner. Therefore, in order to study "How far can the Kashmir conflict 1989-2009 be attributed to 'fundamentalist' religious empowerment?", this study will go beyond the period mentioned before for a strategic investigation, otherwise this study will be reduced to a mere symptomatic Mujahideen/Militant study focusing on the tactics of Militants and the operational response of the authorities. Therefore, this strategic investigation will be done with a view to find the cause of the problem, the growth of fundamentalism and understanding the strategic implications of this conflict in the longer run.

**Literature Survey**

The topic is related with the Kashmir crisis which takes its peak after 1989, so there is paucity of literature but the work done so far which is related with Kashmir problems and crisis will be discussed as under follows:

"*Ethnic Conflict and Secessionism in South and Southeast Asia: Causes, Dynamics and Solutions*" by Rajat Ganguly and Ian Macduff (eds.) 2003 pointed out the main problems of Kashmir. The book is divided into three broad parts, addressing these three interrelated issues and questions connected with ethnic conflicts in South and Southeast Asia.

Presenting a remarkable historical account of the Kashmir problem, Vernon Hewitt argues that, "a large part of the crisis is not because of the inflexibility between India and Pakistan over their claims to the former Princely State, but due to the overwhelming difficulty of defining a stable Kashmiri identity, either within India or Pakistan or within any future independent sovereign state." Besides placing the focus on Kashmiri identity formation in the historical context the author also discusses the legal and procedural aspects of the dispute. But he fails to provide the possible pathways towards a resolution of the crisis. Murtaza Shibli, "*Kashmir: Islam, Identity and Insurgency*" in which he gives more emphasis on the Hizbul Mujahideen Groups. The impact of 9/11 on the

**Fig. 1.2:** Jammu and Kashmir Area

terrorist organization and their behaviour. He also pointed out the Kashmir Conflict is an 'Ethno-religious conflict' with the political struggle and insurgency being informed both by religion and politics.

Indeed, many Kashmiris, both political leaders as well as insurgents have cited a history of humiliation at the hands of India, felt both personally and collectively as a Kashmiri nation, as a reason for choosing the path of violence. This is evident from the arguments of Masood Tantray who was Deputy Chief Commander of HM and the author of several books. While discussing the rationale of armed insurgency, Tantray, in his book *Gawahir-e-Masood* (2006) often characterizes the relationship between India and Kashmir as that of "a slave and master"; explaining Indian behaviour towards Kashmiris along those lines (Tantray, 2006: 3).

Instantiating this long-term sensibility of Kashmiris being forced out of their homes, being subjected to unpaid and forced labour, or various examples of Hindus getting away with only the penalty of a small fine imposed on them even when guilty of the crime of killing a Muslim. In another part of the book, while discussing the Humiliating arrest of the then Kashmiri Prime Minister, Sheikh Abdullah, by the Indian Army on 9th August, 1953, he suggests it created a "Darkness of Mistrust". Azam Inqillabi, one of the oldest Kashmiri resistance fighters and political leader, while discussing "political cataclysm and militant upheaval and insurgency in Kashmir" talks about India leaving "no stone unturned in humiliating and enslaving Kashmiris" (Inqillabi, 2004:44). In another of his article, he talks about the Indians "humiliating and brutalizing the votaries of political resistance movement in the jails and interrogation centres". This humiliation is also evident from the prison diaries of Syed Ali Geelani, the Islamist ideologue and separatist leader when he says, "I grew up under the shadow of Indian serfdom and I will never forget that moment when I was going to... school when an Indian Army Soldier slapped my face without any reason" (Geelani, 1994:199). Talking about an incident in July 1980 during which the Indian Army Soldiers beat up Kashmiris and destroyed properties, he observes that the Indian Army was not "even willing to offer the people a position of animals that are even herded with love. This situation woke up the people here from slumber and they started thinking about the future. I was so influenced by this event that I openly declared that people here are not safe from the occupying Army and therefore, they should get licence and have arms."

Kashmiri's well-known writer/journalist and pro-freedom leader, Mohammad Farooq Rehmani in his commentary in Urdu on Kashmiri resistance, *Azadi Ki Tlash* (1993) seeks to explain the Kashmiri's discontent with Indian rule and their various models of resistance that eventually erupted into insurgency.

A number of works written from the Indian perspective blame either Pakistan or Islamic terrorism for the insurgence. Praveen Swami's new book not only exaggerates Pakistan's role in fomenting insurgency in Kashmir but also overstates the influence of *Jihadi* Islam on the moment in citing the overuse of Islamic symbols by Kashmiris to use Islamic symbolism in their struggle.

Two books about Kashmiri history, focusing primarily on the pre 1947 period, examine the shaping of Kashmiri identity, its relation to religion and its role in popular socio-political discourse and political struggle. Mridu Rai suggests that the intertwining of political and religious mobilization of Muslims was primary in response to the religious nature of the Dogra princely state being resisted, which presided over a Hinduization of political authority, bureaucracy and public space. Chitralekha Zutshi also uncovers the many ways and contexts in which Kashmiri Muslims expressed their regional and religious identity. She further argues that the incorporation of Kashmir into India in 1947 did not mean any improvement so far as the Muslims were concerned.

## Objectives of the Study

Kashmir Valley is an isolated, backward and mountain grit having a distinct geographical entity. Insurgency and political instability prevail here. There are not only problems but there is also beauty in Kashmir. There is unlimited potential for the development of all human as well as natural resources. The development of human and natural resources leads to control on instability and political disturbances and also helps in socio-economic development and brings peace and prosperity in the region.

The present study has certain specific research objectives. They are as follows:

1. Now the issue is not the merger of Kashmir with India, neither to merge with Pakistan or alignment towards China or to achieve independence.
2. The basic issue now is to develop Kashmir socio-economically and development at par with other states of India.
3. The impact of past atrocities on the present crisis in Kashmir Valley.
4. The peace in Kashmir will help the internal and external relation of India with other neighbouring countries.

## Methodology

The underlying idea of the methodology is that of achieving the prospects of peace and minimizing the Kashmir Crisis. This directly implies that regional inter- and intra-disparities should be removed for the maintenance of peace in the region. The main focus of the methodology is to achieve the prospects of peace through socio-economic development and disparity in socio-economic conditions as well as political justice which can be achieved through integrated planning approach. This approach involves a thorough survey of the area through a detailed questionnaire and analysis of different periods as well as comparative study with other states of India. Every chapter in the study have different types of methodologies for the analysis of the problem. The first chapter introduction is based on the significance of the problem. Second chapter discusses with historical background of the study before independence as well as after independence and the period between 1989 and 2009.

Besides this various accords meeting and issues regarding the Kashmir Crisis were discussed and to investigate these problems differently from the work done previously by other authors. Third and fourth chapters are based on the socio-economic comparability of the region with other states of India. The final chapter is based on the questionnaire and the results were first tabulated. The final data is analysed through various techniques, graphs and diagrams for achieving the authentic and reliable results and in bringing the peace prospects of the region on one hand and the social harmony with the country as a whole.

## Spatial Organization of Kashmir and Aspects of Peace

It is evident that accessibility with Kashmir across the region is not posing the entry and exit problem from the Kashmir. Strategically, Kashmir should be treated as a centre of these regions. Advantages and disadvantages are many. Therefore, nation should be careful about the interest of the surrounding regions and nations. If cooperation does not exist a development anti to any nation can surface in a negative manner and peace will be disturbed. Border security, human security, life and economic security will always be in danger if the nations across the region are not taken into account. Kashmir Valley has been a half-closed ecosystem, opening up slowly in space and across time. The Vitasta has been and continues to be the key element of the ecosystem. Kashmir is, indeed, the gift of the Jhelum. It is born of it, made up of the detritus brought down by its numerous tributaries and is united with it through every fibre of its being. The sons of the soil have come to terms with the natural elements of the system, through millennia of settled life, by sticking to the Valley floor and developing slopes, permitting terrace culture linked with indigenous irrigation, and the favourable temperature regimes.

The geographical location of Kashmir is such that it is surrounded by a number of foreign countries. This makes the Kashmir valley very important from strategic angle. As far as the geography of Kashmir is concerned, the valley has River Jhelum flowing through it, along with its tributaries. Geographical location plays an important role and having statistical location.

The space relations of the Valley have historically evolved through the interactive mechanism discussed above. An understanding of these relations is of crucial significance in any meaningful geographical interpretation of the land.

The Valley is located in a region where East, Central, West and South Asia meet and has been consequently in contacts of varying degrees with four major geopolitical elements:

(i) The Indo-Gangetic plain with the geostrategic node at Delhi;
(ii) The land of the Pathans and the Afghans and through it with the extensive realm of the West Asia;
(iii) Central Asia, all along the arc stretching from Balkh and Badakhshan in the west through Dushanbe, Samarkhand and Bokhara to Kashghar, Yarkand and Khotan in the east; and
(iv) Tibet, and through it with China.

Having had a cursory look at the space relations of the Kashmir Valley at the macro level with the geo-political realms of Asia, it may be worthwhile to focus attention on the links with the micro units lying on and along the mountain ramparts across the bounding crest. They may be analyzed in four sections:

### *Across the Pir Panjal Range*

To the south of the Valley, across the Pir Panjal Range, lies that complex web of small worlds of Valleys and side Valleys which, over the centuries, have sustained *thakuriats* and principalities, living by and large, as closed systems, interacting with each other rarely—through wars, feuds and matrimonial alliances—some expanding at the cost of others, some contracting and becoming assimilated and all living under the shadows of the power based in the Indo-Gangetic plain. This multi-tiered system of suzerainties underwent kaleidoscopic changes over time and crystallized into the twenty-two principalities led by the clans.

The role of some of the main passes through which the Valley of Kashmir was linked with the regions across the Pir Panjal range is discussed below:

(a) The construction of the Jawahar Tunnel has for the first time in history provided a safe all-weather link between the Valley and the rest of the world. It is in this direction that the inter-regional bonds are being strengthened and the process of the opening up of the semi-closed system of the Valley is taking place most effectively.

(b) The Budil pass lies on the route which is along an almost straight line connecting Srinagar with Akhnur. It is suitable for pedestrian traffic only but has been quite popular, owing to the short duration of the trip in spite of the difficulties of terrain.

(c) Beyond the snow peak, from where the main ranges turns northwest, lie the passes of Rupri and Darhal, both above 3,900 metres (13,000 feet) and provide the most direct access to Rajouri. Near the Darhal pass lies Nandansar. The route leading to it through the Darhal pass has been used by pilgrims on a considerable scale since ancient times.

(d) The lowest dip in the central part of the whole range is situated about eight kilometres to the north of Nandansar. It is marked by Pir Panjal Pass and in historical context has been most important link with the Valley across the mountain ramparts.

The route which crosses the Pir Panjal pass proper is the most important of these variants and is also known as the Imperial Road or the Mughal Road, connecting Poshiana in the south to Aliabad Serai in the north. Akbar passed through this road thrice.

### *Across the Gorge of the Jhelum*

The gorge of the Jhelum from Baramullah to Muzaffarabad was the tradition zone between the Khasa home lands lying to the west and the projection of Kashmir influence in the east. The dividing line was the

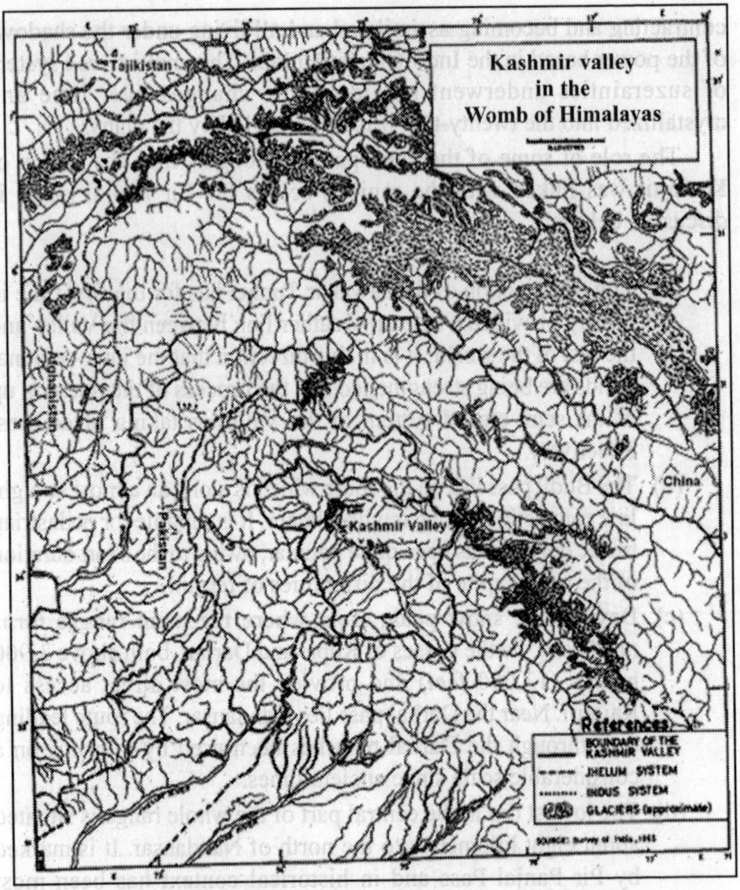


**Fig 1.3:** Spatial Relation of Kashmir

town of Bolyasaka. The portion of the Valley between Muzaffarabad and Bolyasaka bore the old name of Dvaravati.

To the west of the gorge lay the territory of Urasa which occupied the Sindh-Sagar Doab in the present district of Hazara. The Jhelum gorge is the single outlet for the waters of the Valley and has been traditionally one of the most important gateways into it. Nevertheless, this valley was used on a considerable scale during ancient and medieval times. It was well-known to Al Beruni. Apart from the main route which followed the Jhelum from Baramullah to Muzaffarabad, the gorge acted as a feeder for the Haji Pir route which connected the Valley with Poonch. This side route deviates from the main route at Uri and leads across the Haji Pir pass to Poonch.

### *Across the Northern Mountains*

The space relation along the northern mountains can be meaningfully studied under three sub-sections.

(a) At the northwestern corner of this sector lie the ancient territories of Karnah and Drava. Karnah comprised the hill district which lies immediately to the west of Kamraj, that is, the portion of the Kishen Ganga valley above Muzaffarabad and several side valleys drained by the Karnah River and its tributaries. This section was on the whole unimportant in the space relationship of the Kashmir Valley because across the watershed, to the west, lay areas which were both politically and economically unimportant. The Kashmir areas of Samala (Hamal), Uttra (Utter) and Lolaha (Lolab) were, no doubt, in contact with Karnah and Drava across the watershed, so much so that during early Mughal times both were treated as constituent parts of Kamraj. But owing to the low level of development on both sides of the watershed, no important routes were developed.

(b) As has been noted earlier, the course of the Kishen Ganga lies for a long distance above Sardi through an almost inaccessible and uninhabited gorge. Hence, for almost fifty kilometres eastwards, we find no proper route across the mountain. Beyond this gorge lies an important line of communication which connect the Valley with the Dard lands—the region of Gurez, Gilgit, Hunza, Nagar, Ishkuman and Mastuj—each one of them sprawling along the valley of one or the other of the mountainous tributaries of the Indus. The Bandipur Gurez Road now crosses the range by the Tragbal or Razdiangan pass.

From Dudakutta pass up to Zojila the mountains are formidable and have had in ancient and medieval times restricted communication across them. The only line along which communication was established lay between Tilel on the Kishen Ganga and Lahara or Lar in the Sindh valley through the Satsaran pass.

(c) The lowest point along the watershed between the Indus and the Jhelum basins is situated close to the junction of Harmukh with the Nanga Parbat-Nun Kun range. This pass is known by its Ladakhi name of Zojila. Ancient chronicles distinguish between the little and the great Bhuttaland which may be considered to be the same as *Tibet-e- Buzurg* and *Tibet-e-Khurd* of the medieval chronicles.

(d) There is no mention in ancient and medieval chronicles of the Margan pass, which connects the Valley with Maruwardwan. In the southern sector, however, the marbal or the Singhpur pass has played a considerable part in linking the Kashmir Valley with Kishtwar, which has been historically the refuge of defeated factions in the Valley. It is now proposed to build a metallic road on this route. This project, when completed, would further strengthen the links between the Valley and Kishtwar.

As a result of the exploratory probing into the space relations of Kashmir Valley, one comes up with a spatial mosaic of tremendous complexity of a process of systems within systems, each opening up steadily into the one above in the hierarchical order. Since economic development in the area is still in its early stages, the interregional linkages are still weak and the regional structure still fragile. Rapid rates of growth, both in the Valley and the surrounding regions of the country, combined with an imaginative approach towards pluralism in a democratic set-up within the republic alone can hasten the opening up of the semi-closed system through strengthening interdependence to national as well as regional advantage.

# 2
# Historical Background of Peace Process in Jammu and Kashmir

## Introduction

The 'Kashmir dispute' is the oldest unresolved international conflict in the world today. Pakistan considers Kashmir as its core political dispute with India. So does the international community, except India. The exchange of fire between their forces across the Line of Control, which separates Azad Kashmir from Kashmir, is a routine affair. Now that both India and Pakistan have acquired nuclear weapons potential, the possibility of a third war between them over Kashmir, which may involve the use of nuclear weapons, cannot be ruled out. Kashmir may be a cause to a likely nuclear disaster in South Asia, which should be averted with an intervention by the international community. Such an intervention is urgently required to put an end to Indian atrocities in Kashmir and prepare the ground for the implementation of UN resolutions, which call for the holding of a plebiscite to determine the wishes of the Kashmiri people.

## History of Muslim Rulers in Kashmir Valley (11th to 15th Century)

History of Kashmir began with the settlement of the Indo-Aryan people in it in pre-Mahabharata days. It became a centre of Indo-Vedic culture and civilization. Sanskrit literature is replete with references to it. It is often described as "*Nandanvan*" the pleasure garden of Bharat. Unlike many other parts of India, we have recorded history of Kashmir from the earliest times. The oldest of these records is *Nilamat Purana*. It deals with the legends pertaining to the origin of Kashmir, the ordinances of

Nila, the earliest ruler of Kashmir and gives detailed information about its numerous *Nags* or springs and lakes that dotted the whole valley and its surrounding ranges. Other notable sources of its history are: *Kultanimala Kavya* of Damodar Gupta, *Deshopadesha* of Kshemendra, *Vikrama Devacharita* of Bilhan, *Rajtarangini* of Kalhan and chronicle of *Jonrajya* who wrote in 15th century. Kalhan recorded the history of Kashmir from the Mahabharata period but the real beginning of Kashmir's history can be traced to the rule of Mauryan emperor Ashoka who built Srinagar as its capital.

Kashmir was made a centre of Mahayana Buddhism by Kushan emperor, Kanishka. He built a town "*Kanishkapura*," now called Kanspura. It is situated about five miles from Baramullah on the Baramullah-Srinagar road. He also built many Buddhist Viharas and convened the fourth Buddhist council there. Archaeological remains of the Viharas built by him have been found near Harvana Lake. Hun king Mihirgula, occupied the throne of Kashmir for some time after he was driven out of Punjab in the fourth century A.D. He later embraced Shaivism. The most celebrated king of Kashmir was Lalitaditya who ruled over it in the seventh century A.D. He extended his way beyond the valley. He built the famous Sun temple — the Martanda temple — on a plateau overlooking the town of Anantnag and the holy springs of Mattan in the Liddar valley. The ruins of this great temple which was destroyed by Sultan Sikandar in the 14th century point to the glory that was Kashmir at that time.

Avantivarman was another notable ruler of Kashmir who ruled in the 11th century. He built a new capital, Avantipur, mid-way between Anantnag and Srinagar. His Prime Minister, Sayyah, deepened the *Vitasta* from the Wullar lake to Baramullah which helped in reclamation of more land. A new town *Sayyapur* now called Sopore was built on the reclaimed land.

Shadow of Islam first fell on Kashmir in the 11th century when Sultan Mahmood of Ghazani made an unsuccessful attempt to conquer it. But some Muslim adventurers and preachers of Turkish, Persian and Khorasani origin entered the valley in the wake of his invasion. The last effective Hindu ruler of Kashmir was Sahdev who ascended the throne in 1301 A.D. Two Muslim adventurers, Shahmir from Khorasan and Lanker Chak from Gilgit, came to Kashmir during his reign and entered his service. Another foreign adventurer to enter his service was Rinchan, a Buddhist Bhotia from Laddakh. He married queen Kota Rani, daughter of Ramachandra, the commander-in-chief of Sahdev in 1319. He wanted to embrace Shivism but Brahmins refused to accept him. He, then, turned to Islam and took the name Sadaruddin. Rinchan died in 1323 A.D. Udyan Dev, brother of Sahdev, and then ascended the throne. He married Kota Rani and ruled up-to 1338 A.D. After the death of Udyandev, Kota Rani took over the reigns of government. But she could not rule for long. Shahmir, who had entrenched himself in Udyandev's court, staged a coup and took control of the government.

After capturing power, Shahmir made Kota Rani captive. He wanted to marry her but she spurned his offer. She was then forcibly put into the harem of Shahmir. She committed suicide the next morning. Thus, the throne of Kashmir passed into the hands of a foreign Muslim adventurer whose conduct can be compared with that of Haider Ali who usurped the throne of Mysore fourteen centuries later. This marked the beginning of Muslim rule over Kashmir in 1339 A.D.

Fourth ruler of the dynasty was Sikander who is called *But-shikan,* i.e. iconolast because he destroyed almost all Hindu temples of Kashmir including that of Martand and confronted the people with the choice of conversion to Islam or death. Most of the Kashmiri Hindus were converted or killed. A few Brahmin families took shelter in Jammu region across Panchal range. The present Hindus of Kashmir are progeny of those refugees. According to Kashmiri tradition he burnt seven maunds of sacred threads of the murdered Hindus whose bodies were thrown into Dal Lake to form what is now called *Butt-mazar,* i.e. grave of Brahmins. This is a bund which runs across the Dal Lake from Nasim garden to Nishat garden. Zain-ul-Abdin who succeeded Sikander in 1420 AD brought a welcome change. He not only stopped forced conversions but also allowed those Hindus who had fled away to return to their homeland. He appointed Hindus to high places in his court. Jonraj the famous chronicler who continued the chronicle of Kalhan and brought it to date enjoyed his patronage.

Shahmiri dynasty was replaced by Chak dynasty in 1561 AD. Ghazi-chak the founder of this dynasty was a scion of Lanker Chak, the Muslim adventurer from Gilgit who came to Kashmir in the reign of Sahdev. Chaks were Shia. Therefore, Shia sect of Islam got a foothold in Kashmir during Chak rule. Usuf Shah the last effective Chak ruler of Kashmir was defeated by a Mughal army led by Raja Bhagwan Dass, during the reign of Akbar. Usuf Shah died in Patna as an exile. His son, Yakub Shah, ruled over Kashmir for some time but was defeated and displaced by the Mughals in 1686 AD.

## History of Mughal Rulers in Kashmir Valley (16th to 18th century)

Akbar made Kashmir a separate province of Mughal empire. His son Jahangir had special liking for Kashmir. He described it as "*Heaven on earth*" and embellished it with the famous Mughal gardens. The Mughals used Bhimber, Rajouri-Nandi–Marg route for going to Kashmir from Punjab. This area was inhabited by war-like Suddan and Chib Hindu Rajputs many of whom were forcibly converted to Islam under orders of Jahangir. Aurangzeb let loose a reign of terror on Hindus of Kashmir. Later Mughals patronized Kashmiri Brahmins who took to Persian language with gusto. Many of them came down to Delhi and Agra to work as scribes and tutors in the Mughals' households.

Mohammed Shah, one of the later Mughal rulers of Delhi, decreed that Kashmir's Brahmins should be described as Kashmiri Pundits to distinguish them from local Brahmins. This name has stuck with them since then. Mughal rule in Kashmir ended formally in 1752 when Ahamed Shah Abdali annexed it to his kingdom of Kabul. But, beginning of the end of Mughal rule took place in 1739 when Nadir Shah sacked Delhi and gave a body blow to the decadent Mughal Empire. Afghan rule over Kashmir, which is considered to be the cruelest and the worst, lasted till 1819 when it was conquerred by Diwan Mohakam Chand, a General of Maharaja Ranjit Singh. It then became a *Suba* or Province of Lahore Kingdom. Thus Hindu rule returned to Kashmir after a lapse of about five centuries.

## History of Dogras Rule in Kashmir Valley (1845 to 1949)

Kashmir passed into the hands of Raja Gulab Singh of Jammu, a feudatory of Lahore kingdom in 1846. He entered into a treaty with the East India Company in March 1846 as a result of which the British recognized him as *de jure* master of all the hill territories of Lahore Kingdom lying to the east of the Indus and west of the Ravi. This territory was taken over by the British after the first Anglo-Punjab war of 1845 in lieu of war indemnity of Rs.75 lakh which Lahore Durbar was not in a position to pay. Gulab Singh was already *de facto* master of all this territory excepting Kashmir Valley which was a separate province of Lahore Kingdom. Therefore, the only real acquisition of Gulab Singh as a result of this treaty was Kashmir. That is why it is alleged by his critics that he purchased Kashmir for Rs.75 lakh from the British. But this is not correct. The British at that time were in no position to dislodge Gulab Singh and annex this territory to their expanding empire. Gulab Singh had to wage a war against the Governor of Kashmir who under secret instruction from Lahore Durbar, refused to hand over Kashmir to him. He, therefore, got Kashmir by force of arms. After the defeat of the Sikh army at Subraon in February 1846, peace negotiations were opened. Raja Gulab Singh was given full powers to negotiate on behalf of the Lahore Darbar. The British Government was well aware of the resourcefulness of Gulab Singh who was reported to have advised the Lahore Darbar to avoid pitched battles with the British and instead cross the Sutlej and attack Delhi with the help of some picked cavalry regiments. The British were, therefore, very anxious to secure his friendship. He was offered bait that he would be recognized as an independent ruler of Jammu & Kashmir if he withdrew his support from the Lahore Darbar and made a separate deal with the British. Gulab Singh replied that he could not negotiate with the British about his own possessions while he was acting as an envoy for Dalip Singh, the king of Lahore. He continued the negotiations on behalf of the Lahore Darbar which culminated in the Treaty of Lahore signed on 9 March, 1846.

According to this Treaty of Lahore it was agreed by the Lahore Darbar to cede the territory between the Beas and the Sutlej to the British and Pay 15 lakh pounds (Rs. One crore Nanak Shahi) as war indemnity. Lal Singh, the then Prime Minister of the Lahore kingdom, had no love lost for Gulab Singh. He offered to the British the hill territories of the Lahore Kingdom including Jammu & Kashmir in lieu of the indemnity. His idea was "to deprive Gulab Singh of his territory and give the British the option either of holding Kashmir which would have been impossible at that time because of the long distance and intervening independent State of Punjab or to accept a reduced indemnity." This offer, however, suited Gulab Singh. The original offer of making him an independent ruler of Jammu & Kashmir was revised. But now it was conditioned by his taking the responsibility of paying the indemnity which had been made a charge on this territory by the cleverness of Lal Singh. Gulab Singh agreed to pay the money to the British and they recognized him as an independent sovereign. Accordingly, a stipulation was made in the Treaty of Lahore by which Maharaja Dalip Singh of Lahore agreed to 'recognize the independent sovereignty of Raja Gulab Singh in such territories and districts in the hills as may be made over to the said Raja Gulab Singh by a separate agreement between him and the British Government. Seven days later, on the sixteenth of March, 1846, the Treaty of Amritsar was signed between Maharaja Gulab Singh and the British according to which Gulab Singh was recognized as an independent ruler of all the territories already in his possession together with the valley of Kashmir which until then formed a separate province of the Lahore Kingdom. According to the Treaty of Amritsar, the British transferred for safe independent possession to Maharaja Gulab Singh and his heirs all the hilly and mountainous portions with its dependencies situated to the east of the river Indus and West of the river Ravi including Chamba and excluding Lahaul — being part of the territories ceded to the British Government by the Lahore Kingdom. In consideration for this Maharaja Gulab Singh was to pay to the British Rs. 75 lakh in cash. There was stipulation in this Treaty about the British keeping a Resident or an army in Jammu & Kashmir. The Maharaja, however, recognized the Supremacy of the British Government in token of which he was to present annually to the British Government one horse, 12 hill goats and 3 pairs of Kashmiri Shawls. The amount to be paid was reduced to Rs. 75 lakh from one crore because the British decided to retain in their own hands the territory between the Beas and the Ravi which includes the Kangra district of the Punjab because of the strategic value of Nurpur and Kangra forts. The territories of which Gulab Singh was thus recognized as an almost independent ruler also included the area between the Jhelum and the Indus in which Rawalpindi and Islamabad, the capital of Pakistan, are situated. Since this area was too far removed from Jammu, he approached the British to exchange it for certain plain area near Jammu. Thus the Jhelum instead of the Indus became the western border of this kingdom. Gulab Singh died in 1857 and was replaced by Rambir Singh (1857–1885). Two other Maharajas, Partab Singh (1885–1925) and Hari Singh (1925–1949) ruled in succession.

**History before Independence**

Gulab Singh and his successors ruled Kashmir in a tyrannical and repressive way. The people of Kashmir, nearly 80 per cent of whom, were Muslims, rose against Maharaja Hari Singh's rule. He ruthlessly crushed a mass uprising in 1931. In 1932, Sheikh Abdullah formed Kashmir's first political party—the All Jammu & Kashmir Muslim Conference (renamed as National Conference in 1939). In 1934, the Maharaja gave way and allowed limited democracy in the form of a Legislative Assembly. However, unease with the Maharaja's rule continued. According to the instruments of partition of India, the rulers of princely states were given the choice to freely accede to either India or Pakistan, or to remain independent. They were, however, advised to accede to the contiguous dominion, taking into consideration the geographical and ethnic issues. In Kashmir, however, the Maharaja hesitated.

The principally Muslim population, having seen the early and covert arrival of Indian troops, rebelled and things got out of the Maharaja's hands. The people of Kashmir were demanding to join Pakistan. The Maharaja, fearing tribal warfare, eventually gave way to the Indian pressure and agreed to join India by, as India claims, 'signing' the controversial Instrument of Accession on 26 October, 1947. Kashmir was provisionally accepted into the Indian Union pending a free and impartial plebiscite. This was spelled out in a letter from the Governor General of India, Lord Mountbatten, to the Maharaja on 27 October, 1947. In the letter, accepting the accession, Mountbatten made it clear that the State would only be incorporated into the Indian Union after a reference had been made to the people of Kashmir. Having accepted the principle of a plebiscite, India has since obstructed all attempts at holding a plebiscite.

In 1947, India and Pakistan went to war over Kashmir. During the war, it was India, which first took the Kashmir dispute to the United Nations on 1st January, 1948. The following year, on 1st January, 1949, the UN helped enforce ceasefire between the two countries. The ceasefire line is called the Line of Control. It was an outcome of a mutual consent by India and Pakistan that the UN Security Council (UNSC) and UN Commission for India and Pakistan (UNCIP) passed several resolutions in years following the 1947-48 war. The UNSC Resolution of 21st April, 1948—one of the principal UN resolutions on Kashmir—stated that "both India and Pakistan desire that the question of the accession of Jammu and Kashmir to India or Pakistan should be decided through the democratic method of a free and impartial plebiscite". Subsequent UNSC Resolutions reiterated the same stand. UNCIP Resolutions of 3 August, 1948 and 5 January, 1949 reinforced UNSC resolutions.

***Jinnah and Kashmir***

The Quaid-e-Azam Mohammad Ali Jinnah thanked the National Conference leadership for the right royal reception given to him but at the same time said that it was not a reception for his person, but to the All India Muslim League, the party of ten crore Muslims of India of which he was President. This annoyed the Hindu leader so much that he left the stage in distress. According to Mr. Justice Yusuf Saraf, author of "*Kashmiris Fight for Freedom*" the Quaid-e-Azam and his wife seemed to have had visited Kashmir for the first time before 1929. Though this visit was private in nature, yet as a great Muslim leader he felt concerned at the appalling conditions of the Kashmiris at that time too. The second visit of the Quaid-e-Azam was in 1936 during which he hinted to his first visit, saying that he had visited Kashmir ten years earlier too. In 1936 the Quaid-e-Azam addressed a meeting held in connection with Milad-un-Nabi, the birthday of the Holy Prophet (SAW) at the Mujahid Manzil, Srinagar. The Muslim Conference (at that point of time was led by Chaudhry Ghulam Abbas and Sheikh Abdullah) in welcome address to Jinnah appreciated his role as lover of Hindu-Muslim unity. Mr. Jinnah reciprocated the sentiments and said that the Muslims were in majority in Kashmir but it was their duty to ensure that the minority community, that is the Hindus of Kashmir would get justice and fair play at the hands of the majority community of Kashmir Mr. Jinnah, who was once proclaimed as ambassador of Hindu-Muslim unity, had been disillusioned by that time and in his speech regretted that some of the leaders of the majority community in British India had not been able to give such an assurance to the Muslim minority. That showed that the Quaid-e-Azam was not satisfied with the concept of Hindu-Muslim unity in British India. The Muslim Conference, which represented the Muslims of the State in 1936, was converted into National Conference in 1939 as its leaders had come under the influence of Nehru. Chaudhry Ghulam Abbas, who had joined hand with Sheikh Abdullah in 1939 to found National Conference, realized his mistake within three years. He returned to the Muslim Conference, which had been revived by 14 other leaders from Jammu and Kashmir. Soon many others joined the revived Muslim Conference and once again it became a force to reckon with.

The main and the last visit of the Quaid-e-Azam to the State of Jammu and Kashmir took place in 1944. During this visit he attended a reception by the National Conference headed by Sheikh Abdullah. Sheikh Abdullah had thought that with the help of Dogra administration and the active and crafty Hindus he would suppress the pro-Muslim League elements in the State and assure Mr. Jinnah that the Kashmiris, Hindus as well as Muslims, were believers in One Nation Theory of the Congress. A Hindu nationalist Jialal Kilam presented the address of welcome to the Quaid-e-Azam.

The Quaid-e-Azam thanked the National Conference leadership for the right royal reception given to him but at the same time said that it was not a reception for his person, but to the All India Muslim League, the party of ten crore Muslims of India of which he was President. This annoyed the Hindu leader so much that he left the stage in distress.

***Different Ideas regarding Kashmir Dispute***

This historical background of Kashmir Valley, the real bone of contention between India and Pakistan, is of vital importance for proper understanding of Kashmir problems. It points to certain realities which are vital for arriving at a durable settlement of this problem. Because of its geographical situation, Kashmir valley has a distinct geo-political identity different from the territories surrounding it across the Himalayan ranges, which remain snow bound and impassable for four to six months in a year. That is why it has always been a separate kingdom or a separate province of the various Indian empires of which it becomes a part in course of history. Some of its rulers like Lalitaditya did extend their way to the territories beyond the surrounding mountains for some time. But that did not in any way affect the distinct identity and character of Kashmir Valley as such. The second reality to be noted is that Kashmir has always been a part of the Indian state system. Geography, history and culture have made it an inseparable part of Bharat-Khand and Jambu-Dweep now called Hindustan or India. The third fact to be kept in mind is that even though Kashmir came under Muslim rule and most of its people get converted into Islam it never got completely cut-off from its Indo-Vedic cultural moorings. Islam sat rather lightly on its people who continued to cherish their pre-Islamic culture and way of life till recently. Their links with the rest of Hindustan were never snapped. Its holy shrines like Amarnath cave and Holy springs like Mattan and Khir Bhavani continue to attract pilgrims from all over Hindustan. These links were reinforced during 30 years of Sikh rule and 100 years of Dogra rule. Jammu and Kashmir was one of the 500 and odd princely states of India before the British left it for good in 1947. The cultural affinity of Kashmir with the rest of India is evident from its language, art, literature and architecture. All its mosques still look like Buddhist Gompas and temples. None of them has minaret which is an essential feature of mosque architecture all over the world. The only mosque with a minaret in Arab-Persian style was built by Sheik Abdullah at Hazratbal around 1980. Most of the Muslim saints of Kashmir are still called *"rishis."* Kashmiri language, which is directly derived from Sanskrit, was written in Sharda script, a form of Devnagari script till Persian script was imposed on it by Muslim rulers.

Recent developments which have made Kashmir a storm centre of the world and dragged it into the vertex of international power politics, are directly connected with the developments in and about Jammu and

Kashmir State of which it became a part in 1846. Therefore, the story of the making of Jammu and Kashmir State, its relations with the rest of India and British Government and recent socio-political developments in it are very relevant and important for any study of genesis of the Kashmir problem and its changing contours and dimensions over the years.

### *Standstill Agreement*

On 12 August, 1947 the new Prime Minister of Jammu and Kashmir State, Janak Singh proposed by telegram a Standstill Agreement both with Pakistan and India. Pakistan agreed on 15 August. India procrastinated, arguing that the matter needed to be negotiated by an official from the State sent to Delhi. No such official was dispatched for this purpose—no Standstill Agreement ever concluded. The Indian response was certainly a departure from the procedure, which Mountbatten had earlier indicated and it suggested that Indian policy after Independence was going to set out in hitherto uncharted waters. The Maharaja confronted with growing internal disorder (including a full scale rebellion into the Poonch region of the State), sought Indian military help without, if at all possible, surrendering his own independence. On 25 October, 1947, before the Kashmir crisis had fully developed and before Indian claims based on so-called Maharaja's accession to India (which is alleged to have had been signed on 26 October, 1947) had been voiced, Nehru in a telegram to Attlee, the British Prime Minister, declared that: "I should like to make it clear that (the) question of aiding Kashmir... is not designed in any way to influence the State to accede to India. Our view, which we have repeatedly made public, is that (the) question of accession in any disputed territory must be decided in accordance with the wishes of the people, and we adhere to this view." An instrument of Accession of Jammu and Kashmir to India is alleged to have been signed by Maharaja on 26 October, 1947 and the acceptance of this Instrument was made by Governor General of India on 27 October, 1947. Another pair of documents consist of letter from the Maharaja to Mountbatten dated 26 October, 1947 in which Indian military aid is sought in return for accession to India (on terms stated in an allegedly enclosed Instrument) and the appointment of Sheikh Abdullah to head the interim government of State; and a letter from Mountbatten to the Maharaja dated 27 October, 1947 acknowledging the above and noting that, once the affairs of the State have been settled and law and order is restored "the question of the State's accession should be settled by a reference to the people".

### *Fake Instrument of Accession*

The recent research based on the material in archives and sources as the memoirs of Prime Minister Jawaharlal Nehru of India and Prime Minister of Jammu and Kashmir at that time Mehar Chand Mahajan and the recently published correspondence of Jawaharlal Nehru and V.P. Menon's account (The Integration of Indian States) prove beyond any shadow of doubt that these two documents (a) the Instrument of accession, and (b) the letter of the Maharaja to Mountbatten could not possibly have been signed on 26 October, 1947. By that time Maharaja had fled from the capital and during October 26, 1947 he was travelling by road from Srinagar to Jammu. His Prime Minister, M.C. Mahajan who was negotiating with Government of India and senior Indian official concerned in the State matter V.P. Menon were still in New Delhi where their presence was noted by many observers. There was no communication between New Delhi and the travelling Maharaja. Menon and Mahajan set out by air from New Delhi to Jammu at about 10 a.m. on 27 October and the Maharaja learned from them for the first time the result of his prime minister's negotiations in New Delhi in the early afternoon of that date. The earliest possible time and date for their signature would have been the afternoon of 27 October, 1947.

With regard to exchange of letters between Maharaja and Mountbatten, the former seeking military aid and the latter acknowledging the same and promising plebiscite, Alastair Lamb says "It seems more than probable, both were drafted by Government of India before being taken to Jammu on 27 October, 1947 (by V.P. Menon and Jammu and Kashmir Prime Minister M.C. Mahajan whose movements, incidentally, are correctly reported in the *London Times* of 28 October, 1947) after the arrival of Indian troops at Srinagar field. The case is very strong, therefore, that the document, i.e. Maharaja's letter to Mountbatten was dictated to the Maharaja". Government of India published two documents, namely Maharaja's letter and Mountbatten's reply on 28 October, 1947. But the far more important document—the alleged Instrument of Accession was not published until many years later, if at all. It was not communicated to Pakistan at the outset of overt Indian intervention in the State of Jammu and Kashmir, nor was it presented in facsimile to the United Nations in early 1948 as part of Indian reference to the Security Council. The 1948 White Paper in which Government of India set out its formal case in respect to the State of Jammu and Kashmir does not contain the Instrument of Accession as claimed to have been signed by the Maharaja. Instead, it reproduces an unsigned form of Accession such as, it is implied, the Maharaja might have signed. Alastair Lamb writes: "To date no satisfactory original of this Instrument as signed by the Maharaja has been produced; though a highly suspect version, complete with the false date 26 October, 1947, has been circulated by the Indian side since the 1960s. On the present evidence it is by no means clear that the Maharaja ever did sign an Instrument of Accession. There are, indeed, grounds for suspecting that he did no such thing."

## History after Independence

### *Nehru was Criticized as a Betrayal*

India's first Prime Minister Jawaharlal Nehru made a pledge to resolve the Kashmir dispute in accordance with these resolutions. The sole criteria to settle the issue, he said, would be the "wishes of the Kashmir people". A pledge that Prime Minister Nehru started violating soon after the UN resolutions were passed. The Article 370, which gave 'special status' to 'Jammu and Kashmir', was inserted in the Indian Constitution. The 'Jammu and Kashmir Constituent Assembly' was created on 5 November, 1951. Prime Minister Nehru also signed the Delhi Agreement with the then 'ruler' of the disputed State, Sheikh Abdullah, which incorporated Article 370. In 1957, the disputed State was incorporated into the Indian Union under a new Constitution. This was done in direct contravention of resolutions of the United Nations Security Council (UNSC) and UNCIP (United Nations Commission for India and Pakistan) and the conditions of the controversial Instrument of Accession. The puppet 'State' government of Bakshi Ghulam Mohammed rushed through the constitutional provision and the people of Kashmir were not consulted.

In 1965, India and Pakistan once again went to war over Kashmir. A cease-fire was established in September 1965. Indian Prime Minister Lal Bhadur Shastri and Pakistani President Ayub Khan signed the Tashkent Declaration on 1 January, 1966. They resolved to try to end the dispute by peaceful means. Although Kashmir was not the cause of 1971 war between the two countries, a limited war did occur on the Kashmir front in December 1971. The 1971 war was followed by the signing of the Simla Accord, under which India and Pakistan are obliged to resolve the dispute through bilateral talks. Until the early 1997, India never bothered to discuss Kashmir with Pakistan even bilaterally. The direct foreign-secretaries-level talks between the two countries did resume in the start of the 1990s; but, in 1994, they collapsed. This happened because India was not ready even to accept Kashmir a dispute as such, contrary to what the Tashkent Declaration and the Simla Accord had recommended and what the UNSC and UNCIP in their resolutions had stated.

The Pakistan government of Prime Minister Nawaz Sharif, after coming to power in February 1997, took the initiative of resuming the foreign secretaries-level talks with India. The process resumed in March 1997 in New Delhi. At the second round of these talks in June 1997 in Islamabad, India and Pakistan agreed to constitute a Joint Working Group on Kashmir. But soon after the talks, India backtracked from the agreement, the same way as Prime Minister Nehru had done back in the 1950s by violating his own pledge regarding the implementation of UN resolutions seeking Kashmir settlement according to, as Mr. Nehru himself described, "the wishes of the Kashmiri people." The third round of India-Pakistan foreign secretaries-level talks was held in New Delhi in September 1997, but no progress was achieved as India continued dithering on the question of forming a Joint Working Group on Kashmir. The Government led by Prime Minister Atal Behari Vajpaee is neither ready to accept any international mediation on Kashmir, nor is it prepared to seriously negotiate the issue bilaterally with Pakistan.

### *Autonomy*

Sheikh Abdullah is stated to have had a dream of internal autonomy for Jammu and Kashmir within India. This unrealistic dream could never come true and indeed did not. But in the process of dreaming Sheikh Abdullah put the jugular vein of the entire Kashmiri community under the sword of Hindu India. He walked out of prison to become the so-called Prime Minister of Jammu and Kashmir. His honeymoon with Nehru ended soon and he again went to jail in 1953. And for the rest of his life he had been unsuccessfully claiming for pre-1953 status for the State of Jammu and Kashmir, which was never restored. Till 1953 a special permission was required for Indians to enter Kashmir. Till 1953 accession was considered to be conditional. In 1953 India claimed the fraudulent accession of Jammu and Kashmir to be final. Till 1953 the chief executive of Jammu and Kashmir was called Prime Minister and not the chief minister.

During his chief ministership Sheikh Abdullah did keep senior civil posts in the state to be held by Kashmiris and projected this as decentralization policy. But this was more for his personal convenience rather than by conviction or a matter of policy. Kashmiri bureaucrats obviously desired not to be transferred outside the State. Thus they were more submissive and willing to do any dirty job for the chief minister while Indian Administrative Service officers consulted Delhi before executing any apparently extraordinary orders from the chief minister.

As regards Article 370 of the Indian Constitution giving special status to the State of Jammu and Kashmir, it has been amended so many times that it has lost the importance that it was intended for. Autonomy had been consistently eroding. Earlier this year Hindu nationalist party BJP won parliamentary polls in India with election promises to do away with whatever was left of Article 370 for the State of Jammu and Kashmir, repealing personal Law for Muslims in India, constructing Rama temple in place of Babri Mosque pulled down by Hindu fanatics seven years back in Ayodhya and making India a nuclear weapon state. Within 40 days of coming into power of BJP, India with a series of underground nuclear tests had already become the sixth nuclear power state in the world with BJP redeeming one of the pledges. Sheikh Abdullah had returned to power in Jammu and Kashmir State in 1976, of course, without winning anything extra for the state subjects or repairing any damage done to the State's autonomy. His duplicity was more than exposed. In Jammu and Kashmir he was described at clever and cunning man and his slogan of State's self-assertion as mere stunt.

### *Ploy of Resettlement Bill*

A private bill Jammu and Kashmir Grant of Permit for Resettlement Permanent Return to the State Bill (1980) piloted by Abdul Rahim Rather was adopted by the Indian occupied Jammu and Kashmir legislature with the support of the ruling National Conference. This was an enabling provision to grant for permit for resettlement in the State of any person who had been a State subject and migrated to the territories now forming Pakistan (it did not apply to Azad Kashmir) between March 1947 and May 14, 1954. Ostensibly it was intended to give a deceptive impression to the general public that there were many Kashmiri Muslims who had migrated to Pakistan were but now being repentant and dissatisfied with living conditions in Pakistan and wanted to return to the State, which was paradise on Earth. Indeed it was a camouflage in the sense that under its garb the motive was to give permit of residence to those Hindu migrants from Pakistan at the time of Independence and from other places in India subsequently to offset Muslim majority complexion of the state. According to the some Srinagar citizens the real purpose of the bill was to distribute the property left by Muslims in Jammu among favourites of Sheikh Abdullah. The evacuee property had already been given to Hindus and millions of rupees were being received by way of rent and the Bill aimed at finally distributing the booty among the favourites. A provision of the Bill lay down that the applicant for resettlement was to take an oath of allegiance to the Constitution of India and to undertake to faithfully observe the laws of the State and India. In early 1980s militancy was not visible on surface, yet the youth looked conscious and determined to fight their own battle. They admitted that Pakistan had done its outmost for them and had suffered in return. The people in the valley were on the whole Islam-loving and pro-Pakistan. It was a privilege to parade as a Pakistani. They love you. Everybody would offer you a cup of tea. You do not have to introduce yourself. Their just coming to know that you are a Pakistani was enough. Even not very bold persons would come to whisper in your ear: We know you. We are pleased to see you here. They did not wait to be introduced or to introduce themselves and would disappear in the crowd. An attendant in a tourist bungalow said, "We too were very keen on Pakistan. Probably it was not our luck to be Pakistanis". Love for Islam is inexhaustible. On occasion of Shab-e-Bara't mosques were full for the entire night for what they called "Shab" which included Zikar, Naatkhwani and Waaz. The people of Kashmir are engaged in a heroic resistance struggle and have lain down and continue to lay supreme sacrifices to relieve jugular vein of Pakistan and that of their own from enemy's sword as willed by the Quaid-e-Azam.

### *Simla Agreement*

The Simla Agreement was signed between India and Pakistan at 12:40 a.m. on July 3, 1972. It followed from the war between the two nations in the previous year that had led to the independence of East Pakistan (now Bangladesh). The agreement laid down the principles that should govern their future relations. It also conceived steps to be taken for further normalization of mutual relations. Most importantly, it bound the two countries "to settle their differences by peaceful means through bilateral negotiations". The Kashmir dispute again came to the core-issue when India and Pakistan signed the controversial Simla Accord in June 1972 in the wake of the Indo-Pak war in 1971. The accord converted the 1949 UN Ceasefire line into new boundary undefined (LAC) between Pakistan and India which however did not affect the status of the disputed territory, since 1972. "In Jammu and Kashmir, the Line of Control resulting from the cease-fire of December 17, 1971 shall be respected by both sides without prejudice to the recognised position of either side and is not a final agreement pending a final agreement will be further negotiated, Kashmiris also should be included in the Peace process between the two now nuclear rival Nation-states. Neither side shall seek to alter it unilaterally irrespective of mutual differences and legal interpretations. Both sides further undertake to refrain from threat or the use of force in violation of this Line." The agreement also paved the way for diplomatic recognition of Bangladesh by Pakistan. As a gesture of goodwill India decided not to try 90,368 Pakistani prisoners of war for war crimes and released them. The agreement has been the basis of all subsequent bilateral talks between India and Pakistan, though it has not prevented the relationship between the two countries from deteriorating to the point of armed conflict, most recently in the Kargil War. The treaty was signed in Simla, in India, by Zulfiqar Ali Bhutto, the Prime Minister of Pakistan, and Indira Gandhi, the Prime Minister of India.

- 1971-Ceasefire line of control should be treated
- Diplomtic recgnition of Bangladesh
- Release the POW and not treat them as war criminals
- Through bialateral Negotiations (all the problems)

**History after 1989: Characterized as Armed Insurgency**

In 1989, a widespread Armed Insurgency started in Kashmir. Since after 1987 disputed rigged State elections resulted in some of the 'states legislative assembly' 'formed militant wings' later on after the election forming and creating the catalyst for the insurgency which continues to this day furthermore 'in part' fuelled by Afghan Mujahideen in 1989 Timeline of the conflict. India contends that this was largely started by the large number of Afghan Mujahideens who entered the Kashmir valley following the end of the Soviet-Afghan War, though Pakistan and Kashmiri nationalists argue that Afghan Mujahideen did not leave Afghanistan in large numbers until 1992, three years after the insurgency began. Yasin Malik, a leader of one faction of the Jammu Kashmir Liberation Front (JKLF), along with Ashfaq Majid Wani and Farooq Ahmad Dar *alias* Bitta Karatay, was one of the Kashmiris to organize militancy in Kashmir. However since 1995, Malik has renounced the use of violence and calls for strictly peaceful methods to resolve the dispute. He developed differences with one of the senior leader Farooq Papa for shunning the demand for independent Kashmir and trying to cut a deal with Indian Prime Minister resulting in spilt in which Bitta Karatay, Salim Nanhaji and other senior comrades joined Farooq Papa. Pakistan claims these insurgents are Jammu and Kashmir citizens, and they are rising up against the Indian Army in an independence movement. It also says the Indian Army is committing serious human rights violations to the citizens of Jammu and Kashmir. It denies that it is giving armed help to the insurgents.

India claims these insurgents are Islamic terrorist groups from Pakistan-administered Kashmir and Afghanistan, fighting to make Jammu and Kashmir part of Pakistan. It believes Pakistan is giving armed help to the terrorists, and training them in Pakistan. It also says the terrorists have been killing many citizens in Kashmir, and committing human rights violations, while denying that its own armed forces are responsible for the human rights abuses. On a visit to Pakistan in 2006 current Chief Minister of Kashmir Omar Abdullah remarked that foreign militants, who had nothing to do with Kashmir, were engaged in reckless killings and mayhem in the name of religion. Also US Intelligence agencies believe that Al-Qaeda and Taliban are helping organize a terror campaign in Kashmir to foment conflict between India and Pakistan. A 2001 report 'Pakistan's Role in the Kashmir Insurgency' of US Think tank RAND corporation noted that 'More intrinsically, the nature of the Kashmir conflict has been transformed from what was originally a secular, locally-based struggle (conducted via the Jammu Kashmir Liberation Front, JKLF) to one that is now largely carried out by foreign militants and rationalized in pan-Islamic religious terms. In July 2006 Al-Qaeda stated that it had established a wing in Kashmir. Indian government has said militancy is now on the decline. The Pakistani government calls these insurgents, "Kashmiri freedom fighters", and claims that it gives only moral and diplomatic support to these insurgents, though India believes they are Pakistan-supported terrorists from Pakistan administered Kashmir. In October 2008 President Asif Ali Zardari of Pakistan called the Kashmir separatists Terrorists in an interview with *The Wall Street Journal*, these comments by Zardari sparked outrage amongst many Kashmiris, some of whom defied a curfew by the Indian army to burn his effigy. The peacful protest movement has been a 'purely indigenous, purely Kashmiri (Quoted by Washington Post from Mirwaiz Farooq a Kashmiri party leader) 'Ghandi style' (stated by *Wall Street Journal*) peaceful protest movement in Indian Administered Kashmir since 1989. The movement was created for the same reason as the insurgency; the disputed rigged elections in 1987, Kashmir dispute and grievances with the Indian government specifically the Indian Military that has committed human rights violations. This reinforced by the United Nations that has said India has committed Human rights violations.

### *Conflict in Kargil*

In mid-1999 insurgents and Pakistani soldiers from Pakistani Kashmir infiltrated into Jammu and Kashmir. During the winter season, Indian forces regularly move down to lower altitudes as severe climatic conditions make it almost impossible for them to guard the high peaks near the Line of Control. The insurgents took advantage of this and occupied vacant mountain peaks of the Kargil range overlooking the highway in Indian Kashmir, connecting Srinagar and Leh. By blocking the highway, they wanted to cut off the only link between the Kashmir Valley and Ladakh. This resulted in a high-scale conflict between the Indian Army and the Pakistan Army. At the same time, fears of the Kargil War turning into a nuclear war provoked the then-US President Bill Clinton to pressure Pakistan to retreat. Faced with mounting losses of personnel and posts, Pakistan Army withdrew the remaining troops from the area ending the conflict. India reclaimed control of the peaks which they now patrol and monitor all year long.

### *Main Causes of the Kashmir Dispute – Kashmir View*

India's forcible occupation of the State of Jammu and Kashmir in 1947 is the main cause of the dispute. India claims to have 'signed' a controversial document, the Instrument of Accession, on 26 October, 1947 with the Maharaja of Kashmir, in which the Maharaja obtained India's military help against popular insurgency. The people of Kashmir and Pakistan do not accept the Indian claim. There are doubts about the very existence of the Instrument of Accession. The United Nations also does not consider Indian claim as legally valid: it recognizes Kashmir as a disputed territory. Except India, the entire world community recognizes Kashmir as a disputed territory. The fact is that all the principles on the basis of which the Indian subcontinent was partitioned by the British in 1947 justify Kashmir becoming a part of Pakistan: the State had majority Muslim population, and it not only enjoyed geographical proximity with Pakistan but also had essential economic linkages with the territories constituting Pakistan.

### *Main Causes of Kashmir Dispute—Indian View*

Indian viewpoint is succinctly summarized by the Ministry of External Affairs, Government of India. India holds that the Instrument of Accession of the State of Jammu and Kashmir to India, signed by the Maharaja Hari Singh (erstwhile ruler of the State) on 26 October, 1947, was completely valid in terms of the Government of India Act (1935), Indian Independence Act (1947) and international law and was total and irrevocable.

The Constituent Assembly of Jammu and Kashmir had unanimously ratified the Maharaja's Instrument of Accession to India and had adopted a Constitution for the state that called for a perpetual merger of the state with the Union of India. India claims that this body was a representative one, and that its views were those of the Kashmiri people at the time.

United Nations Security Council Resolution 1172 tacitly accepts India's stand regarding all outstanding issues between India and Pakistan and urges the need to resolve the dispute through mutual dialogue and does not call for a plebiscite.

United Nations Security Council Resolution 47 cannot be implemented since Pakistan failed to withdraw its forces from Kashmir which was the first step in implementing the resolution. Now the resolution is obsolete since the geography and demographics of the region have been permanently altered. The resolution was passed by United Nations Security Council under Chapter VI of the United Nations Charter. Resolutions passed under Chapter VI of UN charter are considered non-binding and have no mandatory enforceability as opposed to the resolutions passed under Chapter VII.

India does not accept the two-nation theory that forms the basis of Pakistan and argues that Kashmir, despite being a Muslim-majority state, is in many ways an "integral part" of secular India.

The state of Jammu and Kashmir was provided significant autonomy in the Article 370 of the Constitution of India. India points to the recent state-assembly elections held in phases in November–December 2008. High turnouts were seen in spite of calls for boycott by Kashmiri separatists. The pro-India National Conference party emerged as the winner. Additional Indian viewpoint regarding the broader debate over the Kashmir conflict include:

"India believes that the insurgency and terrorism in Kashmir is deliberately being fuelled by Pakistan to create instability in the region. The Government of India has repeatedly asked the international community to declare Pakistan as a sponsor of terrorism."

"Pakistan is trying to raise anti-India sentiment among the people of Kashmir by spreading false propaganda against India. According to the state government of Jammu and Kashmir, Pakistani radio and television channels deliberately spread "hate and venom" against India to alter Kashmiri opinion."

In a diverse country like India, disaffection and discontent are not uncommon. Indian democracy has the necessary resilience to accommodate genuine grievances within the framework of our sovereignty, unity and integrity. Government of India has expressed its willingness to accommodate the legitimate political demands of the people of the state of Jammu and Kashmir.

India has asked United Nations that it should not be leave unchallenged or unaddressed claims of moral, political and diplomatic support for terrorism, which were clearly in contravention of United Nations Security Council Resolution 1373 which is a Chapter VII resolution that makes it mandatory for member states to not provide active or passive support to terrorist organizations. Specifically, it has pointed out that the Pakistani government continues to support various terrorist organizations, such as Jaish-e-Mohammad and Lashkar-e-Taiba, in direct violation of this resolution.

India points out at various reports by human rights organizations condemning Pakistan for the lack civic liberties in Pakistan-administered Kashmir. According to India, most regions of Pakistani Kashmir, especially Northern Areas, continue to suffer from lack of political recognition, economic development and basic fundamental rights.

All differences between India and Pakistan including Kashmir need to be settled through bilateral negotiations as agreed to by the two countries when they signed the Shimla Agreement on July 2, 1972.

### *Main Causes of Kashmir Dispute—Pakistan View*

Pakistan's claims to the disputed region are based on the rejection of Indian claims to Kashmir, namely the Instrument of Accession. Pakistan insists that the Maharaja was not a popular leader, and was regarded as a tyrant by most Kashmiris, Pakistan also maintains that the Maharaja used brute force to suppress the population. Pakistan also accuses India of hypocrisy, as it refused to recognize the accession of Junagadh to Pakistan and Hyderabad's independence, on the grounds that those two states had Hindu majorities (in fact, India occupied and forcibly integrated those two territories). Furthermore, as he had fled Kashmir due to Pakistani invasion, Pakistan asserts that the Maharaja held no authority in determining Kashmir's future. Additionally, Pakistan argues that even if the Maharaja had any authority in determining the plight of Kashmir, he signed the Instrument of Accession under duress, thus invalidating the legitimacy of his actions.

Pakistan also claims that Indian forces were in Kashmir before the Instrument of Accession was signed with India, and that therefore, Indian troops were in Kashmir in violation of the Standstill Agreement, which was designed to maintain the *status quo* in Kashmir (although India was not signatory to the Agreement, signed between Pakistan and the Hindu ruler of Jammu and Kashmir). From 1990 to 1999 some organizations report that Indian Armed Forces, its paramilitary groups, and counter-insurgent militias have been responsible for the deaths of 4,501 of Kashmiri civilians. Also from 1990 to 1999, there are records of 4,242 women between the ages of 7-70 that have been raped. Similar allegations were also made by some human rights organizations.

In short, Pakistan holds that the popular Kashmiri insurgency demonstrates that the Kashmiri people no longer wish to remain within India. Pakistan suggests that this means that either Kashmir wants to be with Pakistan or independent. According to the two-nation theory which is one of the theories that is cited for the partition that created India and Pakistan, Kashmir should have been with Pakistan, because it has a Muslim majority. India has shown disregard to the resolutions of the UN Security Council, and the United Nations Commission in India and Pakistan by failing to hold a plebiscite to determine the future allegiance of the entire state.

The Kashmiri people have now been forced by the circumstances to rise against the alleged repression of the Indian army and uphold their right of self-determination through militancy. Pakistan claims to give the Kashmiri insurgents moral, ethical and military support.

Recent protests in Indian administered Kashmir show a large number of people showing increased anger over Indian rule with massive rallies taking place to oppose Indian control of the state.

Pakistan also points to the violence that accompanies elections in Indian Kashmir and the anti-Indian sentiments expressed by some people in the state. Pakistan has noted the wide spread use of extra judicial killings in Indian-administered Kashmir carried out by Indian security forces while claiming they were caught up in encounters with militants. These fake encounters are common place in Indian-administered Kashmir and the perpetrators are spared criminal prosecution. These fake encounters go largely uninvestigated by the authorities. Pakistan points towards reports from the United Nations which condemns India for its human rights violations against Kashmiri people. Pakistan President Asif Ali Zardari stated in October 2008 that Kashmiri 'freedom fighters' were terrorists. However, his remarks met with widespread condemnation across Pakistan and Kashmir, including prominent politicians.

The Chenab formula—This was proposed in 1960s, in which Kashmir valley and other Muslim dominated areas north of Chenab river will go to Pakistan, and Jammu and other Hindu dominated region will go to India. It is widely known that the disputed rigged election of 1987 had caused the catalyst for the insurgency in Indian Kashmir and yearning for Independence from India or joining Pakistan.

### Past Autocracy in Kashmir Valley

Jammu and Kashmir came into being as a single political and geographical entity following the Treaty of Amritsar between the British Government and Gulab Singh signed on March 16, 1846. The Treaty handed over the control of the Kashmir State to the Dogra ruler of Jammu who had earlier annexed Ladakh. Thus a new State comprising three distinct religions of Jammu, Kashmir and Ladakh was formed with Maharaja Gulab Singh as its founder ruler. The feudal dispensation in the State, however, was too harsh for the people to live under and towards the end of a hundred years of this rule when their Indian brethren were fighting for independence from the British under the inspiring leadership of Mahatma Gandhi and Pandit Jawaharlal Nehru, the Kashmiris led by a towering personality, the Sher-I-Kashmir Sheikh Mohammad Abdullah, rose against the autocracy. The autocratic rule came down heavily on the people's freedom movement. However, the people laid their lives in the cause of freedom and to uphold the ideals of secularism, equality, democracy and brotherhood. The high point of the movement was July 13, 1931 when 22 protesters were martyred. The event strengthened the movement and contrary to the expectations of the then rulers, the people emerged more determined in their resolution to seek an end to autocratic rule. By the time the rulers could realize the futility of breaking the will of the people with the might of the State, the National Conference, headed by Sheikh Mohammad Abdullah, had become a mass movement and a force to reckon with. It broke the barriers of region and religion and became a popular and secular voice of the people of the State whose collective yearning was freedom from autocracy and the establishment of a popular rule. The suffering Kashmir laboured hard under the oppressive Dogra Yoke. The *begar* (forced labour) is the most painful memory of this oppressed that Kashmiris still possess and relate. The Muslims discriminate in education and social attributes. The other factors are Dogra autocracy, state extract wealth from the poor, Shopian case 1931—in which 22 Kashmiris were killed in police firing on July 13, 1931 are buried. These martyrs for the cause of Kashmir were at the head of a wave of protect and resentment against the oppressions of the Dogra regime. It was, in the opinion of many scholars, the inauguration, of the freedom struggle of Kashmiris against the Dogra rule, and in the opinion of other recent scholars, of the region's history, "The significance of the date drew from the fact that it was the first time that a gathering of Kashmiri Muslims openly challenged the authority of the Maharaja and his government."

After this incident the Maharaja withdrew his offer of audience with the representatives, only adding to the indignation of the people. Subsequently, many leaders were arrested. Sheikh Abdullah and his prominent leaders were lodged first in the Badamibagh Cantonment and after a few days were moved to the Hari Parbat fort under a military guard. The city was placed under curfew and martial law was declared. The imposition of the martial law gave an unprecedented licence to the state troops. "People were forced to kiss the Dogra flag, lick the shoes of Dogra soldiers." Besides all the roads on 13 July, 1931 linking Srinagar and other parts of the state were closed. Telephone and telegram communications were also shut down.

Kashmiris were demanding greater political rights from the Dogra autocracy at a time when the events of the Civil Disobedience Movement were taking place in India. The problem of representation was at heart of the events that culminated in the 1931 massacre. With the onset of Second World War in September 1939, Kashmiri movement generated by July 31 events, became more directionless and meaningless. The Dogra were the allies of the British, and on the ground the hooliganism of the Sheikh Abdullah gained the upper ground with the tacit support of Ayyenger and his backers in New Delhi. The hijacked movements became instruments of collaboration with the Dogra rule.

Besides how deplorable and strange in it that the genocide of Muslims in Jammu in November 1947 has never received acknowledgement or treatment in historiography. On other major issues of heinous crime such as Ghandhi's assassination (1948), Babri Masjid demolition (1992), Bombay carnage (1993), etc., commissions have been instituted which have put the records right, though action was always lacking. The Jammu genocide which, according to many estimates left about 200,000 Muslims dead and as many as uprooted from their homes, is not mentioned any where in academic or political discourse. In Jammu the monumental crime of Muslim genocide took place only because it was state sponsored and later Indian Army too was directly or indirectly responsible for it. The countless massacres which took place in October-November 1947 over a vast region from Kathua to Reasi, Udhampur to Rajouri were not communal acts of violence. All this became possible because it was state sponsored genocide with clear political objective of winning Jammu primarily and Kashmir possible to the Indian side on the strength of the armed might.

The powerful forces responsible for the Jammu genocide were:

- The Dogra Hindu state of Maharaja Hari Singh.
- Armed gangs of the RSS.
- Armed Sikh Jathas from eastern states of Punjab.
- Sardar Patel's Home Ministry and Baldev Singh's Defence Ministry.

Of course, Maharaja Hari Singh and his forces are responsible in major part in what happened in Jammu. When Maharaja left Srinagar, as is being claimed, on or around October 26, 1947, he considered Kashmir as lost. According to historians, right from Udhampur, Hari Singh's wife Maharani Tara Devi incited her coreligionists to kill the Muslims. Joseph Korbel mentioned in his book *Danger in Kashmir* that in 1947 RSS has 400,000 trained cadres supported by 500,000 sympathizers in reserve. In Punjab alone they had 30,000 trained cadres. In October 1947, Jammu and Kashmir was the only place left then where their services were "need". They remained active up to 1949, even when ceasefire was declared by the Security Council.

## Past Atrocities and its Impact on Present

The people of Jammu and Kashmir State remain the target of either Indian military forces or the separatists since first quarter of 20th century. Before the independence atrocities in the Kashmir take the life of thousands of people. A brief chronological account of atrocities in Kashmir that this area has witnessed and its people have suffered since 1925. The Dogra rule, followed by Indian occupation in 1947, is a bleak chapter in the history of Jammu and Kashmir. The Dogra rule, which continued from

1846-1947, is considered as the gloomiest period. Indian armed forces occupied a major part of Jammu and Kashmir on October 27, 1947 that is continuing to date. The Indian troops pursued the policy of suppression in a systematic manner to reduce the overwhelming Muslim majority in occupied Jammu and Kashmir. To achieve this objective Indian troops started the process of mass massacre. There are plenty of events and evidences to support this gory fact. In October 1924 Muslim notables in Srinagar present a memorandum to the British Viceroy regarding the Maharaja's misrule and setting forth popular demands. This is a sequel to a labour strike in the state-run silk factory in which the workers were charged by troops commanded by Hari Singh, then the heir apparent, and their leader tortured to death. In March 1925 the leader of the signatories to the memorandum, Saaduddin Shawl, is deported from the State. In April 1925 first meeting in Lahore (now in Pakistan) of Kashmiri expatriates and other Muslim leaders to muster support for the reformist struggle in Kashmir. In March 1929 Albion Bannerji, a Bengali Christian, resigns as the Maharaja's Prime Minister makes a public statement: "The large Muslim population is governed like dumb-driven cattle... the press is non-existent... the economic conditions are appalling." On the day of 13 July, 1931, the people of Kashmir had been raising their voice against the Dogra usurpation of their land and as a result they faced brutal consequences. On this day a large number of Kashmiris gathered in front of the Srinagar central jail, at a time when the trial of a youth Abdul Qadeer accused of involvement in a case of agitation, was in progress inside the jail. The objective was to demonstrate solidarity with the young man. As the time for obligatory prayer approached a young Kashmiri stood for Azan (Call for the prayer) and the Dogra police opened fire on him, and he got martyred. Thereby, another youth took the place of the martyred young man and started the Azan. He too was shot dead. In this way 22 Kashmiris embraced martyrdom in their efforts to complete the Azan. In June 1947, people of Poonch had launched a no-tax campaign against the heavy taxation of Maharaja. To curb the agitation, Maharaja Hari Singh, the last Dogra ruler of the state, ordered the use of brute military force. in August 26 the protesters were confronted by the Dogra-armed forces. The Dogra troops opened bran-gun fire on the huge crowd of 5,000 civilians, martyring and wounding hundreds of them.

Maharaja Hari Singh fled from Srinagar to Jammu on 26 October, 1947, as the liberation activists were poised in Srinagar's suburbs to capture the city. On reaching Jammu, he issued orders to his troops and police besides the Hindu extremist groups, to kill Muslims found anywhere. The

Muslims were asked to assemble in parade ground in Jammu so that they would be driven to Pakistan in Lorries. While on their way, on October 20, 1947, eight thousand Muslims were massacred at Malatank Jammu. On October 22, 1947 at least 14000 Muslims were massacred at Saniya Jammu and 15,000 Muslims were gunned down near the bridge at Akhnoor.

On November 5 and 6, 1947, more than 100 lorries, loaded with women, children and old men were taken into the wilderness of Kathua forests. Hindu extremists and armed gangs were let loose on these innocent people and an unparallel butchery was perpetrated, killing thousands of them. Women were raped, molested and their valuables looted. All these bloodsheds were taking place in full view of the Indian army, which had by that time occupied a major part of the state. In another act of butchery, a large gathering of 25000 Muslims, in Miran Sahib and Ranbir Singhpora, were machine-gunned. During migration to Pakistan in 1947, nearly 300,000 people were massacred in cold. British daily the *London Times* wrote on October 10, 1947 in a report from its special correspondent in India that the Maharaja, under his own supervision, got assassinated 237,000 Muslims, using military forces in Jammu area. The editor of "*Statesman*" Ian Stephen, in his book "*Horned Moon*" wrote that till the end of autumn 1947, more than 200,000 Muslims were assassinated.

### Atrocities from 1947 to the Present Day

Right from 1947, the fury of mass killings is going on unabated. Kashmiris suffered massacres in 1965 and 1971. Since 1989, India increased its acts of brutalities and people were killed in mass groups. Some of the savage events are as under:

#### *Atrocities in 1990*

- **January 8:** Firing at various places in Srinagar city, 17 people were killed.
- **January 15:** In Handwara town, the Indian army and paramilitary forces shot dead 17 unarmed civilians including one woman when troops opened unprovoked fire on peaceful protesters.
- **January 21:** 55 innocent civilians were killed in the localities of Basantbagh and Gawkadal in Srinagar city by Central Reserve Police Force troops when more than 20,000 people took to the streets, defying curfew.

- **January 22:** The Indian army and paramilitary forces resorted to unprovoked firing at Alamghari Bazar, Srinagar and killed many unarmed civilians. The people had come out unarmed to protest against the military killings at Gaw Kadal in Srinagar.
- **January 25:** 26 civilians were shot dead in Handwara town of Kupwara district. The township was set afire by Border Security Force after the latter was panicked by a bang. Some of the slain persons including women were roasted alive.
- **March 1:** In order to halt massive demonstrations by the people, who were to submit a memorandum to United Nations Military Observers Group on India and Pakistan (UNMOGIP), Indian army opened fire at Tengpora bypass and Zakoora crossing in Srinagar, killing 21 and injured 26 demonstrators, respectively.
- **May 21:** 70 persons were put to death by Central Reserve Police Force troops near Islamia College, Srinagar. The unarmed civilian mourners were carrying the dead body of late Mirwaiz Molvi Muhammad Farooq, prominent liberation leader and father of All Party Hurriyat Conference chairman, Mirwaiz Umar Farooq. More than three hundred people were injured. Five women, one of them pregnant, were killed. Even minors were not spared. The forces did not spare even the coffin-bearers. The dead body of late Mirwaiz was also shot at.
- **August 6:** The troops besieged Mashali Mohalla in Srinagar, raided the houses of local inhabitants and killed innocent civilians. In this incident more than two-dozen people were brutalized, of whom nine died on the spot.
- **August 10:** Border Security Force cordoned off the whole area of Pazipora, Kupwara. The male inmates were ordered to gather in a park for identification parade. The locals objected to let ladies stay at their homes without being accompanied by any male members. Later the forces, in absence of male members, entered the houses and raped and molested a number of ladies. By hue and cry of the ladies, the male members tried to rush to their respective homes in order to rescue the ladies from the clutches of the armed forces. But the troops fired on the unarmed civilians of the locality and killed 25 of them on the spot.
- **September 11:** A civil passenger bus, carrying about fifty persons, was intercepted by the Border Security Force troops. Passengers were fired upon. 22 died on the spot. The bus was set on fire due to which eight persons got burnt alive.

- **October 1:** The BSF personnel in Handwara town of Kupwara district started indiscriminate firing on the unarmed civilians, who were busy in marketing activities, killing 20 of them on the spot.

***Atrocities in 1991***

- **January 19:** The personnel of 42-CRPF opened indiscriminate fire, killing 11 civilians in Magarmalbagh, Srinagar. Most of the victims were waiting for bus and being a busy place; most of the passers-by received bullet shots and died on the spot.
- **January 30:** In Achabal Islamabad, the Indian armed forces opened indiscriminate fire, killing 7 innocent persons.
- **March 11:** At Rakhi Haigam, Sopore, in Baramullah district, Indian armed forces started indiscriminate firing, killing six civilians, including Manzoor Ahmad Dar aged only 12 years.
- **March 16:** The Indian troops cordoned the area in Pishwari Trehgam in Kupwara district. At that time about 12 persons were offering prayers in a mosque within the cordoned area. The forces directed the worshipers to come out of the Mosque but they could not come out as they were engaged in the prayers. The forces entered into the Mosque and started firing. The Imam (Leader of the prayers) did not break the prayers. He was shot in his head. Other persons were dragged in the compound of the Mosque and six more persons were shot dead.
- **May 5:** At Khayam, Khanyar in Sriangar, the troops fired indiscriminately on the pedestrians due to which, five persons including a girl, Aisha, aged three years were killed.
- **May 8:** In Pir Dastgeer, Khanyar locality of down town Srinagar, troops of CRPF, BSF's 2nd and 60th Bn opened fire on thousands of people who were assembled to bury some martyred Kashmiris. 18 civilians were killed. In this incident, one infant aged two years, and his father were also killed.
- **June 11:** The CRPF troops opened indiscriminate fire, having been frightened by the sound of a tire burst, leaving 32 civilians killed in the densely populated area of Chotabazar, Srinagar. The killed included shopkeepers, passers-by, old persons, women and children.
- **September 3:** At Safanagri and Nelora in Pulwama district, the armed forces fired on unarmed civilians and more than 23 got killed.

***Atrocities in 1992***

- **April 2:** In Aloosa village of Bandipore tehsil of Baramullah district, the villagers were kept confined to the village limits for the whole day by the Indian troops, while those out for fishing were fired upon. At least five boatmen were killed in the firing. Many bodies were recovered from the Wular Lake as they had been made to sink by tying heavy stones to their limbs.
- **April 13:** During early hours of the day, BSF troops charged into the area, comprising Mohalla Hajama, Talian, Syed Sultanpora, Mahrajpora, and Chinkipora, started indiscriminate firing which resulted in killing of 13 civilians including one woman.
- **July 2:** There was a tyre burst of a moving vehicle, which created a panic in the crowded market of Lal Chowk, Srinagar. In response the CRPF troops, posted at Hari Singh High Street, fired indiscriminately, killing six civilians.
- **July 6:** The BSF men subjected Ishbar locality in the outskirts of Srinagar to indiscriminate firing and at least 7 civilians were killed.
- **July 13:** Army personnel entered the village of Nasrullahpora, adjacent to Budgam, and started indiscriminate firing, killing ten innocent people.
- **August 15:** In Taj Mohalla of Tral in Pulwama district, BSF troops killed 6 civilians in cold blood. One of them was burnt alive.
- **October 2:** 10 civilians were killed in Handwara town of Kupwara district by BSF troops.
- **December 12:** Indian troops killed 7 civilians in Kishtwar area of Doda district.

***Atrocities in 1993***

- **January 6:** 94 BSF-Bn personnel ran amuck, killing 57 civilians, mostly roasted alive, when they set ablaze 37 residential and 35 commercial structures at Sopore in Baramullah district.
- **April 10:** 47 innocent Kashmiris were burnt alive when BSF set afire, most of the Lal Chowk, Srinagar, destroying 59 houses, 190 shops, 53 godowns and 2 office complexes.
- **July 1:** In Baba Reshi area of Baramullah district, the troops

started indiscriminate firing and killed 9 civilians who had come to the shrine.

- **July 30:** In Hangubutch, Pulwama district 12 civilians were killed and 100 injured. A magisterial probe was announced but never completed.
- **August 1:** Sub-inspector Ajmer Singh of BSF, 60Bn along with three of his subordinates, killed a couple Abdul Rashid Dar and Hajra after barging into their residence in Daribal, Srinagar. Their critically injured son Hilal succumbed to wounds in hospital. After thousands of people took to the streets in anti-India demonstration, the police and army resorted to firing, killing 10 of them.
- **August 14:** Indian secret agents dragged out passengers from a bus on Sarthal link road in Kishtwar, Doda and sprayed them with bullets, killing 14 civilians.
- **October 22:** Troops of BSF, 7Bn opened fire on a procession in Bijbehara town of Islamabad district, killing 50 and injuring 100 civilians.
- **November 20:** At Aadipora, in Sopore area of Baramullah district, the BSF personnel opened fire and killed five persons including a woman.
- **November 24:** In Sangrama in Baramullah district, the BSF troops fired indiscriminately and killed seven unarmed civilians.
- **December 22:** At Bulbul Nowgam in Shangas area of Islamabad district, the Indian troops fired indiscriminately, killing six civilians.

### *Atrocities in 1994*

- **January 24:** Indian troops killed 18 Kashmiris in Kupwara.
- **May 10:** In Bandipora BSF troops, during crack-down, arrested 9 persons in presence of the locals, took them to a military camp in Bandipora where they were killed and their dead bodies were handed over to their relatives.

### *Atrocities in 1995*

- **February 10:** BSF opened fire in narrow business street, in Gad Kocha, Srinagar, killing 6 shopkeepers and injuring 38 others.

*Atrocities in 1996*

- **January 5:** Indian armed agents massacred 15 Kashmiris, 10 of them belonging to one family, in Barshala village of Doda district.
- **June 8:** In Kamlari village of Doda district, Indian armed agents killed eight civilians.

*Atrocities in 1997*

- **March 20:** Seven civilians were killed in Sangrampura (Budgam).
- **April 7:** A group of Indian secret agents swooped on Sangurampora village, in Beerwa outskirts in Budgam district, and shot dead seven Kashmiris.
- **April 18:** 27 civilians were killed in Prankote in Udhampur district in Jammu region.
- **September 19:** In mortar shelling by BSF, 11 villagers were killed in remote village of Arin in Baramullah district.

*Atrocities in 1998*

- **January 26:** Indian agents swooped Wandhama village of Ganderbal tehsil in Srinagar district and massacred 26 Kashmiris.
- **June 19:** 25 civilians were killed in Chapnari area of Doda district in Jammu region.
- **June 28:** In Madwa, Doda 9 villagers were massacred by 26-Rashtriya Rifles, on the *Eid* (Muslim festival) day.
- **July 28:** 16 civilians were killed in two villages of Doda District in Jammu region.
- **August 3:** Twenty civilians were killed in Sailain village of Surankote, Poonch. The dead included seven children.
- **August 8:** 35 labourers were killed in Kalaban on Jammu-Himachal Pradesh border.

*Atrocities in 1999*

- **February 20:** Four civilians were killed at Muraputta-Rajouri, nine at Barlyara-Udhampur and seven at Bllala-Rajouri in Jammu.

- **February 20:** In Baljaralan hamlet of Udhampur district, Indian armed agents killed 10 civilians. Apparently, the same group reappeared in Mora Pota in Budhal belt, and killed 4 members of a family.
- **June 29:** Indian troops and their agents dragged out 17 civilians, including 5 women 7 children, in twin hamlets of Morha Bichai and Sahotri in Poonch and killed them.
- **June 30:** Fifteen labourers were killed in Anantnag district of south Kashmir.

***Atrocities in 2000***

- **February 28:** Five civilians were killed near Qazigund in Anantnag district of Kashmir.
- **March 17:** Indian secret agencies killed 7 truck drivers near a BSF camp at Qazigund in Islamabad district.
- **March 20:** 35 civilians were massacred at Chatisinghpora in Anantnag.
- **March 24:** Five innocent civilians, missing since March 24, 2000, were killed in custody and subsequently roasted by army at Brakpora in Islamabad district.
- **March 30:** 7 protestors were killed by SOG troops near Pathirbal in Islamabad district, who were demanding dead bodies of Brakpora massacre.
- **May 14:** Five teenagers, arrested from Sopore, were killed by Indian troops in Tangdar area of Kupwara district.
- **August 1:** 35 Amarnath Yatris (pilgrims) were killed by Indian secret agencies and CRPF troops at Pahalgam in Islamabad district.
- **August 1:** 31 civilians were massacred at Pahalgam in Anantnag.
- **August 1:** 27 labourers were gunned down in Qazigund and Achabal in Anantnag.
- **August 2:** Seven people of one family were killed in frontier district of Kupwara in North Kashmir.
- **August 2:** 11 civilians were killed in Doda district of Jammu.

***Atrocities in 2001***

- **February 3:** Indian secret agencies killed 7 Sikhs at Mahjoornagar in Srinagar.

- **February 10:** At Kotchatwal in Bhudal area of Rajouri district, 12 civilians including 6 kids and 4 women were killed by Indian troops and their secret agencies.
- **March 17:** Eight people were massacred near Atholi in Doda.
- **March 21:** At Mandi in Poonch district, the Indian troops used helicopters and gun ships and killed 10 Kashmiris.
- **March 31:** At Doru, Islamabad, 7 Kashmiri drivers were killed by Indian troops.
- **July 21:** 13 civilians were killed at Sheshnag in Anantnag.
- **July 22:** 12 people were massacred in Cheerji and Tagood in Doda district of Jammu.
- **August 4:** 15 villagers were killed in Ludder-Sharotid Har area of Doda.
- **August 6:** Indian agents killed 7 civilians in Sajjar village of Atholi, in Kistwar tehsil of Doda district.
- **December 8:** 10 unarmed civilians, including women and children, were killed in the indiscriminate military firing in Baramullah.

***Atrocities in 2002***

- **January 6:** 6 civilians were killed at Luddu and Ramsu, Doda.
- **January 20:** 11 civilians were killed at Behra, Poonch.
- **January 21:** Indian troops killed 14 persons including 8 children of 3 families, at Salwa village in Maindher area of Poonch in Rajouri district.
- **February 16:** 8 civilians were killed at Nirala Rajouri.
- **May 14:** 36 civilians were killed at Kaluchak, Jammu.
- **July 13:** 28 civilians were massacred at Kasimpura in Jammu.
- **August 5:** Nine pilgrims were killed in Nuwan Pehalgam in Islamabad district.

***Atrocities in 2003***

- **March 24:** 24 civilians were massacred including 11 women and 2 children at Nadimerg village of Pulwama.
- **October 22:** Seven members of a family were shot dead when armed Indian agents opened indiscriminate firing at a wedding ceremony in Domail area of Doda district.

### *Atrocities in 2004*

- **April 5:** Seven civilians were killed at Pahalgam in Islamabad.

### *Atrocities in 2006*

- **May 01:** 35 civilians were killed at Basantgarh in Udhampur and Kulhanag in Doda district.

**Table 2.1:** Atrocities by Indian Troops from 1990-2008

| *Years* | *Total killings* | *Tortured/ Injured* | *Arrested* | *Kidnapped/ Missing* | *Women gang Raped/ Molestation* |
|---|---|---|---|---|---|
| 1990 | 428 | 2021 | 1120 | 1130 | 432 |
| 1991 | 680 | 2200 | 1130 | 1232 | 644 |
| 1992 | 928 | 2400 | 1137 | 1319 | 722 |
| 1993 | 1012 | 2405 | 1120 | 905 | 514 |
| 1994 | 1122 | 3105 | 1445 | 1653 | 312 |
| 1995 | 802 | 3308 | 1320 | 1489 | 105 |
| 1996 | 540 | 3860 | 1667 | 1205 | 144 |
| 1997 | 620 | 3790 | 1820 | 1020 | 187 |
| 1998 | 780 | 3546 | 2005 | 924 | 195 |
| 1999 | 554 | 3025 | 1632 | 832 | 119 |
| 2000 | 800 | 4087 | 2220 | 1026 | 120 |
| 2001 | 600 | 2927 | 1416 | 989 | 93 |
| 2002 | 604 | 2507 | 1002 | 514 | 104 |
| 2003 | 600 | 2578 | 932 | 232 | 90 |
| 2004 | 504 | 2480 | 1416 | 323 | 87 |
| 2005 | 650 | 2500 | 1320 | 387 | 73 |
| 2006 | 667 | 2578 | 1221 | 210 | 85 |
| 2007 | 642 | 2045 | 1016 | 107 | 68 |
| 2008 | 538 | 4824 | 1408 | 44 | 93 |

*Source:* Kashmir Media Service.

**Table 2.2:** Total Cases of Atrocities from January 1989 to June 2010

| | |
|---|---|
| Total Killings | 93,274 |
| Custodial Killings | 6,969 |
| Civilians Arrested | 117,345 |
| Structures Arsoned/Destroyed | 105,861 |
| Women Widowed | 22,728 |
| Children Orphaned | 107,351 |
| Women gang-raped / Molested | 9,920 |

**Table 2.3:** Cases of Atrocities in the Month of June 2010

| | |
|---|---|
| Total Killings * | 33 |
| Men | 29 |
| Women | 0 |
| Children | 4 |
| Custodial Killings | 0 |
| Tortured/Critically Injured | 572 |
| Civilians Arrested | 228 |
| Structures Arsoned/Destroyed | 16 |
| Disappeared | 0 |
| Women Widowed | 2 |
| Children Orphaned | 4 |
| Women gang-raped / Molested | 8 |

* *Source*: Kashmir Media Service.

**Table 2.4**: Total number of militancy related killings (1986-1997)

| | |
|---|---|
| Kashmiri Pandits | 765 |
| Muslims | 8360 |
| Hindus | 554 |
| Sikhs | 259 |
| Christians | 2 |
| Buddhists | — |
| Foreigners | 11 |
| **Total** | **9951** |

It is clear from the Table 2.4 that the highest number of militancy related killings were of Muslims recorded 8360 person out of total 9951. Kashmiri Pandits with 765 were the second in terms of militancy related killing, while Hindus 554, Sikhs 259, foreigners 11.

**Table 2.5:** Number of Killings by Militants (1986-1997)

| | |
|---|---|
| Kashmiri Pandits | 430 |
| Muslims | 3478 |
| Hindus | 233 |
| Sikhs | 111 |
| Christians | — |
| Buddhists | — |
| Foreigners | 1 |
| **Total** | **4253** |

Table 2.5 shows that Muslims are the in highest numbers to be killed by militants recorded 3478 out of total 4253 persons. While Kashmiri

Pandits killed by the militants were 430, Hindus 233 and Sikhs 111. While only one foreigner was killed by militants.

**Table 2.6:** Number of cross firing Casualties (1986-1997)

| | |
|---|---|
| Kashmiri Pandits | — |
| Muslims | 1424 |
| Hindus | 3 |
| Sikhs | 40 |
| Christians | — |
| Buddhists | — |
| Foreigners | 1 |
| **Total** | **1468** |

It is clear from Table 2.6 that out of total 1468 cross-firing casualties, Muslims with 1424 were the highest to be recorded, while all other religious groups have either very low or even no cross-firing causalties to be recorded.

**Table 2.7:** Number of Bomb Blast Casualties (1986-1997)

| | |
|---|---|
| Kashmiri Pandits | 5 |
| Muslims | 248 |
| Hindus | 73 |
| Sikhs | 25 |
| Christians | 2 |
| Buddhists | — |
| Foreigners | — |
| **Total** | **353** |

In case of Bomb Blast Causalties also the ratio of Muslims recorded highest having 248 out of total 353 cases, while Hindus 73, Sikhs 25 and Pandits 5 were on the second, third and fourth number respectively.

**Table 2.8**: Number of Dead Bodies Recovered (1986-1997)

| | |
|---|---|
| Kashmiri Pandits | 88 |
| Muslims | 1075 |
| Hindus | 43 |
| Sikhs | 8 |
| Christians | — |
| Buddhists | — |
| Foreigners | — |
| **Total** | **1214** |

Muslims were of the highest numbered (1075) out of the total 1214 dead bodies recovered during this period. Kashmiri Pandits with 88 were the second and Hindus with 43 and Sikhs 8 were on the third and fourth number.

**Table 2.9:** Number of Deaths due to Critical Injuries (1986-1997)

| | |
|---|---|
| Kashmiri Pandits | 60 |
| Muslims | 573 |
| Hindus | 43 |
| Sikhs | 9 |
| Christians | — |
| Buddhists | — |
| Foreigners | — |
| **Total** | **685** |

Number of deaths due to critical injuries were the highest among the Muslims, i.e. 573 out of the total 685, where as Kashmiri Pandits with 60 cases and Hindus with 43 were on the second and third respectively. There was no such case recorded among the Christian, Buddhists and Foreigner.

**Table 2.10:** Number of Rape Victims Killed (1986-1997)

| | |
|---|---|
| Kashmiri Pandits | 22 |
| Muslims | 352 |
| Hindus | 16 |
| Sikhs | 44 |
| Christians | — |
| Buddhists | — |
| Foreigners | — |
| **Total** | **434** |

Out of the total 434 rape victims killed the highest were of Muslims 352. While among other religion Sikhs with 44 were on the second, Kashmiri Pandits with 22 on the third, Hindus with 16 person on the forth respectively. There were no such case recorded among Christen, Buddhists and Foreigners.

**Table 2.11**: Number of Kidnapped Victims Killed (1986-1997)

| | |
|---|---|
| Kashmiri Pandits | 124 |
| Muslims | 885 |
| Hindus | 109 |
| Sikhs | 16 |
| Christians | — |
| Buddhists | — |
| Foreigners | 08 |
| **Total** | **1142** |

In case of kidnapped victims killed from 1986-1997, out of total 1142 cases Muslims were the highest which recorded 885, whereas Kashmiri Pandits kidnapped victims killed were 124, Hindus 109, and Sikhs 16. It is also interesting to note that among the kidnapped victims killed, there were 8 foreigners too.

**Table 2.12:** Number of Brutal Killing (1986-1997)

| | |
|---|---|
| Kashmiri Pandits | 10 |
| Muslims | 69 |
| Hindus | 21 |
| Sikhs | — |
| Christians | — |
| Buddhists | — |
| Foreigners | 1 |
| **Total** | **101** |

Table 2.12 depicts that 69 out of the total 101 Brutal killing cases by militants were of the Muslims. In this case Hindus were on the second number with 21 persons, Kashmiri Pandits on the third with 10 persons and 01 foreigner also included among this type of killing.

**Table 2.13:** Number of Deaths due to Strangulation (1986-1997)

| | |
|---|---|
| Kashmiri Pandits | 8 |
| Muslims | 72 |
| Hindus | 2 |
| Sikhs | 4 |
| Christians | — |
| Buddhists | — |
| Foreigners | — |
| **Total** | **86** |

Among the number of deaths due to strangulation also Muslims recorded highest. In this type of killing of the total 86 cases 72 were Muslims, where as 8 Kashmiri Pandits, 4 Sikhs and only 2 cases of Hindus strangulation deaths were recorded. There was no such case of death among the other groups such as Christian, Buddhists and Foreigners.

**Table 2.14:** Number of Deaths due to Hanging (1986-1997)

| | |
|---|---|
| Kashmiri Pandits | 18 |
| Muslims | 147 |
| Hindus | 9 |
| Sikhs | 2 |
| Christians | — |
| Buddhists | — |
| Foreigners | 1 |
| **Total** | **177** |

Muslims were the highest sufferers among the deaths due to hanging. The number of Muslims in this type of killing were 147 out of the total 177 cases. Whereas Kashmiri Pandits killed due to hanging were 18, Hindus 9 and only 2 Sikhs were hanged to death. Only one foreigner was hanged to death during this period.

**Table 2.15:** Number of Victims Burnt to Death (1986-1997)

| | |
|---|---|
| Kashmiri Pandits | — |
| Muslims | 37 |
| Hindus | 2 |
| Sikhs | — |
| Christians | — |
| Buddhists | — |
| Foreigners | — |
| **Total** | **39** |

The cases of burnt to death were the lowest among all type of killing due to militancy related problems. Muslims here are also outnumbered, while negligible cases were recorded among other religious groups.

**Table 2.16:** Number of Rape Cases (1986-1997)

| | |
|---|---|
| Kashmiri Pandits | 18 |
| Muslims | 16029 |
| Hindus | 70 |
| Sikhs | 86 |
| Christians | — |
| Buddhists | — |
| Foreigners | 1 |
| **Total** | **16204** |

Out of the total rape cases 16029 were the Muslim women to be victims out of the total 16204. It is clear from the table that Muslim women are the highest sufferers among all the religious groups. Sikh women with 86 were on the second number, while Hindus with 70, Kashmiri Pandits with 18 and foreigner 1 are on the second, third, fourth, and fifth number respectively.

**Table 2.17:** Number of Critically Wounded Cases (1986-1997)

| | |
|---|---|
| Kashmiri Pandits | 108 |
| Muslims | 3058 |
| Hindus | 638 |
| Sikhs | 56 |
| Christians | 1 |
| Buddhists | 2 |
| Foreigners | 3 |
| **Total** | **3866** |

It is clear from Table 2.17 that number of critically wounded cases were recorded highest among the Muslims 3058 persons out of the total 3866. The second highest critically wounded were Hindus which were 638. The other critically wounded cases were 108 Kashmiri Pandits, 56 Sikhs, 3 foreigners, 2 Buddhists, and only one Christian were recorded among the critically wounded cases.

**Table 2.18:** Number of Wounded Victims (1986-1997)

| | |
|---|---|
| Kashmiri Pandits | 30 |
| Muslims | 3255 |
| Hindus | 4 |
| Sikhs | 13 |
| Christians | 2 |
| Buddhists | — |
| Foreigners | — |
| **Total** | **3304** |

The number of wounded victims was also highest among the Muslims which were 3255 of the total 3304 persons. The other religions cover 30 Kashmiri Pandits, 13 Sikhs, 4 Hindus and 2 Christians. There was no case of wounded victims among the Buddhists and Foreigners.

**Table 2.19:** Number of Kidnappings (1986-1997)

| | |
|---|---|
| Kashmiri Pandits | 66 |
| Muslims | 659 |
| Hindus | 204 |
| Sikhs | 61 |
| Christians | — |
| Buddhists | — |
| Foreigners | 10 |
| **Total** | **1000** |

Out of the total kidnapping cases 659 were the Muslims of the total 1000. 204 were Hindus, 66 were Kashmiri Pandits and 61 were Sikhs and the foreigners were 10 out of the total 1000 persons.

**Table 2.20:** Number of Kidnapped Victims Released/Rescued/Escaped (1986-1997)

| | |
|---|---|
| Kashmiri Pandits | 10 |
| Muslims | 260 |
| Hindus | 104 |
| Sikhs | 17 |
| Christians | — |
| Buddhists | — |
| Foreigners | 06 |
| **Total** | **397** |

The total number of the kidnapped victims released/rescued or escaped during this period were 397. Out of which 260 were the Muslims, 104 were Hindus, 17 were Sikhs, 10 were Kashmiri Pandits and 6 were foreigners.

**Table 2.21:** Number of Missing Persons (1986-1997)

| | |
|---|---|
| Kashmiri Pandits | 56 |
| Muslims | 400 |
| Hindus | 100 |
| Sikhs | 44 |
| Christians | — |
| Buddhists | — |
| Foreigners | 04 |
| **Total** | **604** |

Out of the total 604 cases of missing, Muslims were more than 400. In this category 100 Hindus were also recorded, while the number of missing Kashmiri Pandits was 56, Sikh 44 and 4 Foreigners.

Thus it is clear from the above discussion that only Muslim religious group is the highest victims of atrocities.

**Chronology of Kashmir Freedom Movement**

- Chronology 1924-1947
- Chronology 1948-1964
- Chronology 1965-1972
- Chronology 1973-1989
- Chronology 1990-1994
- Chronology 1995-1998

**October 1924** Muslim notables in Srinagar present a memorandum to the British Viceroy regarding the Maharaja's misrule and setting forth popular demands. This is a sequel to a labour strike in the state-run silk factory in which the workers were charged by troops commanded by Hari Singh, then the heir apparent, and their leader tortured to death.

**March 1925** The leader of the signatories to the memorandum, Saaduddin Shawl, is deported from the State.

**April 1925** First meeting in Lahore (now in Pakistan) of Kashmiri expatriates and other Muslim leaders to muster support for the reformist struggle in Kashmir.

**March 1929** Albion Bannerji, a Bengali Christian, resigns as the Maharaja's Prime Minister makes a public statement: "The large Muslim population is governed like dumb-driven cattle... the press is non-existent... the economic conditions are appalling."

**April 1931** A police official stops the *khutba* or sermon at a congregational religious service of Muslims in Jammu on the ground that it alludes to the Quranic passages about Moses and the Pharaoh and thus indirectly advocates sedition. It was protested by worshippers in Jammu led by Ghulam Abbas in Srinagar and major towns.

**June 1931** At a large public meeting in Srinagar, 11 representatives are chosen to conduct a movement against the Maharaja's repression: these include Sheikh Abdullah, Ghulam Abbas, Saaduddin Shawl and Mirwaiz Muhammad Yusuf Shah.

**13 July 1931** Unarmed Muslims gather at Srinagar jail demanding right to attend trial being held in camera of a political prisoner charged with sedition for speech at June meeting. Police firing leaves 21 dead. Beginning of mass agitation Ghulam Abbas arrested the same day, Sheikh Abdullah the next, along with three other leaders.

**July-August 1931** Maharaja's government claims that popular movement is instigated by "outside elements" and announces policy of not permitting speeches creating hatred against the regime. Leaders released on condition of "good behaviour".

**August 1931** All India Kashmir Committee formed in Lahore to organise support for Kashmir freedom movement. Led by Muhammad Iqbal, renowned poet-philosopher and Bashiruddin Mahmud, head of the Ahmediyya community. Meanwhile, All India Muslim League adopts resolution commending "the gallant struggle carried on both inside and outside Kashmir for rights of humanity in the State".

**September 1931** Kashmir leaders rearrested. On 24 September, large number of young men parade in the streets of Srinagar armed with spears and knives— "this is all we have and we will fight the Maharaja's soldiers". Maharaja responds by display of military armour in the city the next day. Law promulgated providing for flogging as punishment for political activity. Ordinary citizens bludgeoned by soldiers if they fail to shout '*Maharaja ki jai*' — victory to the Maharaja.

**In October 1931** British Viceroy urges Maharaja to adopt conciliatory policy. Leaders released and asked to present demands, which they do on 19 October. *Excerpts*: "We demand same liberties as obtain in British India... equality of rights regardless of religion... better terms for labour... a representative form of government... the State cannot claim proprietary rights over land merely because Kashmir was purchased from the British." November 1931—January 1932 No tax campaign in Mirpur. Armed encounters in Kotli between Maharaja's soldiers and local militants. Collapse of Maharaja's administration in areas now in Azad Kashmir. British Indian government intervenes, moves troops to Jammu and Mirpur. A Muslim political party in Punjab—Jamaat-i-Ahrar—launches movement for unarmed "civil invasion" of the State. Around 30,000 people arrested to prevent crossing of border. Meanwhile, on British urging, a Reforms Commission is appointed, headed by a British official (Douglas Glancey) and consisting of four public representatives: two Muslim (including Ghulam Abbas), and two Hindu (including Prem Nath Bazaz). Commission recommends limited reforms, including establishment of legislative assembly. Kashmiri Pandits denounce their representative, Prem Nath Bazaz, for supporting reforms. Hindu newspapers in India condemn movement in Kashmir as evidence of "dishonourable Muslim communalism". A delegation of Hindu leaders in India meets Viceroy stressing the strategic importance of Kashmir to India against a "pan-Islamic wave".

**October 1932** First mass organisation in the State — the Jammu and Kashmir Muslim Conference—established. At session in Srinagar, Sheikh Abdullah elected President and Ghulam Abbas General Secretary.

**In January 1934** Mass protests against limitation of franchise to three per cent of the population for proposed legislative assembly and restrictions on assembly's powers. At meeting of Muslim Conference held in Sialkot (now in Pakistan) Ghulam Abbas designated "dictator" of the campaign. Abdullah distances himself from the campaign. Abbas arrested.

**In September 1934**, State legislative assembly established by Maharaja. Muslims constituting 77 per cent of population allotted 32 seats in a house of 75, out of which 21 to be elected and 11 nominated by Maharaja. Muslim Conference captures 20 seats.

**October 1935** Abbas elected President of Muslim Conference. With Hindu leaders attending as observers at annual convention, Abbas appeals to non-Muslims "to join in the struggle for emancipation of our country". Muslim Conference members of State Assembly (19 out of 21 elected members) resign in protest against Assembly's restricted powers.

**May 1936** M.A. Jinnah visits Srinagar. Though visit private, both factions of Muslim Conference (led respectively by Abdullah and Mirwaiz Yusuf Shah) invite him to address large public meetings organized in his honor. Jinnah counsels promoting harmony between Muslim majority and Hindu minority.

**September 1937** Abdullah again elected President of Muslim Conference. Urges "a common platform" of Muslims and non-Muslims and demands that State representatives to the Indian federation (contemplated in Government of India Act of 1935 before the demand for the establishment of a separate federation of Muslim majority states—Pakistan—was formulated by M.A. Jinnah in 1940) be chosen by the people and not nominated by the Maharaja.

**In June 1938** Working Committee of Muslim Conference recommends change in name and constitution of party. Abbas opposes move which is deferred for one year.

**October 1939** Special session of Muslim Conference decides to convert party into National Conference. Abbas endorses move on conditions that, *inter alia*, (a) it will not mean affiliation with Indian National Congress against Muslim League; (b) non-Muslims will participate in campaign for representative government; and (c) Conference will continue to seek end of discrimination against Muslims. Some prominent Hindu leaders, including Prem Nath Bazaz, join National Conference but Hindu masses keep aloof.

Maharaja's Prime Minister, Gopalaswamy Ayyangar—a Hindu bureaucrat from Madras—promulgates constitution on 7 September, 1939 providing not only for Maharaja's unrestricted veto over legislative assembly's enactments but also for any enactment by Maharaja himself to be considered as if made by assembly. Abdullah establishes understanding with Ayyangar that, in return for refraining from any active campaign for responsible government, he will be supported in his fight against his political opponents—former leaders of Muslim Conference. On his advice, National Conference members abstain from vote on bill abolishing discrimination against Muslims in arms licences; Abdullah cultivates closer relations with Congress leaders, particularly Jawaharlal Nehru, criticizes Muslim League but later disclaims remarks.

**In 1940-41** Some Hindu leaders resign from National Conference alleging "oppressive communal atmosphere". Jawaharlal Nehru visits Kashmir (30 May, 1940) and appeals to Hindus to support National Conference and its struggle for responsible government. Enthusiastic welcome accorded to Nehru by Abdullah and his following is marred by hostile demonstrations by others. A handbill widely circulated by students asks 'Where were you, Mr. Nehru, in 1931? You claim to be a Kashmiri; how come you have been silent all through our testing struggle?' Gopalaswamy Ayyangar, Prime Minister since 1937, quits on 9 April, 1943. 'Deliverance Day' observed by dissident sections of National Conference. Bazaz, virtually co-founder with Abdullah, also resigns, expressing disillusionment. Abbas re-establishes Muslim Conference pleading as ground non-fulfilment of conditions set for conversion of party into National Conference. Protests against Ayyangar's statement that Kashmir would be first to accede to Indian Union.

**In 1944** National Conference issues radical manifesto called "new Kashmir" contemplating drastic social and economic measures. At the same time—as against Muslim Conference position of non-cooperation with Maharaja's government, agrees to inclusion of one nominee of National Conference in Maharaja's cabinet. M.A. Jinnah visits Kashmir on joint invitation of Muslim Conference and National Conference.

Attempts to bring about reconciliation, advises maintaining single Muslim representative organization which, on the basis of full safeguards for rights of non-Muslim minorities, should arrive at an "honorable" settlement with their representative.

# 3

# Human Resources Development of Kashmir Valley

## Human Resources Development – Deprivation and Peace Prospect

Human resources—a term used to describe the individuals who comprise the workforce of an organization, although it is also applied in labour economics too, for example, business sectors or even whole nations. Human resources is also the name of the function within an organization charged with the overall responsibility for implementing strategies and policies relating to the management of individuals (i.e. the human resources). This function title is often abbreviated to the initials.

Human resources are a relatively modern management term, coined in the 1960s. The origins of the function arose in organizations that introduced 'welfare management' practices and also in those that adopted the principles of 'scientific management'. From these terms emerged a largely administrative management activity, co-ordinating a range of worker related processes and becoming known, in time as the 'personnel function'. Human resources progressively became the more usual name for this function, in the first instance in the United States as well as multinational corporations, reflecting the adoption of a more quantitative as well as strategic approach to workforce management, demanded by corporate management and the greater competitiveness for limited and highly skilled workers.

In organizations, it is important to determine both current and future organizational requirements for both core employees and the contingent workforce in terms of their skills/technical abilities, competencies, flexibility, etc. The analysis requires consideration of the internal and external factors that can have an effect on the resourcing, development, motivation and retention of employees and other workers. In Kashmir Valley the educated youth are wandering on the roads from morning till evening they could not get any job. This leads to the unrest among the youth in Kashmir Valley. The manpower is available in abundance but not fully utilized in that particular part. Besides, the corruption which is main hindrance in the development of the human resource in the Kashmir Valley. Corruption is in every section of administration as well as in every sphere of life which make a great unrest among the youths.

External factors are those largely out with the control of the organization. These include issues such as economic climate and current and future labour market trends (e.g., skills, education level, government investment into industries etc.). On the other hand, internal influences are broadly controlled by the organization to predict, determine, and monitor for example the organizational culture, underpinned by management style, environmental climate, and the approach to ethical and corporate social responsibilities. In Kashmir Valley there is lack of private sector, the government could not help to established the private firms for generation of employment this also leads the barrier in the development of human resources in Kashmir Valley. The most important industry which is smokeless and needs less infrastructure and capital to develop is not full developed and less attention where given by government bodies for further development. Besides, this the abundant sources of water bodies are found in the Valley of Kashmir which generate the hydroelectricity not only for India but also for surrounding countries for export but that is also not fully developed. Only due to the political system and corruption these sectors are not fully developed.

## Growth of Population and Religious Distribution

The State has registered a net addition of 13.71 lakh persons raising the population from 46.16 lakh in 1971 to 59.87 lakh in 1981 and today (2011) it is about 55 lakh alone in Kashmir Valley. The state population contributes less than one per cent of the country's population. Nevertheless, the rate of growth observed during the last two decades at 29.65 and 29.69 per cent has been substantially higher than the national growth rates of 24.80 and 25 per cent respectively. Thus, the decadal growth rate of population in the state that was around 10 per cent in the preceding three decades has almost trebled in the last two decades. The annual growth rate of 2.97 per cent during 1971-81 is the highest the state has ever experienced.

### *Religious Distribution of Population*

Jammu and Kashmir is the only state in India that has a Muslim majority population. Though Islam is practiced by about 67 per cent of the population of the state and by 97 per cent of the population of the Kashmir Valley, the state has large communities of Buddhists, Hindus and Sikhs. In Jammu, Hindus constitute 65 per cent of the population, Muslims 31 per cent and Sikhs 4 per cent; In Ladakh, Buddhists constitute about 46 per cent of the population, the remaining being Muslims.

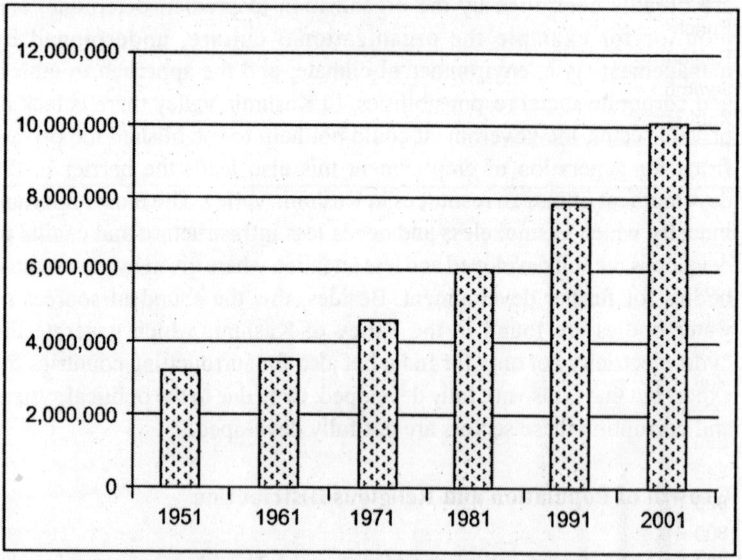


**Fig. 3.1:** Population Growth 1951-2001

The people of Ladakh are of Indo-Tibetan origin, while the southern area of Jammu includes many communities tracing their ancestry to the nearby Indian states of Haryana and Punjab, as well as the city of Delhi. In totality, the Muslims constitute 67 per cent of the population, the Hindus about 30 per cent, the Buddhists 1 per cent, and the Sikhs 2 per cent of the population. Vaishno Devi temple located in the state is one of the holiest Hindu temples dedicated to Shakti.

**Table 3.1:** Sex-wise Distribution of Population in Jammu & Kashmir

| *Districts* | *Male* | *Female* |
|---|---|---|
| Kupwara | 3,41,303 | 3,09,090 |
| Baramula | 6,41,816 | 5,54,964 |
| Srinagar | 6,49,491 | 5,52,956 |
| Badgam | 3,26,050 | 3,03,259 |
| Pulwama | 3,35,544 | 3,17,063 |
| Anantnag | 6,10,007 | 5,62,427 |
| Leh | 64,306 | 52,926 |
| Kargil | 64,955 | 54,352 |
| Doda | 3,63,526 | 3,28,403 |
| Udhampur | 3,99,686 | 3,43,823 |
| Punch | 1,94,213 | 1,78,400 |
| Rajauri | 2,57,336 | 2,25,948 |
| Jammu | 8,50,302 | 7,38,470 |
| Kathua | 2,89,391 | 2,60,693 |

**Fig. 3.2:** Sex-wise Distribution of Population in Jammu & Kashmir

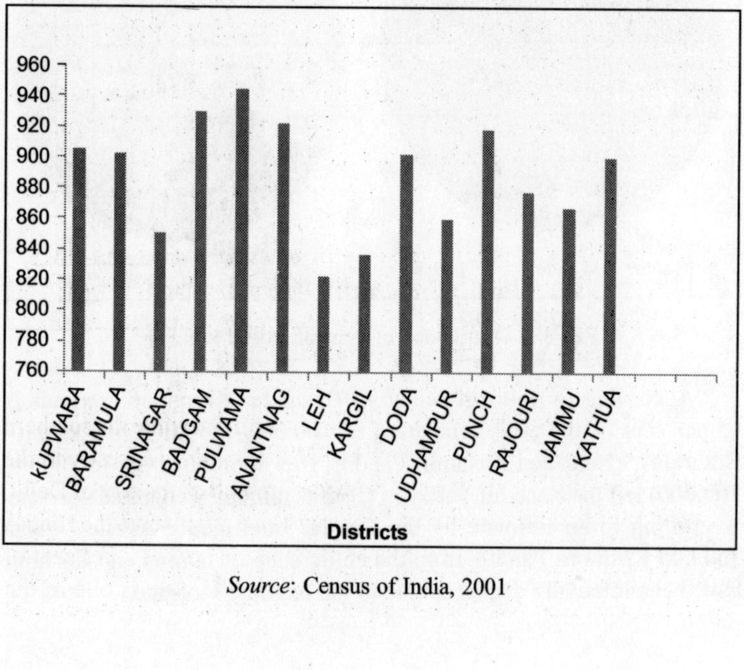


*Source*: Census of India, 2001

**Table 3.2:** Distribution of Population on Religion Basis

| *Division* | *Population* | *% Muslim* | *% Hindu* | *% Sikh* | *% Buddhist/ Other* |
|---|---|---|---|---|---|
| Kashmir (53.9%) | 5,476,970 | 97.16% | 1.84% | 0.88% | 0.11% |
| Jammu (43.7%) | 4,430,191 | 30.69% | 65.23% | 3.57% | 0.51% |
| Ladakh (2.3%) | 236,539 | 47.40% | 6.22% | – | 45.87% |
| Jammu & Kashmir | 10,143,700 | 66.97% | 29.63% | 2.03% | 1.36% |

*Note*: There are roughly 1.5 million refugees from Indian Administered Kashmir in Azad Kashmir and Pakistan. An estimated 50,000-100,000 Kashmiri Muslims and 150-300,000 Kashmiri Pandits have been internally displaced due to militancy.

*Source*: Statistics calculated from the 2001 Census of India District Profiles.

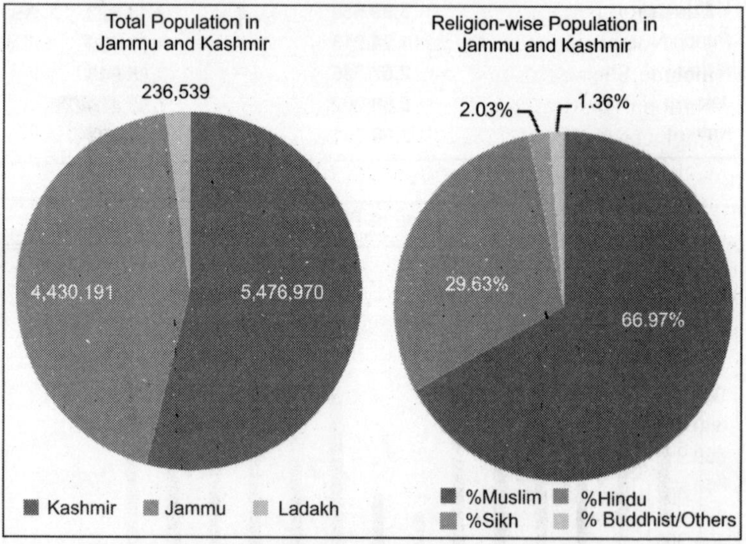


**Fig. 3.3:** Distribution of Population and Religion

According to political scientist Alexander Evans, approximately 95 per cent of the total population of 160,000—170,000 of Kashmiri Brahmins, also called Kashmiri Pandits, (i.e. approximately 150,000 to 160,000) left the Kashmir Valley in 1990 as militancy engulfed the state. According to an estimate by the Central Intelligence Agency, about 300,000 Kashmiri Pandits from the entire state of Jammu and Kashmir have been internally displaced due to the ongoing violence.

**Educational Status**

In 1970, the state government of Jammu and Kashmir established its own education board and university. Education in the state is divided into primary, middle, higher secondary, college and university level. Jammu and Kashmir follows 10+2 pattern for education of children. This is handled by Jammu and Kashmir State Board of School Education (abbreviated as JKBOSE). Various private and public schools are recognized by the board to impart education to students. Board examinations are conducted for students in Class VIII, X and XII. In addition there are various Kendriya Vidyalayas (run by the Government of India) and Indian Army schools that also impart secondary school education. These schools follow the Central Board of Secondary Education pattern.

Notable higher education or research institutes in Jammu and Kashmir include Sher-e-Kashmir Institute of Medical Sciences, Soura, Srinagar, National Institute of Technology, Srinagar, Government College of Engineering and Technology of Jammu and the Government Medical College of Jammu. University-level education is provided by University of Jammu, University of Kashmir, Sher-e-Kashmir University of Agricultural Sciences and Technology of Jammu, Sher-e-Kashmir University of Agricultural Sciences and Technology of Kashmir, Shri Mata Vaishno Devi University, Islamic University of Science & Technology, and Baba Ghulam Shah Badhshah University.

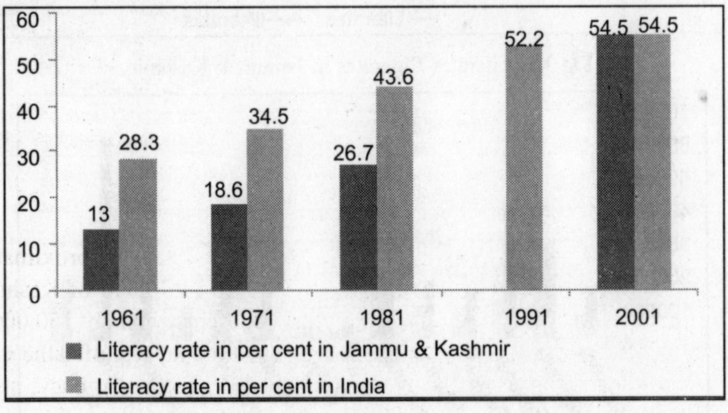


**Fig. 3.4:** Literacy Rate–India & Jammu & Kashmir

**Table 3.3:** District-wise Literacy Distribution

| *Districts* | *Literates* | *Illiterates* | *Districts* | *Literates* | *Illiterates* |
|---|---|---|---|---|---|
| Kupwara | 232557 | 417836 | Kargil | 60803 | 58504 |
| Baramula | 447075 | 722705 | DODA | 274425 | 417504 |
| Srinagar | 641267 | 561180 | Udhampur | 343429 | 400080 |
| Badgam | 226167 | 403142 | Punch | 156398 | 216215 |
| Pulwama | 281518 | 371089 | Rajouri | 234228 | 249056 |
| Anantnag | 463197 | 709237 | Jammu | 1070574 | 518198 |
| Leh | 68248 | 480954 | Kathua | 307370 | 242714 |

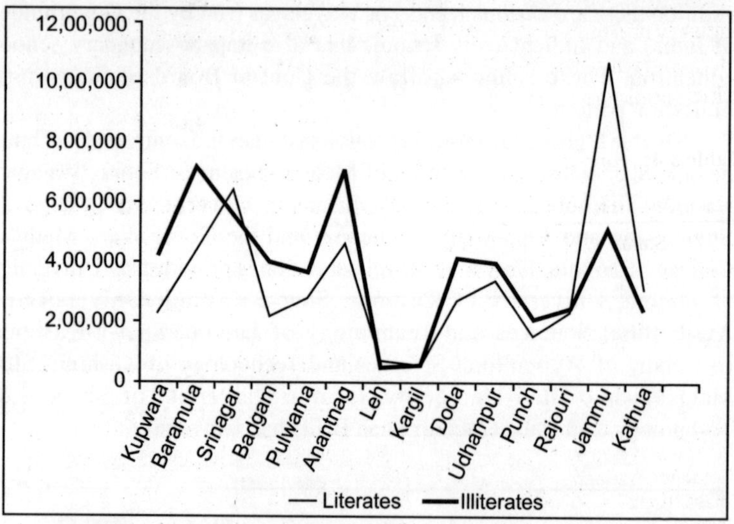


**Fig 3.5:** Literates-Illiterates in Jammu & Kashmir

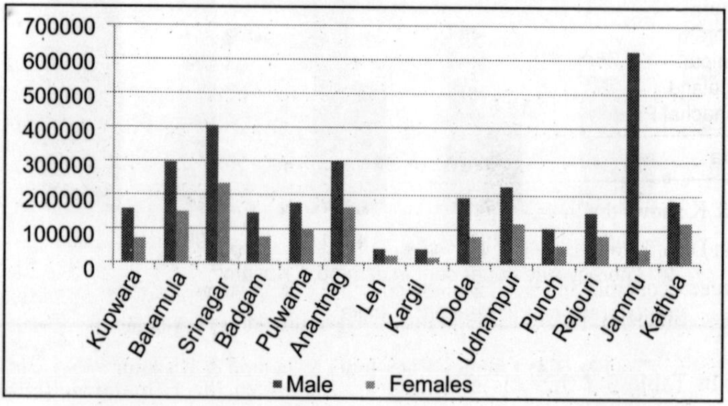


**Fig. 3.6:** Sex-wise Literacy Distribution—Jammu & Kashmir

## Human Development Index of Himalayan States of India

The Human Development Index (HDI) is a summary measure of human resource development. It measures the average achievements in a country in three basic dimensions of human development, viz. healthy life, knowledge and standard of living. These three quality measures are supported by quantitative parametres such as life expectancy at birth, literacy/education and per capita GDP respectively.

Apart from the below, many other indicators of development such as gender disparity, socio-economy, urban settlements, economic growth, industry and commerce, workforce, eco-tourism, micro credits and yield of foodgrains, etc., also depict stages of human resource development, which could be assessed from Tables 3.4 and 3.5.

**Table 3.4:** Human development indicators in the Himalayan Region States and State of J & K

| *States* | *Female workers Participation Rate* | *Literacy percentage#* | | | *Infant Mortality Rate* | *Per capita income at current prices (Rs.) (p)* |
|---|---|---|---|---|---|---|
| | | *Males* | *Females* | *Total* | | |
| | | | *2001* | | *2000-01* | |
| Jammu and Kashmir | 21.96 | 65.75 | 41.82 | 54.46 | 50 | 12399 |
| Himachal Pradesh | 43.69 | 86.02 | 68.08 | 77.13 | 60 | 18920 |
| Uttarakhand | 27.09 | 84.01 | 60.26 | 72.28 | 50 | N.A |
| Sikkim | 38.59 | 76.73 | 61.46 | 69.68 | 49 | 15550 |
| Meghalaya | 35.02 | 66.14 | 60.41 | 63.31 | 58 | 13114 |
| Tripura | 21.02 | 81.47 | 65.41 | 73.66 | 41 | 14348 |
| Mizoram | 47.63 | 90.69 | 86.13 | 88.49 | 21 | N.A. |
| Manipur | 40.51 | 77.87 | 59.70 | 68.87 | 23 | N.A. |
| Nagaland | 38.25 | 71.77 | 61.92 | 67.11 | N.A. | N.A. |
| Arunachal Pradesh | 36.45 | 64.07 | 44.24 | 54.74 | 44 | 14587 |
| **India** | **25.65** | **75.85** | **54.16** | **65.38** | **68** | **16072** |

# J & K shows the lowest figures.

*Note*: Data from Assam and West Bengal hills are not available.

*Source*: Economic Survey of Maharashtra 2002-03, Directorate of Economic and Statistics, Planning Department, Government of Maharashtra.

In Table 3.4 there is a comparison between the Himalayan states with Jammu and Kashmir because both the regions have the same

**Table 3.5:** Ranking of Some selective Indicators of Human Development Index, 2001

| S. No | States | Growth Rate 1991-2001 | Density of Population | % of urban pop. | Total Literacy Rate | Female Literacy Rate | Sum of Ranks | Human development index |
|---|---|---|---|---|---|---|---|---|
| 1. | Andhra Pradesh | 3 | 13.5 | 10 | 22 | 20 | 68.5 | 48.93 |
| 2. | Arunachal Pradesh | 19 | 28 | 19 | 25 | 24 | 115 | 82.14 |
| 3. | Assam | 11 | 9 | 25 | 18 | 18 | 81 | 57.86 |
| 4. | Bihar | 22 | 2 | 27 | 28 | 28 | 106 | 76.42 |
| 5. | Chhattisgarh | 10 | 20 | 20 | 17 | 19 | 86 | 61.43 |
| 6. | Goa | 4 | 8 | 1 | 3 | 3 | 19 | 13.57 |
| 7. | Gujarat | 14 | 15 | 5 | 9 | 15 | 58 | 41.43 |
| 8. | Haryana | 20 | 7 | 8 | 14 | 17 | 66 | 47.14 |
| 9. | Himachal Pradesh | 8 | 22 | 28 | 5 | 4 | 67 | 47.86 |
| **10.** | **Jammu & Kashmir** | **23** | **25** | **14** | **26** | **26** | **114** | **81.43** |
| 11. | Jharkhand | 16 | 10 | 17 | 27 | 27 | 97 | 69.29 |
| 12. | Karnataka | 7 | 13.5 | 6 | 16 | 16 | 58.5 | 41.79 |
| 13. | Kerala | 1 | 3 | 12 | 1 | 1 | 18 | 12.86 |
| 14. | Madhya Pradesh | 17 | 17 | 11 | 19 | 22 | 86 | 61.43 |
| 15. | Maharashtra | 15 | 11 | 4 | 4 | 5 | 39 | 27.86 |
| 16. | Manipur | 26 | 23 | 15 | 13 | 14 | 91 | 65.00 |
| 17. | Meghalaya | 25 | 24 | 21 | 21 | 11 | 102 | 72.86 |
| 18. | Mizoram | 24 | 27 | 2 | 2 | 2 | 57 | 40.71 |
| 19. | Nagaland | 28 | 21 | 22 | 15 | 9 | 95 | 67.86 |
| 20. | Orissa | 6 | 16 | 24 | 20 | 21 | 87 | 62.14 |
| 21. | Punjab | 13 | 5 | 7 | 10 | 8 | 43 | 30.71 |
| 22. | Rajasthan | 21 | 18 | 16 | 23 | 23 | 102 | 72.14 |
| 23. | Sikkim | 27 | 26 | 26 | 11 | 10 | 100 | 71.43 |
| 24. | Tamil Nadu | 2 | 6 | 3 | 7 | 7 | 25 | 17.86 |
| 25. | Tripura | 5 | 12 | 23 | 6 | 6 | 52 | 37.14 |
| 26. | Uttaranchal | 12 | 19 | 13 | 8 | 12 | 64 | 45.71 |
| 27. | Uttar Pradesh | 18 | 4 | 18 | 24 | 25 | 89 | 63.57 |
| 28. | West Bengal | 9 | 1 | 9 | 12 | 13 | 44 | 31.43 |

*Source*: 2005 world population data sheet of Population Reference Bureau, Washington.

physiographic, topography and same other physical features. The first human development indicator which we take into account is women work participation. The female workers participation in Jammu and Kashmir is below National Average. The national average is 25.65 per cent while in Jammu and Kashmir only 21.96 per cent female workers participation rate is found while the surrounding states like Himachal Pradesh and Uttarakhand are having more female workers participation as compared even to national average. Besides this only Tripura has below national average female work participation in Himalayan region.

Among these major indicators of socio-economic development Jammu and Kashmir State's ranking is one of the lowest which shows the major cause of realizing the lower status (Socio-economic). The sense of awareness is not desirable for a healthy attachment with nation. Even per head income as compared to all the mountain states of India is lowest in spite of a very high potential for generating the income and employment.

The another basic important indicator of Human Development is literacy rate and it has been found from Table 3.6 that only Jammu and Kashmir and Arunachal Pradesh are having both female as well as male literacy rate below national average. Besides this the per capita income is also lowest in Jammu and Kashmir as compared with the states listed in Table 3.4

Table 3.6 shows the gender disparity index in 1991 of the states of the Himalayan region and which is compared with the India. The Table 3.7

**Table 3.6:** HDI and Gender Disparity Index (1991) in the States of the Himalayan Region and State of J & K

| *State* | *Rural* | *Urban* | *Combined* | *Gender disparity index* |
|---|---|---|---|---|
| Jammu and Kashmir | 0.364 | 0.575 | 0.402 | 0.740 |
| Himachal Pradesh | 0.442 | 0.700 | 0.469 | 0.858 |
| Sikkim | 0.398 | 0.618 | 0.425 | 0.647 |
| Meghalaya | 0.332 | 0.624 | 0.365 | 0.807 |
| Tripura | 0.368 | 0.551 | 0.389 | 0.531 |
| Mizoram | 0.464 | 0.648 | 0.548 | 0.770 |
| Manipur | 0.503 | 0.618 | 0.536 | 0.815 |
| Nagaland | 0.442 | 0.633 | 0.486 | 0.729 |
| Arunachal Pradesh | 0.300 | 0.572 | 0.328 | 0.776 |
| **India** | **0.340** | **0.511** | **0.381** | **0.676** |

*Note*: Data for Uttarakhand and hills of Assam and West Bengal are not available.

*Source:* Rajya Sabha Unanswered Question No. 5459 dated 17.5.2002.

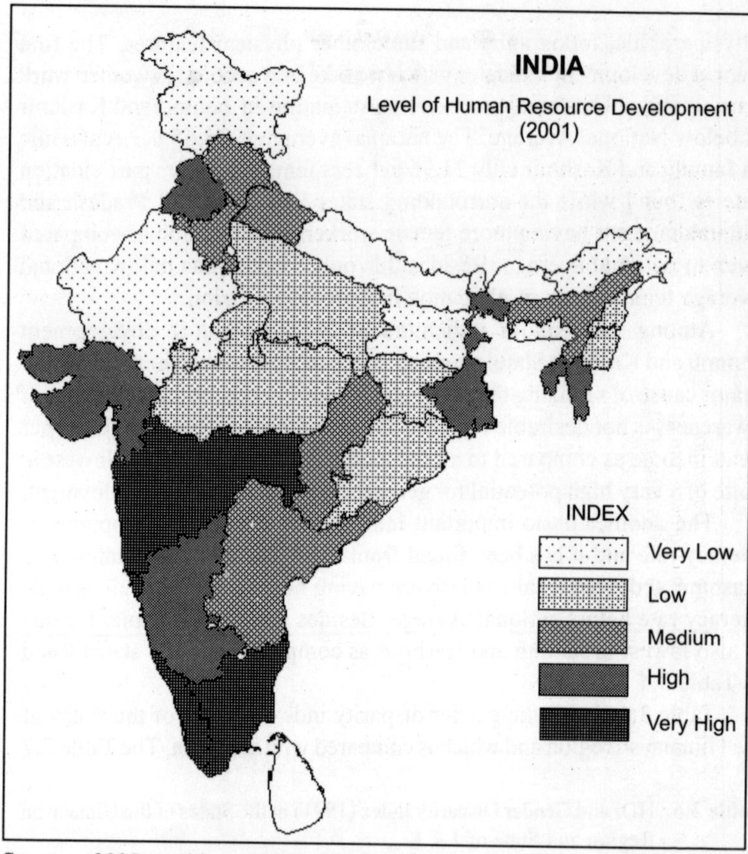


*Source*: 2005 world population data sheet of population reference bureau, Washington

**Fig. 3.7:** India—Level of Human Resource Development, 2001

shows the socio-economic indicators of Himalayan region states in which total population, sex ratio, urban population decennial growth of population and percentage of total workers and workers engaged in the agricultural sector.

In Jammu and Kashmir only 24.88 per cent population is urban remaining is rural. The sex ratio is lowest as compared to the other Himalayan region states. Only 25.19 per cent of main workers are engaged in work remaining population is unemployed and this leads to the disturbance and unrest among the youth which creates lot of other social

**Table 3.7:** Selected Socio-economic indicators of the Himalayan Region State and State of J & K

| *State* | *Population (in lakhs)* | *Density of population* | *% of urban population to total population* | *% of state population to all India population* | *Decennial growth rate of population (%) 1991-2001* | *Sex ratio* | *% of main workers to total population* | *% of Agricultural workers to total workers* |
|---|---|---|---|---|---|---|---|---|
| Jammu and Kashmir | 100.70 | 99 | 24.88 | 0.98 | 30.46 | 900 | 25.19 | 50.10 |
| Himachal Pradesh | 60.77 | 109 | 9.80 | 0.59 | 17.53 | 970 | 33.36 | 68.65 |
| Uttarakhand | 84.80 | 159 | 25.59 | 0.83 | 20.27 | 964 | 27.39 | 58.03 |
| Sikkim | 5.40 | 76 | 11.10 | 0.05 | 32.98 | 875 | 39.31 | 56.34 |
| West Bengal Hills | 16.06 | 510 | 34.44 | 0.16 | 23.54 | 943 | 29.73 | NA |
| Meghalaya | 23.06 | 103 | 19.63 | 0.22 | 29.94 | 975 | 32.21 | 65.89 |
| Assam Hills | 9.99 | 65 | 15.11 | 0.10 | 22.74 | 915 | 28.44 | 69.94 |
| Tripura | 31.91 | 304 | 17.02 | 0.31 | 15.74 | 950 | 28.41 | 50.92 |
| Mizoram | 8.91 | 42 | 49.50 | 0.09 | 29.18 | 938 | 40.83 | 59.77 |
| Manipur | 23.89 | 107 | 24.12 | 0.23 | 30.02 | 978 | 31.68 | 57.38 |
| Nagaland | 19.89 | 120 | 17,74 | 0.19 | 64.41 | 900 | 35.63 | 68.03 |
| Arunachal Pradesh | 10.91 | 13 | 20.34 | 0.11 | 26.21 | 901 | 37.71 | 62.30 |
| **India** | **10270.15** | **324** | **27.78** | **100** | **21.34** | **933** | **30.55** | **58.40** |

*Source:* Economic Survey of Maharashtra 2002-03, Directorate of Economic and Statistics, Planning Department, Government of Maharashtra.

and economic problems. Tripura and Jammu and Kashmir are only the states in this region where the total percentage of the agricultural workers is less as compared to the other states of this region.

## Rural/Urban Population and Settlements

Urbanization is a natural consequence of economic changes that take place as a country develops. At the same time, urbanization helps to contribute to the growth process at large. This is manifest in the increasing contribution of urban sector to national income. Although only about one-fourth of India's people live in towns and cities, more than 4,500 places are classified as urban. In general, the proportion is higher in the agriculturally prosperous regions of the northwest, west, and south than in the northeastern rice-growing parts of the country, where the population capacity is limited by generally meagre crop surpluses.

Table 3.8 shows that the number of towns in the Himalayan region states varies from state to state. The maximum towns are found in Uttarakhand and after that it is in Jammu and Kashmir. Besides the other states are having very less number of towns. There is also a variation in the type of towns. But the urbanization is the indicator of development and Jammu and Kashmir has second highest number of towns in Himalayan Region states.

### *Rural and Urban Population*

As against one-third in Maharashtra and West Bengal and one-fourth in Karnataka, only one-fifth of the population in J&K resides in urban areas. 23.83 per cent population has been recorded as urban in the state against the National Average of 25.72 per cent. Jammu city has recorded very rapid growth and presently ranks as the 48th biggest city in the country. Besides, the cities of Jammu and Srinagar, other important towns are the district headquarters of Anantnag, Pulwama, Budgam, Baramulla, Kupwara, Udhampur, Kathua, Rajouri, Poonch, Doda, Leh and Kargil. The remaining towns continue to have many rural features and pursuits reflecting the state's predominant Agro-pastoral economy.

## Major Trends of Human Resources in Kashmir Valley

To know the business environment an organization operates in, three major trends must be considered:

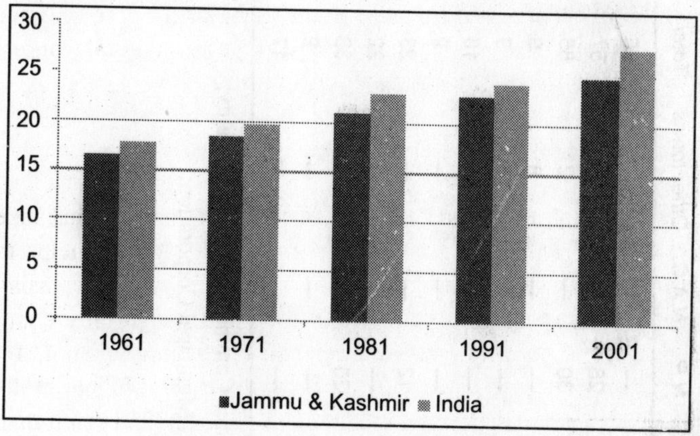


**Fig. 3.8:** Proportion of Urban Population

1. ***Demographics***: The characteristics of a population/workforce, for example, age, gender or social class. This type of trend may have an effect in relation to pension offerings, insurance packages etc.
2. ***Diversity***: The variation within the population/workplace. Changes in society now mean that a larger proportion of organizations are made up of "baby-boomers" or older employees in comparison to thirty years ago. Advocates of "workplace diversity" simply advocate an employee base that is a mirror reflection of the make-up of society in so far as race, gender, sexual orientation, etc.
3. ***Skills and Qualifications***: As industries move from manual to more managerial professions so does the need for more highly skilled graduates. If the market is "tight" (i.e., not enough staff for the jobs), employers must compete for employees by offering financial rewards, community investment, etc.

In the Valley of Kashmir the workforce according to the demographic character is abundant. Maximum workforce is in between the age of 17 and 35 years and abundant educated workforce is found but without getting any job. Or they are just wandering on the roads without earning a penny. This creates a great unrest among the youth.

Secondly, there is diversity in the youth population in the sense of literacy rate and education system. Even the female literacy is good as compared with the other states of India. This means enough availability

**Table 3.8:** Number of towns in the Himalayan Region State (2001) and state of J & K

| *State/region* | *C.T.* | *C.B.* | *T.C.* | *M.C.* | *M.B.* | *M.Cl* | *M.* | *M. Corp.* | *N.P* | *N.A.C.* | *Other towns* | *Total* |
|---|---|---|---|---|---|---|---|---|---|---|---|---|
| Jammu and Kashmir | 2 | 2 | 5 | 3 | — | — | — | — | — | 63 | — | 75 |
| Himachal Pradesh | 1 | 7 | — | 4 | — | 16 | — | 1 | 28 | — | — | 57 |
| Uttarakhand | 12 | 9 | — | 32 | — | — | — | 1 | 30 | — | 2 | 86 |
| Sikkim | 1 | — | — | — | — | — | — | — | — | — | 8 | 9 |
| West Bengal Hills | — | — | — | — | — | — | 3 | 1 | — | 1 | 4 | 9 |
| Meghalaya | 6 | 1 | 3 | — | 4 | — | 2 | — | — | — | — | 16 |
| Assam Hills | — | — | 9 | — | — | — | — | — | — | — | — | 9 |
| Tripura | 10 | — | — | — | — | 1 | — | — | 12 | — | — | 23 |
| Mizoram | 21 | — | — | — | — | — | — | — | — | — | 1 | 22 |
| Manipur | 5 | — | — | — | — | 7 | — | — | 20 | — | 1 | 33 |
| Nagaland | 1 | — | 8 | — | — | — | — | — | — | — | — | 9 |
| Arunachal Pradesh | 17 | — | — | — | — | — | — | — | — | — | — | 17 |

C.T.: Census Town; C.B.: Cantonment Board/Cantonment; T.C.: Town Committee/Town Area Committee; M.: Municipality;
M.B.: Municipal Board; M.C.: Municipal Committee; M.Cl.: Municipal Council; M.Corp.: Municipal Corporation;
N.P.: Nagar Panchayat; N.A.C.: Notified Area Committee/Notified Area Council

*Source:* Census 2001.

of workforce is available but due to political injustice and corruption this leads to the handicapness in the development of the human resource in Kashmir Valley.

Thirdly, there is abundance of skilled workforce in every part of Kashmir Valley with diversity in every work, e.g. Craft, Shawls, Paper Machine, besides this lot of hand work is found in the Valley of Kashmir. But due to ignorance of the Government bodies and the corrupted political system totally eroded the skilled works in Kashmir Valley.

The state-wise absolute figures relating to total population and total workers for the years 1991-2001 can be seen in Table 3.9. It may be noted that, Uttarakhand, Jharkhand and Chhattisgarh have been included in the respective states from which these were carved out after the 1991 Census, to make the data pertaining to Uttar Pradesh, Bihar and Madhya Pradesh comparable.

From Table 3.9 it has pointed out that in 1991 the total workforce at all India level was 37.48 per cent while Jammu and Kashmir has the lowest per cent of workforce as 19.82. During the crisis period certain aids, packages were provided and new incentives were given to the people and in 2001 the workforce increased and reach up to 25. 21 per cent while the over all Indian is having 39. 20 per cent of workforce. Besides, this after analyzing the table Jammu and Kashmir is only the state where workforce out of total population is very less in both the decades. This injustice in the workforce was a big reason for the crisis in Kashmir.

## Employment Scenario in Jammu and Kashmir

Unemployment is one of the important social issues of serious concern in the present times, both at the national as well as state level. Jammu and Kashmir has been facing the problem of unemployment since long. The population of the state has increased from 59.87 lakh in 1981 to 101.44 lakh in 2001. The number of workers also recorded increase of about 39 per cent during the above said period but the share of main and marginal workers in the total workforce remained constant, further classification of the workers during 2001, shows that 42.40 per cent of the total workers are cultivators, 6.56 per cent are agricultural labourers and the remaining 51.04 per cent are engaged in other activities including the household industries. Female workers constitute 28.61 per cent of the total workforce.

In Jammu and Kashmir employment exchange maintain qualification-wise data of unemployment persons who register themselves with these exchanges and also make possible efforts for their placements. As on the

**Table 3.9**: State-wise Distribution of Population and Workforce, 1991-2001

| Sl. No. | States | *State-wise distribution of Population and Workforce 1991-2001* | | | | | |
|---|---|---|---|---|---|---|---|
| | | *Total Population (1991)* | *Total Workforce (1991)* | *% age of workforce* | *Total Population (2001)* | *Total Workforce (2001)* | *% of work-force* |
| 1. | Andhra Pradesh | 66,508,008 | 29,963,648 | 45.05 | 76,210,007 | 34,893,859 | 45.78 |
| 2. | Arunachal Pradesh | 864,558 | 399,782 | 46.24 | 1,097,968 | 482,902 | 43.98 |
| 3. | Assam | 22,41,432 | 8,10,915 | 36.17 | 26,65,528 | 95,70,33 | 35.9 |
| 4. | Bihar (including Jharkhand) | 86,374,465 | 27,777,071 | 32.15 | 109,944,338 | 38,083,636 | 34.63 |
| 5. | Delhi | 9,420,644 | 2,980,461 | 31.63 | 13,850,507 | 4,545,234 | 32.81 |
| 6. | Gujarat | 41,309,582 | 16,620,519 | 40.23 | 50,671,017 | 21,255,521 | 41.94 |
| 7. | Haryana | 16,463,648 | 5,103,470 | 30.99 | 21,144,564 | 8,377,466 | 39.61 |
| 8. | Himachal Pradesh | 5,170,877 | 2,214,379 | 42.82 | 6,077,900 | 2,992,461 | 49.23 |
| 9. | Jammu and Kashmir | 7,718,700 | 15,30,200 | 19.82 | 10,069,917 | 25,38,905 | 25.21 |
| 10. | Karnataka | 44,977,201 | 18,886,798 | 41.99 | 52,850,562 | 23,534,791 | 44.53 |
| 11. | Kerala | 29,098,518 | 9,146,118 | 31.43 | 31,841,374 | 10,283,887 | 32.29 |
| 12. | M.P. (including Chhattisgarh) | 66,181,170 | 28,340,485 | 42.82 | 81,181,826 | 35,473,390 | 43.69 |
| 13. | Maharashtra | 78,937,187 | 33,910,366 | 42.90 | 96,878,627 | 41,173,351 | 42.49 |
| 14. | Manipur | 1,837,149 | 774,904 | 42.17 | 2,166,788 | 945,213 | 43.6 |
| 15. | Meghalaya | 1,774,778 | 757,322 | 42.67 | 2,318,822 | 970,146 | 41.83 |
| 16. | Nagaland | 1,209,546 | 516,237 | 42.68 | 1,990,036 | 847,796 | 42.60 |
| 17. | Orissa | 31,659,736 | 11,882,762 | 37.53 | 36,804,660 | 14,276,488 | 38.78 |
| 18. | Punjab | 20,281,969 | 6,261,989 | 30.87 | 24,358,999 | 9,127,474 | 37.47 |
| 19. | Rajasthan | 44,005,990 | 17,104,372 | 38.86 | 56,507,188 | 23,766,655 | 42.0 |
| 20. | Sikkim | 406,457 | 168,721 | 41.51 | 540,851 | 263,043 | 48.63 |
| 21. | Tamil Nadu | 55,858,946 | 24,194,343 | 43.31 | 62,405,679 | 27,878,282 | 44.6 |
| 22. | U.P.(including Uttarakhand) | 139,112,287 | 44,799,280 | 32.20 | 174,687,270 | 57,117,860 | 32.69 |
| 23. | West Bengal | 68,077,965 | 21,914,774 | 32.19 | 80,176,197 | 29,481,690 | 36.77 |
| | **India** | **815,479,910** | **305,705,090** | **37.48** | **990,922,527** | **388,475,159** | **39.20** |

*Source*: Census of India 2001, Primary Census Abstract.

last day of 2006, 2007 and 2008 the following position of unemployed persons was noted on the live registers of the employment exchanges.

The number of registered illiterate unemployed in the year 2007 was 4030 whereas the number in the year 2008 has been increased to 4167 thereby registering a growth of 3.40 per cent. The number of literate unemployed (literate below metric) has recorded an increase of about 5.41 per cent during the year 2008.

Unemployment among the registered educated people has recorded a rising trend. The educated unemployed population has been recorded as 82,619 in the year 2007 and 89,796 in the year 2008 recording an increase of 8.69 per cent. The overall number of registered unemployed in the state during 2007 was 1,11,564 persons which have increased to 1,20,228 persons in the year 2008, showing an increase of about 9.91 per cent. The ground level position was not so because the statistics of employment exchanges, however, does not provide accurate picture of unemployment in the state.

The training institutions and other skill training centres have no doubt been meeting a significant part of the requirements of the skilled manpower of the organized industry. It, however, seems necessary that the process of restructuring and reorientation of their courses is required to be more expeditious with a view to quickly respond to the labour market so that the growth rate of unemployed shows a substantial decrease. This would result in a positive signal towards growth of skilled employment creation and consequent absorption. Efforts have to be towards that this skilled trait does not pile up which will distort the overall employment and unemployment scenario. Rapid expansion of education, particularly of higher education, has also contributed to mismatch in labour market. High private rates of return on higher education, to a large extent resulting from low private cost, is an important reason for the rush for higher education despite high incidence of educated unemployment. Self-employment and casual labour continued to play a pivotal role in rehabilitation of the unemployed.

### *Growth of Employment in Unorganized Sector*

According to the economic survey of Jammu and Kashmir there are 3.24 lakh enterprises in the state which are engaged in different economic activities. The total number of persons working in these enterprises was recorded to be 7.52 lakh, more or less equally distributed in rural and urban areas, i.e. 51.53 per cent in urban areas and the remaining 48.47

**Table 3.10:** Year-wise/Qualification-wise break up of unemployed registered with Employment Exchange

| S. No. | Category | Registered unemployed | | | | (Unit in Nos.) | |
|---|---|---|---|---|---|---|---|
| | | 2006 | | 2007 | | Growth in Unemployment during 2007 | No. of Registered unemployed as on 31st Dec. 2008 |
| | | Number | %age of total | Number | %age of total | | |
| A. Illiterate unemployed | | | | | | | |
| (I) | Illiterate | 9369 | 8.5 | 4030 | 3.61 | (–) 56.98 | 4167 |
| B. Literate Unemployed Below Matric | | | | | | | |
| (i) | Below Matric | 25384 | 23.20 | 24916 | 22.33 | (–) 1.84 | 26265 |
| C. Educated Unemployed Matric and above | | | | | | | |
| (i) | Total (C) | 74630 | 68.22 | 82619 | 74.05 | (+) 10.70 | 89796 |
| **Grand Total** | | **109383** | **100.00** | **111564** | **100.00** | **(+)1.99** | **120228** |

*Source*: Jammu and Kashmir Digest of Statistics, 2007-08.

per cent in the rural areas. The average annual growth rate in employment in the said enterprises during 1998 to 2005 was 6.82 per cent. With this annual average growth rate in employment in such enterprises that Jammu and Kashmir State is on top. However, this momentum needs to be kept going. Some of the prerequisites for ensuring that the present rate of the growth in the small and medium economic enterprises continues during the Eleventh Five Year Plan include, provision of quality power, especially to small and household industrial units including handlooms, provision of connectivity to all villages to improve trade avenues in the rural areas and promotion of horticulture to tap the employment avenues available in this sector.

This is the well-known fact that almost 70 per cent of the population of the state of Jammu and Kashmir is directly or indirectly dependent on agriculture and its allied sectors including horticulture, which contributes to be a subsistence sector. In addition to agriculture and its allied sectors, the sectors which have been employing large chunk of population include small scale industries, handicrafts, and handlooms. The number of persons employed is indicated in Table 3.11.

As per the data analysis, number of workers employed in handicraft and Horticulture/Agriculture sector has remain constant in the year 2006-07 and 2007-08 as there has been no additional absorption of the human components in these sectors. Handloom sector has shown decline in employment over the years. Substantial employment growth was absorbed in small enterprises which help to tackle the task of unemployment to some extent by expending employment base. As regards village and Khadi industries, the employment scenario has drastically reduced from 69,468 to 43,850, thereby registering a negative growth of 37.13 per cent.

**Table 3.11:** Number of workers engaged in various sectors during 2006-07 and 2007-08

| *S. No.* | *Sector* | *Units* | *Number of workers* | |
|---|---|---|---|---|
| | | | 2006-07 | 2007-08 |
| 1. | Handicrafts | Lakhs | 3.50 | 3.50 |
| 2. | Handlooms | | | |
| | Units | Nos. | 2378 | 2334 |
| | Organized sectors (Co-operative Societies) | Nos. | 15280 | 15301 |
| | Unorganized Sector | Nos. | 22000 | 22000 |
| 3. | Small Scale Industries | Nos. | 225963 | 232915 |
| 4. | Village and Khadi industries | Nos. | 69468 | 43850* |
| 5. | Shops and establishments | Nos. | 229999 | 249225 |
| | Shops and establishments | Nos. | 177814 | 187068 |
| | Employee | Nos. | 52185 | 62157 |
| 6. | Horticulture/Agriculture | Lakhs | 25.00 | 25.00 |

*Including partially employed persons

*Source:* J&K Directorate of Economic and Statistics 2007-08.

## Unemployment Scenario in Jammu and Kashmir

The quinquennial survey on employment-unemployment carried out by the National Sample Survey Organization provides estimates on various characteristics pertaining to employment and unemployment at the national as well as state level.

The term used for measuring unemployment is the 'unemployment rate' defined by National Sample Survey Organization as the number of person's unemployed per 1000 persons in the labour force (which include both the employed and unemployed). For the calculation of unemployment rate, person-days as per the current daily status approach is followed. This infect gives the unutilized position of labour force. Thus it is a more refined indicator of employment situation in the population than the 'proportion unemployed' which is merely the number of unemployed per thousand persons in the population as a whole.

The latest National Sample Survey 2005 constitutes an important source of information on unemployment. The unemployment rates for the state in comparison to nation are given in Table 3.12.

**Table 3.12:** Unemployment Rate* for Jammu and Kashmir State/All India

| S. No. | Area | J&K | | | All India | | |
|---|---|---|---|---|---|---|---|
| | | Male | Female | Person | Male | Female | Person |
| 1. | Rural | | | | | | |
| | Usual Principal Status | 5.1 | 0.6 | 4.7 | 2.5 | 2.2 | 2.4 |
| | Current Weekly Status | 6.5 | 0.3 | 5.0 | 4.3 | 3.3 | 4.0 |
| | Current Daily Status | 7.9 | 0.5 | 6.7 | 8.3 | 7.5 | 8.1 |
| 2. | Urban | | | | | | |
| | Usual Principal Status | 6.7 | 11.7 | 7.3 | 4.8 | 7.9 | 5.4 |
| | Current Weekly status | 7.0 | 8.1 | 7.1 | 5.8 | 7.7 | 6.1 |
| | Current Daily Status | 7.6 | 8.7 | 7.7 | 7.9 | 10.1 | 8.3 |
| 3. | Combined (Rural Urban) | | | | | | |
| | Usual Principal Status | 5.4 | 3.5 | 5.2 | 3.1 | 3.0 | 3.1 |
| | Current Weekly status | 6.6 | 1.2 | 5.4 | 4.7 | 3.9 | 4.5 |
| | Current Daily Status | 7.9 | 1.8 | 6.9 | 8.2 | 7.9 | 8.1 |

*Unemployment Rate per 100 persons

*Source:* Jammu and Kashmir National Sample Survey Organization.

The unemployment indicators have been worked out at three basic principles indicated below:

(i) Usual Principal Status (UPS) – indicator of chronically unemployed.

(ii) Current Weekly Status (CWS) – indicator of chronic and seasonal unemployment.

(iii) Current Daily Status (CDS) – indicator of unemployment on a day of conduct of survey.

The analysis of the above information reveals that the combined (male female) unemployment rate at rural level in the state is comparatively higher than that of national unemployment rate as per usual principal status and current weekly status whereas in case of current daily status the indicator is high at all India level than that of Jammu and Kashmir state. The higher unemployment rate indicators highlights that employment situation is worse at the ground level. At the rural level the indicators in respect of females is better than that of the males. At the national level the indicator is better for males than females.

In the state at urban level, the overall unemployment rate is comparatively higher than that of national level unemployment rate as per current principal status and current weekly status whereas the indicator as per the current daily status is high at all India level than that of Jammu and Kashmir state. In case of females at rural level their position of employment is worse than that of males in the state as well as at national level when the indicator is analyzed. When we combined the rural urban level, the unemployment status as per usual principal status is 5.2 which is less than the indicator for urban areas (7.3) and higher than rural (4.7). Similarly, the indicator as per the current weekly status is 5.4 which are more than rural areas (5.0) and less than urban areas (7.1). The indicator as per current daily status is 6.9 which is higher than the indicator for rural areas (6.7) and in urban areas (7.7) as well. While analyzing the indicators at state level, the chronic unemployed situation exists in urban areas with the indicator standing at 7.3 per cent as per usual principal status.

**Table 3.13:** Comparison between Unemployment Rate of Jammu and Kashmir State for 61st and 62nd round of National Sample Survey Organization

| *NSS Round* | *Male* | | | *Female* | | | *Combined (Male+Female)* | | |
|---|---|---|---|---|---|---|---|---|---|
| | *UPS* | *CWS* | *CDS* | *UPS* | *CWS* | *CDS* | *UPS* | *CWS* | *CDS* |
| 61st | | | | | | | | | |
| Rural | 2.1 | 4.7 | 5.8 | 6.3 | 2.9 | 4.7 | 2.6 | 4.2 | 5.6 |
| Urban | 3.8 | 4.0 | 4.6 | 15.6 | 12.2 | 15.2 | 5.3 | 5.3 | 6.0 |
| 62nd | | | | | | | | | |
| Rural | 5.1 | 6.5 | 7.9 | 0.6 | 0.3 | 0.5 | 4.7 | 5.0 | 6.7 |
| Urban | 6.7 | 7.0 | 7.6 | 11.7 | 8.1 | 8.7 | 7.3 | 7.1 | 7.7 |
| Combined | 5.4 | 6.6 | 7.9 | 3.5 | 1.2 | 1.8 | 5.2 | 5.4 | 6.9 |

From analysis of the above Table 3.13, it was revealed that unemployment rate under usual principal status has increased from 61st National Sample Survey round to 62nd round for males. The analysis as per other principles, i.e. current weekly status and current daily status also collaborate the findings usual principal status for males.

There has been improvement in the indicator under usual principal status from 61st round to 62nd round of National Sample Survey and the trend has been observed positive in Current Weekly Status and Current Daily Status for females as well.

The strides made in female employment at state level have been nullified by the downfall of indicators in respect of males, thereby resulting into overall deterioration of the indicator at the state level as per all the three principles of unemployment, exhibiting that the employment situation becoming dismal with the passage of time.

As per the findings of 62nd round of National Sample Survey 2005-06 reports, unemployment rate in respect of Jammu and Kashmir state, has been worked out to be 5.2 per cent (95.4 per cent for males and 3.5 per cent for females) which is on higher side when compared to all India figures of 3.1 per cent (3.1 per cent for males and 3.0 per cent for females) and the neighbouring states, viz. Himachal Pradesh, Haryana, Delhi and North-eastern states which are having lower unemployment rate of 3.5 per cent, 3.9 per cent, 2.4 per cent and 4.8 per cent respectively. However, Punjab is the only state which has higher unemployment rate, with the indicator standing at 5.4 per cent as per usual principal status pattern. The female unemployment rate in respect of Punjab is 13.1 per cent which is quite higher than Jammu and Kashmir State (3.5%), all other neighbouring states and all India level. Male unemployment rate of Jammu and Kashmir State is on the higher side than its neighbouring states, north eastern states and all India level.

Unemployment rate in urban areas is higher than rural areas, not only in Jammu and Kashmir state but also in its neighbouring states/ North Eastern states and at all India level. Unemployment rate of 7.3 per cent in urban areas of Jammu and Kashmir State is on the higher side when compared to its neighbouring states. Male unemployment rate (6.7%) in urban areas of Jammu and Kashmir State is on the higher side when compared to its neighbouring states. Further, Punjab is the only neighbouring state with female unemployment rate of 13.2 per cent followed by the Jammu and Kashmir state (11.7%). In all other neighbouring states and all India level, the female unemployment rate is on the lower side in urban areas.

In rural areas, Punjab is the only neighbouring State with higher unemployment rate of 5.4 per cent followed by Jammu and Kashmir State (4.7%) as compared to the adjoining States/All India level. Punjab is the only neighbouring state with female unemployment rate of 13 per cent which is quite higher than Jammu and Kashmir State (0.6%), all other neighbouring States and all India level. Male unemployment rate of Jammu and Kashmir State in rural areas is 5.1 per cent which is on the higher side than its neighbouring states and all India level.

**Table 3.14:** Unemployment Rate as per Usual Principal Status in Jammu and Kashmir State in comparison with the neighbouring States/North-Eastern States/All India as per 62nd round of National Sample Survey

| *State* | *Rural* | | | *Urban* | | | *Rural+Urban* | | |
|---|---|---|---|---|---|---|---|---|---|
| | *Male* | *Female* | *Person* | *Male* | *Female* | *Person* | *Male* | *Female* | *Person* |
| Jammu & Kashmir | 5.1 | 0.6 | 4.7 | 6.7 | 11.7 | 7.3 | 5.4 | 3.5 | 5.2 |
| Himachal Pradesh | 3.8 | 2.2 | 3.1 | 3.3 | 8.2 | 4.4 | 3.7 | 2.4 | 3.5 |
| Punjab | 4.5 | 13.0 | 5.4 | 4.4 | 13.2 | 5.6 | 4.5 | 13.1 | 5.4 |
| Haryana | 4.6 | 0.1 | 3.9 | 3.8 | 6.0 | 4.1 | 4.4 | 1.5 | 3.9 |
| Delhi | 1.5 | 0.0 | 1.4 | 2.4 | 3.8 | 2.5 | 2.3 | 3.5 | 2.4 |
| North/East States | 3.9 | 3.9 | 3.9 | 5.9 | 16.6 | 9.0 | 4.3 | 5.9 | 4.8 |
| All India | 2.5 | 2.2 | 2.4 | 4.8 | 7.9 | 5.4 | 3.1 | 3.0 | 3.1 |

### *Unemployment among Youth and Educated*

As per the Census 2001, the literacy rate of the State stands at 55 per cent, which has increased further to 65.67 per cent as per Survey results of literacy rate 2008 conducted by Directorate of Economics and Statistics. The estimated mid-year population (7 years and above) of State is 93.872 lakh persons out of which 61.647 lakh persons are literate. With the annual average growth rate of 1.81 per cent in population, the literacy is growing at an annual average growth rate of 2.126 per cent, which results in addition to the educated youth year after year. This situation requires creation of ample opportunities in terms of employment avenues in the state or otherwise increase in literacy rate and number of literates will culminate into higher unemployment ratios.

With the increase in population and number of educated persons in the State, the avenues of employment generation have not increased proportionately. High incidence of unemployment among the youth and the educated has emerged as an area of concern in the State. The data on employment and unemployment generated from the latest round of NSS surveys—61st round, covering the period July 2004 to June 2005, has revealed the incidence of unemployment among youth and educated at the national level and for the state as follow:

**Table 3.15:** Unemployment youth and educated at national level

| | 1993-94 | | 1999-2000 | | 2004-05 | |
|---|---|---|---|---|---|---|
| | Educated# | Youth* | Educated# | Youth* | Educated# | Youth* |
| **Rural** | | | | | | |
| Male | 4.0 | 3.5 | 9.0 | 7.5 | 7.1 | 6.2 |
| Female | 13.6 | 4.2 | 22.3 | 11.7 | 20.2 | 8.9 |
| Person | 5.0 | 3.7 | 10.0 | 7.9 | 8.3 | 6.8 |
| **Urban** | | | | | | |
| Male | 6.5 | 18.7 | 6.9 | 15.6 | 6.2 | 11.2 |
| Female | 21.6 | 33.6 | 19.4 | 27.6 | 31.6 | 31.8 |
| Person | 8.8 | 21.9 | 8.2 | 17.1 | 9.0 | 14.7 |

\# educated: Persons who have attained an educational level of secondary and above including those completed diploma/certificate courses. Normally one can attain this educational level including those years or above. Thus, the data given for education is restricted to person of age between 15 years and above.

*Youth: Persons aged between 15 and 29 years.

*Source:* NSS Survey—61st round.

Table 3.15 reveals that there has been improvement in the employment situation at rural level, as the unemployment indicator has shifted from 10 to 8.3 per cent while as at Urban level slight deterioration in the employment situation in the State from the year 1999-2000 to 2004-05 has been observed as the unemployment rate among educated in the State increased from 8.2 to 9.0 per cent. The unemployment rate among the Youth has, however, improved from 7.9 to 6.8 per cent at rural level while at urban level it has improved from 17.1 to 14.7 per cent during 1990-2000 to 2004-05

As per the data analysis, the area of concern is the urban sector, especially female folk, which has resulted into increase in the indicator. The data on unemployment scenario at urban level, especially for female education and female youth from the period 1999-2000 to 2004-05 show grim situation.

This shows that the unemployment rate of urban educated females increased from 19.4 to 31.6 per cent, registering an increase of 63.4 per cent from 1999 to 2000, an increase of 15.2 per cent over the same period.

### *Approaches Towards Employment Generation*

The objective of the State Government of providing at least one productive job per family is hard to be achieved primarily through providing government jobs but employment opportunities need to be created primarily through two routes:

1. Accelerating the rate of Economic growth of the state.
2. More effective implementation of employment oriented scheme and programmes (broad based inclusive growth scheme).

The following 8 sectors of economy have been identified for generation of employment:

(i) Agriculture (including horticulture, floriculture, food processing and animal husbandry)
(ii) Handloom and handicrafts
(iii) Industries (including small scale industries and rural industries)
(iv) Tourism and Travel
(v) Education and Health
(vi) Large infrastructure projects (Roads and Railways)
(vii) Information Technology and Telecommunication
(viii) Construction Sector

The economy of Jammu and Kashmir has suffered from disturbed conditions prevailing in the State for almost two decades. It would, therefore, be necessary to put the economy back on the rails to enable the average person to get employment opportunities. This would require giving fillip to the economic activities that have traditionally been the mainstay of the State's economy and continue to hold significant potential for growth and employment. Such activities include Agriculture (including Horticulture), Food Processing, Handicraft and Handloom, Tourism etc. It would be equally necessary to ensure diversification of the State economy, especially expanding the industrial base by promoting private capital inflow into the State through various incentives and concessions in the initial stage. The special industrial package announced for Jammu and Kashmir has been a step in the right direction.

While preparing any plan for sustainable employment generation, it has to be kept in view that the prospects of any large scale expansion in the public sector jobs are not very bright. Even if steps are taken to fill all the gaps in man power required to deliver public service in crucial areas such as Health and Education, the contribution of government jobs at the margin would not be more than 15-16 per cent, and even this one sixth contribution to the total increment in employment would be 10 one time contribution. Taken together with the jobs in other formal establishments, the share of regular salaried jobs in the employment generation programmes is not expected for proving sustainable. Therefore, other avenues would have to be explored for providing sustainable employment to the people of the State. Extending support to entrepreneurs to set up small and medium enterprises for self-employment would appear to be most effective and durable way of doing this. A large number of workers in Jammu and Kashmir have traditionally been self-employed in activities such as Handloom and Handicrafts, Tourism, Horticulture, Food Processing etc. The distributed conditions prevailing in the state have suffered loss of employment, majority are working at very low level of income and productivity. Also, in many of the identical areas, especially horticulture and food processing 10 large potential for growth lies untapped waiting to be exploited.

Different sectors and sub-sectors of the State's economy would require different kinds of intervention for the revival/growth depending upon the nature of the activity, the impediments to growth and the institutions that are place to encourage or promote growth. Specific interventions through Government schemes and the special employment programmes (PMRY, REGP, SGSY and JK self-employment Scheme) would be important for giving better employment orientation to growth.

In the interest of a balanced economic growth and development, a conscious attempt has to be made to dovetail the interventions envisaged at the sectoral level to the need for reducing the gender gap on the other. At the stage of monitoring of the employment programme also, the need to strike these balances would have to be given due attention and midcourse corrections, if necessary, applied.

### *Potential for Employment Generation*

Additional productive employment opportunities in the future would be generated mainly in the service and manufacturing sectors and policy initiatives are needed to support this. The intention in the 11th Five Year Plan is to boost, in particular labour intensive manufacturing sectors such as food processing, leather products, foot wears and textiles. And service sectors such as tourism and construction. Construction sector would generate substantial additional employment. Tourism—both domestic as well as international—may provide possibilities for employment generation in the hotel, catering, entertainment and travel sectors as well as 10 market for handloom and handicrafts.

The State of J&K has certain inherent strengths that can be utilized to improve the income of its people and to provide gainful employment opportunities on sustainable basis, which are:

(a) A very strong base of traditional skills not found elsewhere;
(b) Untapped natural resources; and
(c) A natural environment which has been very profitably utilized by other countries for high income environment friendly tourism industry.

### Employment Policy

In order to sustain growth and employment in its economy, the State Government should articulate an Employment Policy focusing on:

1. Improving the productivity of, and thereby income of those engaged in industries based on traditional skills,
2. Shifting the agricultural workforce to high value-added/high income Agriculture/ Horticulture;
3. Transforming the service industry in the State, driven by Tourism, from informal and low income to modern by setting up a world

class tourism infrastructure, largely on the basis of private investment and entrepreneurship;

4. Creating a vibrant self-employed professional workforce, which does not depend on government jobs, or for off take of its services
5. By government alone.

**The Employment Policy will also have the focus on various economic initiatives:**

1. Improve the skills of local labour force such that it is utilized better by the local enterprise, reducing the need to improve skilled and professional man power;
2. Development of institutions that
   - Facilitates growth of productivity of tiny, micro and small units; focus at the clusters of existing artisans and cottage industries;
   - Focus at creation of infrastructure of better productivity at such other locations where bulk of workforce is deployed;
   - Harness the economies of scale of many small units operating in proximity by providing infrastructure for marketing;
   - Facilitates research and development into the production, techniques and methods and equipment used by those working in such existing units; and
   - Promote high income self-employment, and are sensitive to creation of employment opportunities for women in more productive, better income and modern industries and services.

# 4

# Economic Resource Development of Jammu & Kashmir

## Economic Resource Development

Jammu and Kashmir State is full of natural resources of great economic potential. The physiographic location imposes a number of constraints, particularly in agriculture and allied sectors. The initial land-use pattern in the state was purely agriculture. It has changed over a period of time to agri-horticultural silvi-pastoral. Although, the net area sown has remained more or less same - 7.31 lakh hectare in 1990-91 to 7.33 lakh hectare in 1999-2000, the area under fruit and vegetable cultivation has marginally increased over the same period of time. In respect of fruit, it has gone up from 176.30 thousand hectares in 1990-91 to 213.73 thousand hectares in 1998-99. Vegetables have shown a marginal increase, from 14,000 hectares in 1990-91 to 14,930 hectares in 1999-2000. Rice, the staple crop, is planted in May and harvested in late September. Maize is the second-most important crop. The best soil for maize is reclaimed swamp and enormous crops are raised from the black peaty land, which lies under the banks of river Jhelum. In the high villages occupied by the Gujjar grazers, very fine crops of maize are grown. Other important summer crops are millet, pulses (legumes such as peas, beans and lentils), cotton and tobacco. Wheat and barley are the chief spring crops. Foodgrains production has shown an increase from 13664 thousand quintals in 1990-91 to 15253 quintals in 1998-99. Many temperate fruits are also grown. Large orchards in the vale of Kashmir produce apples, pears, peaches, walnuts, almonds and cherries. In addition, it is the largest producer of saffron in the Indian subcontinent. Artificial floating gardens on the lakes are favourable for the cultivation of flowers and vegetables.

**Tourism Development**

The year-wise distribution is interesting and also quite revealing of the touristic strengths of the State and revealed that the trend is inclining due to the natural as well as cultural factors and due to some political as well as other factors tourist flow declines. From 1975 onwards the trend of tourists was inclining up to 1982 (Fig. 4.1).

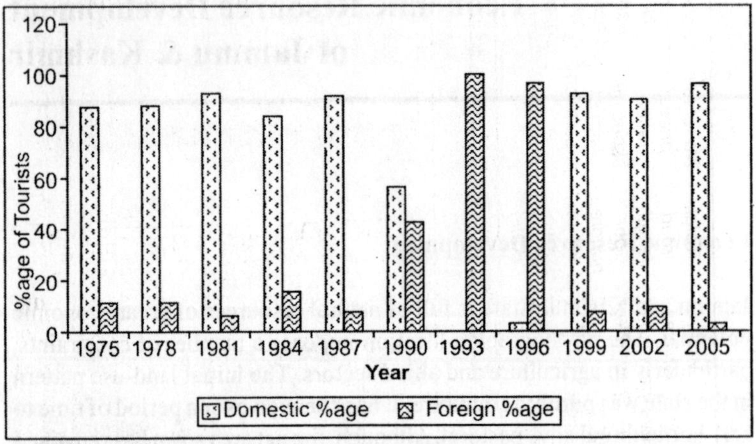


*Source*: Department of Tourism, Jammu and Kashmir.

**Fig. 4.1:** Variation in Tourist Arrivals in Kashmir Valley

Both the domestic as well as the international tourists are inclining but in the year 1983 it again declines up to 1985. During 1980s Kashmir Valley received 89.9 per cent domestic tourists while as the Ladakh region received only 7.2 per cent tourists in average in the same period. Onwards 1977 the proportions of domestic as well as foreign tourists are relatively unchanged.

In 1984 a drop in the total number of tourists was observed, primarily due to the political conditions and insurgency in the neighbouring states like Punjab. Tourist could not avail of the only land route at that time as it passed through this state because of its closure to foreigners due to prevailing terrorism. Again the tourism market developed in the Valley up to 1988 and due to insurgency started from 1989, tourism industry there virtually collapsed, which leads to the unique stimulant for tourism growth in Himachal Pradesh and other neighbouring states of the Jammu

**Table 4.1:** Industry and Commerce in the Himalayan Region States

| *States* | *Per capita gross output in industries (Rs.) (p)* | *Per capita value added in industries (Rs.) (p)* | *Domestic consumption of electricity per capita (kwh) (p)* | *Industrial consumption of electricity per capita (kwh) (p)* | *Motor vehicles per lakh of pop. (No.)* | *Total road length per hundred km of area (kms)* | *No. of fair prices/ ration shops per lakh of population* | *Schedule commercial banks: No. of banking officers per lakh of population* | *Schedule commercial banks: Deposit per capita (Rs.)* | *Schedule commercial banks: Bank credit per capita (Rs.)* |
|---|---|---|---|---|---|---|---|---|---|---|
| | 2000-01 | 2000-01 | 1999-2000 | 1999-2000 | 31-03-00 | 31-03-99 | 2001 | 31-03-2002 | 31-03-2002 | 31-03-2002 |
| Jammu & Kashmir | 1342 | 159.0 | 127.38 | 42.64 | 2201 | 11 | 29 | 8.0 | 11414 | 4102 |
| Himachal Pradesh | 10802 | 2179.0 | 94.02 | 157.91 | 2505 | 53 | 58 | 12.7 | 14042 | 3235 |
| Uttrakhand | 5812 | 1155.0 | N.A. | N.A. | N.A. | N.A. | 31 | 9.8 | 13507 | 3141 |
| Sikkim | N.A. | N.A. | 92.18 | 31.25 | 2271 | 26 | 155 | 8.4 | 14420 | 2309 |
| Meghalaya | 466 | 65.0 | 61.17 | 49.02 | 2596 | 41 | 36 | 7.6 | 8400 | 1514 |
| Tripura | 971 | 405.0 | 28.95 | 11.51 | 1425 | 148 | 104 | 5.6 | 5802 | 1297 |
| Mizoram | N.A. | N.A. | 101.25 | 1.50 | 2327 | 23 | 76 | 8.5 | 5459 | 1412 |
| Manipur | 74 | 8.0 | 38.52 | 4.50 | 3278 | 51 | 21 | 3.1 | 2485 | 634 |
| Nagaland | 485 | 36.0 | 55.44 | 15.04 | 7651 | 123 | 94 | 3.3 | 5006 | 625 |
| Arunachal Pradesh | N.A. | N.A. | 56.61 | 6.08 | 1971 | 22 | 46 | 6.2 | 6768 | 1065 |
| **India** | **9111** | **1417.0** | **75.15** | **107.00** | **4794** | **77** | **N.A.** | **6.3** | **10468** | **6523** |

*Source:* Economic Survey of Maharashtra, 2002-03, Directorate of Economics & Statistics, Planning Department, Government of Maharashtra.

**Table 4.2:** Foodgrain production and yield per hectare in the Himalayan States of India

| *States* | *Yield per ha. (in kg.) (P)* | | | | | *Food Grain Production per capita (kg.)* | *Consumption of fertilizers per ha. of cropped area (kg.)* | *% of gross irrigated area to gross cropped area (p)* | *Net area sown per cultivator (ha) (p)* | *Average daily factory employment per lakh of population (No.) (p)* |
|---|---|---|---|---|---|---|---|---|---|---|
| | *Total cereals* | *Total pulses* | *Total food-grains* | *Cotton (lint)* | *Sugar-cane* | | | | | |
| | *1998-99 to 2000-01* | | | | | *2000-01* | | *1998-99* | | *2000* |
| Jammu & Kashmir | 1555 | 581 | 1488 | 113 | 21400 | 109.8 | 60.00 | 41.4 | N.A. | N.A. |
| Himachal Pradesh | 1760 | 414 | 1754 | N.A. | 27264 | 237.4 | 36.58 | 18.8 | 0.5 | (R) 1447 |
| Sikkim | 1344 | 867 | 1324 | N.A. | N.A. | 187.0 | 7.61 | 12.6 | 1.0 | N.A. |
| Meghalaya | 1473 | 763 | 1501 | 144 | 10667 | 86.8 | 15.39 | 20.8 | 0.5 | N.A. |
| Tripura | 2038 | 582 | 2020 | 209 | 47871 | 163.6 | 20.17 | 13.5 | 0.9 | 973 |
| Mizoram | 1777 | 1761 | 1820 | 494 | 5267 | 137.5 | 12.78 | 9.0 | 0.6 | N.A. |
| Manipur | 2290 | N.A. | 2686 | 227 | 67278 | 155.6 | 106.47 | 14.7 | 0.4 | N.A. |
| Nagaland | 1322 | 757 | 1208 | 227 | 52704 | 135.1 | 1.53 | 25.5 | 0.8 | N.A. |
| Arunachal Pradesh | 1101 | 978 | 1090 | N.A. | N.A. | 183.9 | 2.44 | 14.4 | 0.8 | N.A. |
| **India** | **1808** | **601** | **1646** | **214** | **70972** | **188.8** | **87.56** | **39.2** | **1.3** | **1139** |

*Source:* Maharashtra Economic Survey of Maharashtra 2002-03, Directorate of Economics & Statistics, Planning Department, Government of Maharashtra.

and Kashmir. Security forces restricted travel to and from the area on numerous occasions.

Travel was strongly discouraged by the Indian Government and various national governments throughout the decade and both the tourists and businesses catering to them have left Jammu and Kashmir, and many relocated to Himachal Pradesh. While the well-publicized conflict has a significant deterrent quality, other specific events such as periodic attacks on, and deaths of, pilgrimage tourists and the abduction and the murder of foreign tourists, have rung the death knell for tourism in Kashmir for the time being.

Similarly, in 1990 disturbed political conditions in the Valley contributed to a sharp decline in the total tourist arrivals from 5,57,974 in 1989 to 10,722 a drop of more than 70 per cent. There was also increase in the number of tourists visiting the Valley in 1987 over the previous year, mainly due to a major avalanche around Zojila in November 1986 causing a great human tragedy. During 1992 there is sharp increase in the tourist flow in Kashmir Valley, as it was the Monkey year, which occurred every twelve years in Ladakh.

The conflict in Jammu and Kashmir also has limited access to the high profile tourist destination of Ladakh. This is because the primary overland route passes through highly conflicted areas in Kashmir such as Srinagar, Drass and Kargil. This has resulted in the shift of that travel to the secondary overland route, namely NH 21 through Kullu-Manali. Himachal Pradesh is thus a beneficiary of conflict through a shift in tourist destinations, businesses and traffic.

In the Valley tourism industry remain at the bottom till 1997 and again when insurgency get under control tourist flow increases day by day and cross 1 lakh on 2000 A.D. A record number of 6.10 lakh tourists, including 4.60 lakh Amarnath pilgrims, have visited Kashmir Valley this summer so far, thereby crossing the record of 7.22 lakh tourists in 1988, when the highest number had been registered. The officials here claimed that the increase in Amarnath pilgrims over the years had led to the increase. With the increase in pilgrim tourists, the message had gone across that the situation was improving in the state, which led to the flow of more tourists.

The Tourism Minister said that various areas were being developed for tourist attractions across the Valley and added that Kashmir Valley would once again be entirely a "tourist destination". He said demands were coming in from different areas of the Valley for developing spots of tourist attraction. Due attention was being paid to different areas for

**Table 4.3:** Year-wise Break-up of Domestic and Foreign Tourist Arrivals in Kashmir Valley (1975-2005)

| Year | Domestic | %age | Foreign | %age | Total |
|---|---|---|---|---|---|
| 1975 | 162676 | 87.98 | 22214 | 12.01 | 184890 |
| 1976 | 286412 | 88.26 | 38078 | 11.73 | 324490 |
| 1977 | 387817 | 87.73 | 54223 | 12.26 | 442040 |
| 1978 | 443342 | 88.19 | 59323 | 11.80 | 502665 |
| 1979 | 498067 | 90.59 | 55680 | 10.12 | 549747 |
| 1980 | 548491 | 92.25 | 46026 | 7.74 | 594517 |
| 1981 | 598555 | 93.18 | 43745 | 6.81 | 642300 |
| 1982 | 560987 | 92.90 | 42851 | 7.09 | 603838 |
| 1983 | 398428 | 90.64 | 41101 | 9.35 | 439529 |
| 1984 | 192684 | 84.08 | 36458 | 15.91 | 229142 |
| 1985 | 465599 | 92.45 | 38015 | 7.54 | 503614 |
| 1986 | 536598 | 90.99 | 53118 | 9.00 | 589716 |
| 1987 | 664081 | 92.02 | 57537 | 7.97 | 721618 |
| 1988 | 662097 | 91.69 | 59938 | 8.30 | 722035 |
| 1989 | 490212 | 87.85 | 67762 | 12.14 | 557974 |
| 1990 | 6095 | 56.84 | 4627 | 43.15 | 10722 |
| 1991 | 1400 | 22.26 | 4887 | 77.73 | 6287 |
| 1992 | 1175 | 11.38 | 9149 | 88.61 | 10324 |
| 1993 | 0 | 0 | 8026 | 100 | 8026 |
| 1994 | 500 | 5.09 | 9314 | 94.90 | 9814 |
| 1995 | 322 | 3.77 | 8198 | 96.22 | 8520 |
| 1996 | 375 | 376 | 9592 | 96.23 | 9967 |
| 1997 | 7027 | 43.54 | 9111 | 56.45 | 16138 |
| 1998 | 99636 | 90.67 | 10247 | 9.32 | 109883 |
| 1999 | 200162 | 92.11 | 17130 | 7.88 | 217292 |
| 2000 | 104337 | 93.23 | 7575 | 6.76 | 111912 |
| 2001 | 66732 | 91.92 | 5859 | 8.07 | 72591 |
| 2002 | 24670 | 90.18 | 2686 | 9.81 | 27356 |
| 2003 | 182205 | 95.31 | 8959 | 4.68 | 191164 |
| 2004 | 358095 | 95.05 | 18634 | 4.94 | 376729 |
| 2005 | 585702 | 96.74 | 19680 | 3.25 | 605382 |

*Source:* Department of Tourism, Jammu and Kashmir.

tourism development while famous spots like Pahalgam, Gulmarg and Sonamarg were also being given adequate attention. Sonamarg tourist spot, about 100 kms from here, falling on the Srinagar-Ladakh National Highway, being one of the major staging posts for the Ladakh region, also got developed over time. The Gurez area, about 80 kms from Bandipore in north Kashmir, which remains cut off from the rest of the Valley for six months of winter, is also being developed as a tourist destination.

Mr. Mir said that the Chief Minister, Mr. Mufti Mohammad Sayeed, had given instructions to explore possibilities for developing Bungus Valley in north Kashmir as an Eco-Tourist Resort. Replying to the questions, the Tourism Minister also pointed out that Wullar Lake in north Kashmir had been brought under tourism revival plan under Prime Minister's reconstruction package.

In 2001 due to again political issues and other minor factors tourist flow to the Valley declines but during 2003 onwards it again developed because other factors also stimulate tourism in the Valley like diversification of outdoor recreation activities and attractions and the growth of commercial horticulture and as well, increasingly used for movie and video productions.

The Valley of Kashmir being described "Paradise on the Earth". Both domestic as well as foreign tourists visit the Valley since time immemorial. The domestic tourists are confined to the Pilgrimage centres like Amarnath, Kher Bhawani and other shrines. Besides this the Valley has enormous tourist potential due to its scenic beauty, climatic conditions, and adventurous sports, ruins and relics of pre-historical and cultural has a great attraction for domestic as well as foreign tourists.

It has been observed that the all tourist scene of the Valley is dominated by domestic tourists. These tourists are coming from the rich parts of the country. However, the number of foreign tourists is very dismal which is given in Table 4.3.

Since 1975, there has been a tremendous increase in foreign as well as domestic tourists. Table 4.3 as well as the Figure 4.1 reveals that the proportionate share of domestic and foreign tourists in 1975 was 88.98 per cent and 12. 01 per cent respectively. In 1985 the proportionate share of domestic tourists increased further to 92.45 per cent and proportionate share of foreign tourists decreased to 7.54 per cent. In 1990 the proportionate share of domestic tourists have declined and reached 0 per cent in 1993 while the foreign tourists arrivals get increased in the same period. The starting 1990s were reverse trend in the domestic as well as in foreign tourist arrivals in the Valley of Kashmir whereas the later years recover from this as is given in Table 4.3. In starting 1990s due to infiltration and other political issues the Kashmir was in turmoil. So, no one domestic tourist was interested to take the risk and visit the Valley. This period was also known as "Dark age" in tourism sector in Kashmir Valley. Only 8026 foreign tourists visit the Valley in 1993 and make 100 per cent foreign arrivals in the Valley. But after 1996 the normalcy prevails in the Valley and the proportionate share of domestic tourists began to increase again and share of foreign tourists decreased continuously and the respective share of domestic tourists was 96.74 per cent and foreign tourists was only 3.25 per cent in 2005.

***Year-wise growth of Houseboats in Kashmir Valley***

Growth and performance of any industry is an important dimension irrespective of its significance in the macro perspective (Neil and Young, 1979). The optimization of the growth may be goal, an instrument to achieve some other goals like, maximization of profits, sales, economies of scales and so on. The growth of houseboat industry in Kashmir Valley is largely depends on the flow of tourists, which itself depend upon the supply of tourist products. Supply of tourist product is greatly influenced by the level of development of other constituent activities in the region, i.e. transport, development of tourist spots, travel and communication facilities, marketing, entertainment, travel agencies, courier services, etc. the growth of the houseboat industry involves the development of un-coordinated sector, in order to achieve coordinated results by breaking the vicious circle somewhere (Anand, 1976).

The analysis of growth pattern of houseboat industry has been examined under two sections. The first section intends to analyze the pattern of growth of houseboat industry in the Kashmir Valley, by taking

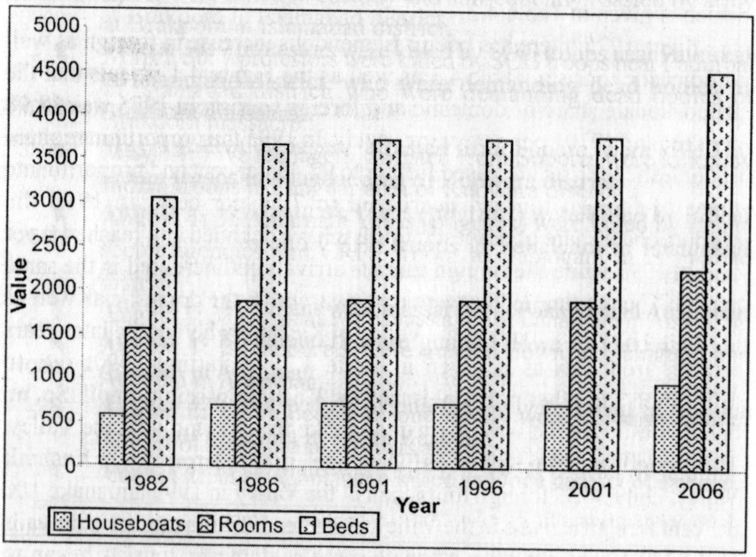


*Source:* Jammu and Kashmir Tourism Department

**Fig. 4.2:** Year-wise Growth of houseboats in Kashmir Valley

simple average method. The second section deals with growth incongruity with regard to different classes of houseboats. It examines the growth of A, B, C, D and E category houseboats.

Table 4.4 indicates that total number of houseboats, operating in the hospitality industry, the number of rooms and number of available beds increased consistently throughout the period. The number of houseboats, rooms and beds has increased to 985, 2285 and 4536 respectively up to ending June 2007 from 584 houseboats, 1563 rooms and 3054 beds in the year 1982.

The rate of growth varies during the different interval periods ranging from 1982-2006. The highest growth before 2000 was found in between 1982 and 1986 ranging from 121 houseboats, 322 rooms and 618 beds. But after 2000 the highest growth was found in 2006. The growth from 2001 to 2006 was ranging from 250 houseboats, 369 rooms and 752 beds. However, the lowest growth is found in the year from 1991 to 1996 4 houseboats, 3 rooms and 12 beds. The average rooms per houseboat computed are 2.31 and average beds per houseboat are 4.60.

**Table 4.4:** Growth of Houseboats in Kashmir Valley

| *Year* | *Houseboats* | *Rooms* | *Beds* |
|---|---|---|---|
| 1982 | 584<br>— | 1563<br>— | 3054<br>— |
| 1986 | 704<br>(121) | 1885<br>(322) | 3672<br>(618) |
| 1991 | 730<br>(25) | 1909<br>(24) | 3734<br>(62) |
| 1996 | 734<br>(4) | 1912<br>(3) | 3746<br>(12) |
| 2001 | 735<br>(1) | 1916<br>(4) | 3784<br>(38) |
| 2006 | 985<br>(250) | 2285<br>(369) | 4536<br>(752) |

*Note:* Figures in parenthesis indicate growth.

*Source:* Jammu and Kashmir Tourism Department.

## *Class-wise Growth of Houseboats in Kashmir Valley*

In the year 1978, Government of Jammu and Kashmir has passed an Act, which is called—The Tourist Act. This Act, however, was put enforce from 1982, with some amendments, wherein the prescribed categories of houseboats have to be duly registered by the Department of Tourism of Jammu and Kashmir as such classifications are granted to the hotel category by virtue of said Act. The houseboats are actually categorized into five groups like Deluxe, A class, B class, C class and D class. But Tourism Department categorized houseboats into three categories.

They combine the deluxe as well as A class and combine the C and D class. Table 4.5 shows that the period of two decades, i.e., 1982-2005, there has been constant growth in the different categories of houseboats—the number of A category houseboats increased from 378 to 490 with corresponding room capacity from 1083 to 1345 and bed capacity from 1694 to 2662. A category of houseboats also refer good type of accommodation and good services to its guest occupant, as well (Fig. 4.3). The growth in terms of A class houseboats, rooms and beds varies between highest 87, 209 and 868 respectively during 1982 to 1986 to the lowest of 2, 4 and 4 respectively, during the period from 1996 to 2001.

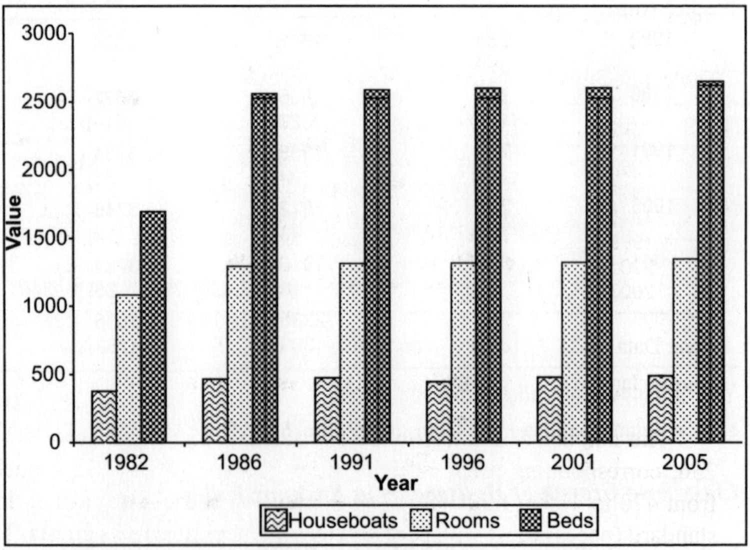


*Source*: Jammu and Kashmir Tourism Department.

**Fig. 4.3:** Growth of A Category House boat in Kashmir Valley

**Table 4.5:** Growth of A Category Houseboats in Kashmir Valley

| *Year* | *Houseboats* | *Rooms* | *Beds* |
|---|---|---|---|
| 1982 | 378 (–) | 1083 (–) | 1694 (–) |
| 1986 | 465 (87) | 1292 (209) | 2562 (868) |
| 1991 | 475 (10) | 1312 (20) | 2588 (26) |
| 1996 | 447 (2) | 1316 (4) | 2600 (12) |
| 2001 | 479 (2) | 1320 (4) | 2604 (4) |
| 2005 | 490 (11) | 1345 (25) | 2652 (48) |

*Source:* Jammu and Kashmir Tourism Department.

The B category houseboats also refer to medium standard accommodation and services to its tourist. Like A category houseboats, the growth of B category houseboats is not very impressive in the valley. The number of B category houseboats increased from 97 to 205, corresponding room capacity from 226 to 480 and bed capacity from 440 to 930. Table 4.6 shows that the highest growth for houseboats, rooms and beds was 78,184 and 350 respectively during the period from 2001 to 2007 and the lowest growth 1, 1 and 2 respectively during the period from 1996 to 2001.

**Table 4.6:** Growth of B Category Houseboats in Kashmir Valley

| *Year* | *Houseboats* | *Rooms* | *Beds* |
|---|---|---|---|
| 1982 | 97 (–) | 226 (–) | 440 (–) |
| 1986 | 124 (27) | 209 (64) | 568 (128) |
| 1991 | 124 (–) | 290 (–) | 568 (–) |
| 1996 | 126 (2) | 295 (5) | 578 (10) |
| 2001 | 127 (1) | 296 (1) | 580 (2) |
| 2007 | 205 (78) | 480 (184) | 930 (350) |

*Note*: Data of 2007 is upto 1st Aug. 2007.

*Source*: Jammu and Kashmir Tourism Department.

The number of C category houseboats has increased from 109 to 256, corresponding room capacity from 226 to 386 and bed capacity from 470 to 1150 (Table 4.7). The C category houseboats refer to low standard (necessaries) with poor services and facilities to its guests. The services are informal. In comparison to the growth of B category houseboats, the growth of C category houseboats is slightly impressive. The growth in terms of C class houseboats, rooms and beds varies between

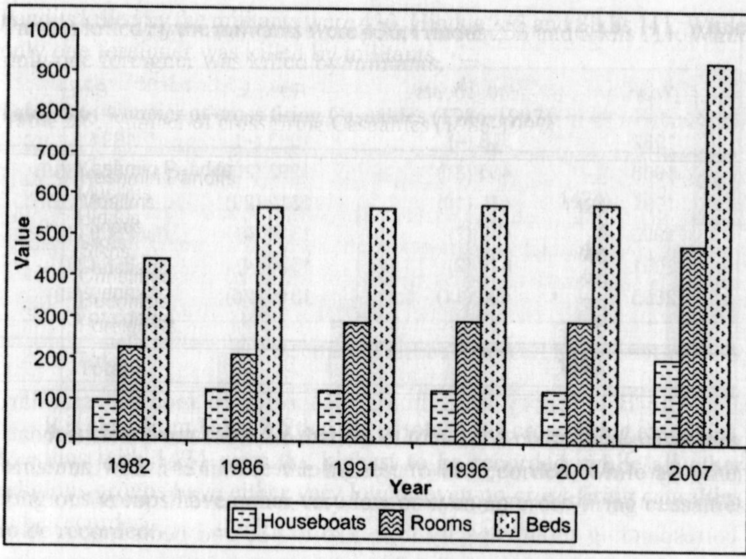


*Source*: Jammu and Kashmir Tourism Department.

**Fig. 4.4:** Growth of B Category House Boats in Kashmir Valley.

**Table 4.7:** Growth of C Category Houseboats in Kashmir Valley

| *Year* | *Houseboats* | *Rooms* | *Beds* |
|---|---|---|---|
| 1982 | 109 (–) | 226 (–) | 470 (–) |
| 1986 | 126 (17) | 290 (197) | 570 (100) |
| 1991 | 128 (2) | 295 (5) | 578 (8) |
| 1996 | 128 (–) | 295 (–) | 578 (–) |
| 2001 | 129 (1) | 296 (1) | 585 (7) |
| 2007 | 256 (127) | 386 (90) | 1150 (565) |

*Source:* Jammu and Kashmir Tourism Department

highest 127, 90 and 556 respectively during 2001 to 2007 to the lowest of 1, 1 and 7 respectively, during the period from 1996 to 2001.

## Tourist Accommodation in Houseboats and their Distribution in Different Water Bodies in Kashmir Valley

Many tourists are attracted to Srinagar by the charm of staying on a

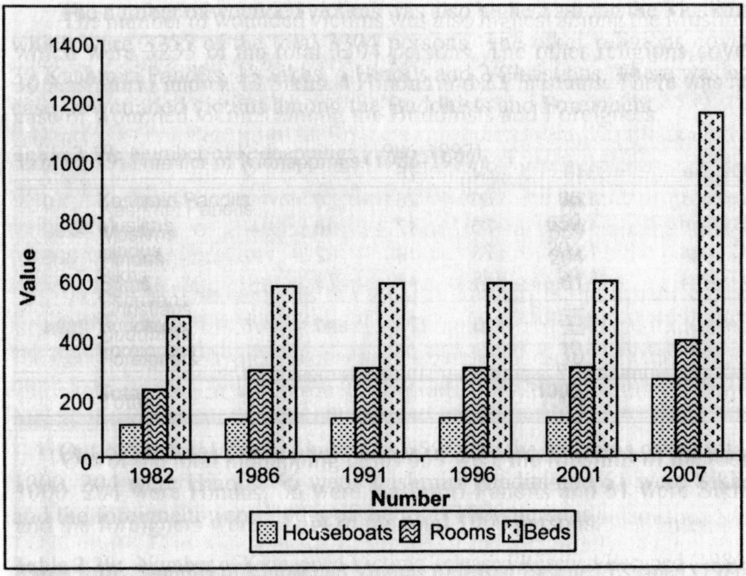


*Source*: Jammu and Kashmir Tourism Department.

**Fig. 4.5:** Growth of C Category Houseboats in Kashmir Valley

houseboat, which provides the unique experience of living on the water in a cedar-panelled elegant bedroom, with all the conveniences of a luxury hotel. Srinagar's thousand or so houseboats are moored along sections of the Dal and Nageen Lakes and River Jhelum, each decorated fancifully and named romantically.

The State Tourism Department has classified the houseboats into five categories as shown in Table 4.8 after 2001. As a general rule, houseboats in the Dal are of all categories, from Deluxe through to D class, while those in the Nageen are largely luxury class and those in the Jhelum largely economy class. This, however, is a generalization. Most houseboats on the Nageen and the Jhelum are situated on the banks of the lake, and can be accessed directly from land without the help of a *shikara*, while all those on the Dal require a *shikara* to get to and from the land. Maximum number of houseboats is found in Dal Lake. The Deluxe Category is dominated in the Dal Lake while as in the D class houseboats are dominated in the river Jhelum.

**Table 4.8:** Distribution of Houseboats in Different Water Bodies

| *Houseboat Category* | *No. of Houseboats* | *Dal Lake* | *Nageen Lake* | *River Jhelum* | *Naseem Bagh* | *Other Locations* | *Total Number of Rooms* |
|---|---|---|---|---|---|---|---|
| Deluxe | 349 | 264 | 76 | 5 | 4 | — | 1007 |
| A class | 129 | 89 | 28 | 10 | 1 | 1 | 310 |
| B class | 124 | 85 | 17 | 16 | — | 6 | 299 |
| C class | 134 | 78 | 9 | 32 | — | 15 | 306 |
| D class | 351 | 186 | 43 | 79 | — | 43 | 772 |
| **Total** | **1087** | **709** | **173** | **142** | **5** | **65** | **2694** |

*Source*: Jammu and Kashmir Tourism Department, 2007.

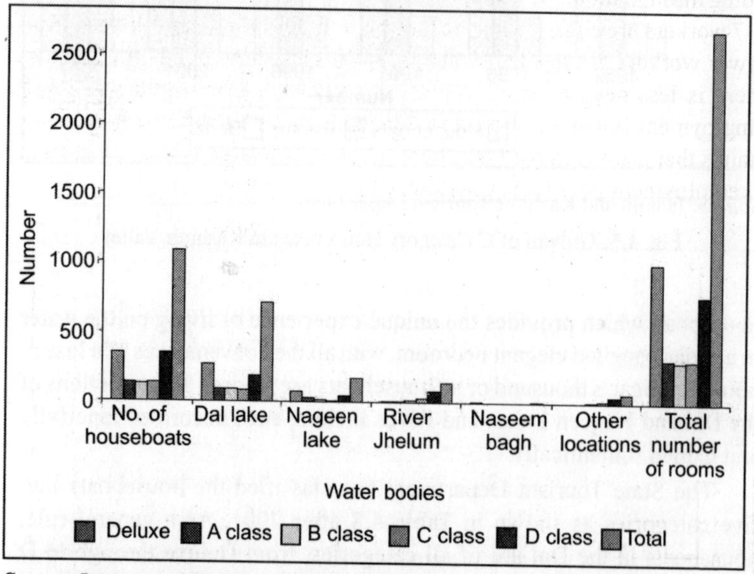


*Source*: Jammu and Kashmir Tourism Department.

**Fig 4.6:** Distribution of Houseboats in Different Water Bodies

## *Employment Potential in Houseboats in Kashmir Valley*

Houseboat owners are giving preference in employing their family members in the houseboats. However, it has been seen that few high standard houseboats employ other than their family members. Table 4.9

**Table 4.9:** Employment Potential in a Houseboat in Kashmir Valley

| Nature of Post | Volume |
|---|---|
| Calendar | 1 |
| Waiter | 2 |
| Cook | 1 |
| Helper | 1 |
| Guide | 2 |
| **Total** | **7** |

*Source:* Based on Field Survey, 2007.

reveals that a houseboat can provide employment to seven persons. After going through the survey of more than 100 houseboat owners, on average 6-7 workers are engaged in a houseboat only for Deluxe and A class. But fewer workers are needed in the B and C class houseboats. In D class there is less need of workers only 1-3 persons. The whole details of employment potential and other things given are in Table 4.9. So this stands that growth in the houseboats is directly related with the increase in employment potential in Kashmir Valley.

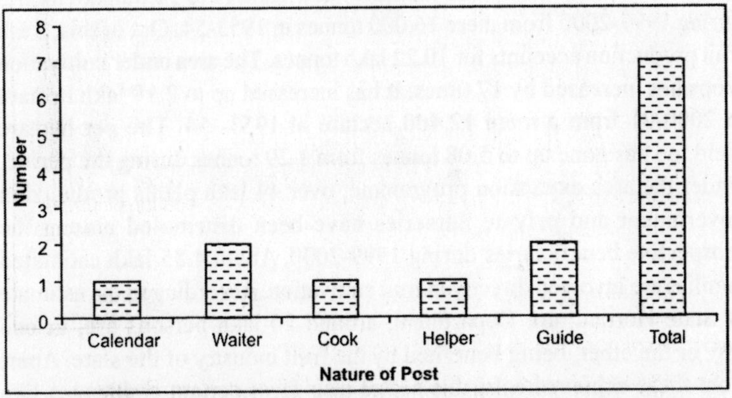


*Source:* Based on Field Survey, 2007.

**Fig. 4.7:** Employment Potential in a House Boat in Kashmir Valley

## Other Resource Development

### *Agricultural Development*

The peculiar geographical situation and inadequacy of infrastructure in

Jammu and Kashmir has restricted the development of agriculture and the possibility of land productivity. The outputs of agricultural products are not increasing in proportion to the cost involved in the farming. The agricultural activity is, therefore, considered to be an uneconomic occupation. In the absence of non-availability of employment opportunities in other sectors, the workforce is forced to depend mainly on agricultural activities. In the context of stagnation in agricultural production, which is not helpful in creating an increasing level of employment opportunities in the region, horticulture is a viable option for exploration.

It occupies an important position in the farming system of the state. Besides, the state has suitable climatic zones for growing temperate, sub-tropical and tropical fruits throughout the year. Temperate fruits like apple, pear, peach, plum, apricot, cheery, walnut, etc., grown at elevation of 1000 to 3000 metres above sea level are important cash-fetching fruits of the state. These fruits not only supplement the diet of the local people, but also form an important item of export to other parts of India.

The Post-Independence era witnessed substantial progress in respect of production and area coverage under horticulture but still needs special attention. Fruit production in the state has increased to 11.05 lakh tonnes during 1999-2000 from mere 16,000 tonnes in 1953-54. Out of this, fresh fruit production accounts for 10.22 lakh tonnes. The area under cultivation crops has increased by 17 times. It has increased up to 2.19 lakh hectare in 2000-01 from a mere 12,400 hectare in 1953- 54. The per hectare yield too has gone up to 5.08 tonnes from 1.29 tonnes during the period. Under the area expansion programme, over 44 lakh plants produced in government and private nurseries have been distributed among the prospective beneficiaries during 1999-2000. About 4.85 lakh estimated families are involved directly in fruit cultivation. According to the estimate of State Horticulture Department, around 20 lakh persons are, in one way or the other, being benefited by the fruit industry of the state. Apart from these achievements, this sector also faces certain challenges like the average land holding size (0.76 hectare) being small for the commercialization of the horticulture activity. Due to unavailability of packaging and processing facilities, 30 per cent of the total fruit produced get wasted. Inadequate marketing facility is also one of the reasons for low productivity. Through certain changes in the development perspective of the Department of Horticulture, this sector could become one of the important sectors in the State economy. The returns from the growth in the apple production should be one of the motivational factors for the growth of horticulture in the region.

### *Area under Horticulture*

The growth and expansion of area under horticulture in the state has been high during the past three decades. Out of the total area under orchards in the state, approximately 90 per cent is concentrated in the valley, for the obvious reason of climate, and soils being conducive to the cultivation of a wide variety of fruits.

The area under orchards is far less in comparison to the area under agriculture. During 1998-99, total area under agriculture was 30.38 per cent; however, total land under the orchards was only 3.02 per cent. The data (Table 4.10) show that still there is a huge area to be explored for horticulture. The agricultural land can be utilized for the purpose of horticulture, because the gestation period in the case of the major varieties of fruit trees is minimum 4-5 years. Moreover, the plantation of fruits trees along with crops like maize, vegetables, fodder, wheat and pulses does not affect crops during the gestation period. Even after the gestation period, some of these crops can be cultivated along with the fruits. Thus it is quite possible that even if the area under these crops does not increase or even remain stable, the area under fruits

**Table 4.10:** Area under different land-use types

| *Land-use type* | *Area in 1000 ha (1984-85)* | *Percentage of area (1984-85)* | *Area in 1000 ha (1998-99)* | *Percentage of area (1998-99)* |
|---|---|---|---|---|
| Forest | 658 | 27.19 | 658 | 27.23 |
| Net area sown | 722 | 29.53 | 734 | 30.38 |
| Land put to non agriculture use | 339 | 14.00 | 291 | 12.04 |
| Barren land | 227 | 9.37 | 291 | 12.04 |
| Permanent pastures and other grazing grounds | 125 | 5.37 | 126 | 5.21 |
| Land area under miscellaneous trees and other groves | 109 | 4.50 | 73 | 3.02 |
| Cultivable waste | 143 | 5.90 | 139 | 5.75 |
| Fallow other than current fallow | 8 | 0.33 | 8 | 0.33 |
| Current fallow | 91 | 3.75 | 96 | 3.97 |

*Source*: *Digest of Statistics*, Jammu and Kashmir, 1999-2000.

could increase. Most of the land available for horticulture is in Anantnag, Pulwama, Srinagar, Badgam, Baramulla and Kupwara (Table 4.11). In the case of Baramulla, Anantnag and Pulwama the area under orchards shows an increasing trend. According to the Godbole Report, the area under orchards in the State was 31,000 acre in 1949-50. It had quadrupled to 1.40 lakh acre by 1970-71. These figures were, however, contradicted by the record of revenue department, which put the area under orchards at 34,000 acre in 1972-73.

The discrepancy arose as large areas converted into orchards were still shown as fallow in the agriculture revenue records. However, Table 4.11 shows that from 1983-84 to 1998-99, there was a minimal increase in the total area. The estimates of agricultural census (1985-86) reveal that the total area under orchards has gone up to 1.48 lakh hectare; 0.64 lakh under apple, 0.33 lakh under walnuts, 0.17 lakh under almonds, 0.30 lakh under crops like cherry, peach, plum, apricot, etc., and 0.04 lakh under mangoes. The State has the largest potential for production of quality temperate horticultural crops. It has created a niche in production of apple, pears, and dry fruits, i.e. almond and walnut.

**Table 4.11:** District-wise Distribution of Area under Orchards and Vegetables

*(Area in 1000 ha)*

| *District* | *Orchards & Vegetables (1983-84)* | *Orchards & Vegetables (1998-99)* |
|---|---|---|
| Anantnag | 7.03 | 10.28 |
| Pulwama | 11.91 | 13.87 |
| Srinagar | 5.80 | 5.47 |
| Badgam | 5.34 | 7.86 |
| Baramulla | 14.58 | 20.27 |
| Kupwara | 4.76 | 5.22 |
| Leh | 0.31 | 0.29 |
| Kargil | 0.12 | 0.34 |
| Jammu | 2.16 | 1.37 |
| Udhampur | 0.28 | 0.48 |
| Doda | 0.73 | 0.51 |
| Kathua | 0.33 | 0.22 |
| Rajouri | 0.02 | 0.06 |
| Poonch | 0.07 | 0.06 |

Among temperate fruits, apple, walnut and almond rank first, second and third respectively in area and production, covering 64.05 per cent, 27.31 per cent and 8.65 per cent of area and 909583, 86263 and 9879 metric tonnes of production respectively. Earlier, apples contributed a major share of total fruit production in the state. But recently a perceptible diversification of fruit has been seen in the walnut cultivation, which has a very high export potential. The potential for foreign exchange earnings on account of walnut export is estimated at Rs.500 crore annually if production technology is further refined and updated according to international standards.

Table 4.12, shows that the districts Baramulla, Anantnag and Pulwama ranked first, second and third respectively in apple production, whereas the districts of Anantnag, Kupwara and Pulwama ranked first, second and third respectively in walnut production. Production of almonds is concentrated in the districts of Pulwama and Budgam. Cherry production is concentrated mainly in district Srinagar for reasons of close proximity to main market, airport and processing units. Pear, plum and peach are concentrated in the districts of Budgam and Srinagar.

**Table 4.12:** District-wise Production of Fruits for the Year 2001-02

*(Production in tonnes)*

| *Districts* | *Apple* | *Pear* | *Citrus* | *Mango* | *Others Fruits* |
|---|---|---|---|---|---|
| Anantnag | 161182 | 7138 | 0 | 0 | 660 |
| Pulwama | 121900 | 3999 | 0 | 0 | 0 |
| Srinagar | 36100 | 2798 | 0 | 0 | 598 |
| Budgam | 45537 | 4079 | 0 | 0 | 12 |
| Baramullah | 469300 | 2079 | 0 | 0 | 1780 |
| Kupwara | 60000 | 1134 | 0 | 0 | 329 |
| Leh | 3350 | 7 | 0 | 0 | 0 |
| Kargil | 350 | 5 | 0 | 0 | 0 |
| Jammu | 0 | 0 | 1892 | 2623 | 3071 |
| Udhampur | 2150 | 1370 | 2705 | 300 | 2211 |
| Doda | 6193 | 1864 | 55 | 0 | 377 |
| Kathua | 1180 | 2853 | 6041 | 3309 | 1111 |
| Rajouri | 125 | 125 | 727 | 825 | 784 |
| Poonch | 2216 | 7499 | 177 | 0 | 403 |

*Source:* Department of Horticulture Srinagar, 2002.

### *Employment Opportunities in the Horticulture Sector*

The cultivation of fruits is labour intensive and requires a significantly higher labour force starting from the stage of planting the trees to the point of its marketing. The manpower requirement in the cultivation and marketing of apples as well as field crops is met by employing paid workers and even the support of family members. This sector not only provides direct employment but it also establishes linkages of various kinds. Apart from labour and capital inputs, the sector generates demand for a wide variety of ancillary activities such as servicing of inputs, packing material, pruning and cutting of branches and transportation of fruit from orchard sites to the fruits centres in the towns and cities of the valley. These ancillaries, have in turn, generated wage employment particularly in horticulture belts. However, according to the estimates of the Horticulture Department, around 20 lakh people are employed in this sector. In a study conducted by the Giri Institute of Development Studies, Lucknow, it is mentioned that the cultivation of apples is providing 77 per cent higher man-days of employment (95 per cent higher in case of paid workers and 71 per cent in case of family workers) as compared to the cultivation of agricultural crops.

The proportion of paid workers in the cultivation of apple increases with the increase in the size of orchards. So there is a need to allocate substantial resources from rural development to the programmes of horticulture so that total area could expand, as rural development programmes are mostly oriented towards creating job opportunities. Horticulture development would prove to be the best investment in this direction as a one-time investment made in plantation programmes would continue to provide job opportunities for years to come.

### *Handloom and Handicraft*

Kashmir is known throughout the world as much for its arts and crafts as for its scenic beauty and bracing climate. Its crafts range from woollen textiles of fleecy soft texture of matchless excellence in weaving, hand-woven carpets of the finest warp and weft, to the exquisite designs worked on papier-mâché, wood work, silverware, etc. They are products of unique craftsmanship. The skill of the craftsmen and their capacity for intricate workmanship are assets, which can help development on a much larger scale. Moreover, as an export oriented sector, it is instrumental in foreign exchange earnings worth crore of rupees annually.

In a state where handicrafts have already proved their worth and where there are vast areas so remote as to make it impossible for major modern industries to be set up, a vigorous policy for developing handicrafts can be specially rewarding. The capital investment in handicrafts is low, their employment potential high and their location can be in the remotest parts of the state.

Like handicrafts, the handloom industry is also the oldest traditional cottage industry in the state. The importance of this sector lies in the fact that it has enormous employment potential; it does not consume scarce resources, does not cause pollution and is environment friendly. The social cost benefit ratio, therefore, of all investment in this sector goes up manifold. J&K is famous for the weaving of specialized fabrics like pashmina and kani shawls, silken, woollen and cotton fabrics.

A Namda is warm, colourful, inexpensive floor covering made out of pressed felt. Rectangular, oval or round, embroidered in chain stitch, Namdas are found mainly in Srinagar and Kupwara district.

Gabba is the common man's carpet made on the outskirts of Anantnag town and nearby villages. Traditionally pieces of waste blankets were sewn together and embroidered. Today barrack blankets are used. Gabbas are embroidered or appliquéd in geometric patterns in brilliant primary colours. Srinagar, Anantnag and Baramulla are the main production centres.

The Handloom Development Corporation has fabrics such as dosooti, a heavy cotton with double twisted yarn, mostly used for Kashmir's famous crewel embroidery. Samba in the Jammu region produce cotton sheets called Masnads or Jajams popularly used for floor coverings. Quilt covers, bedspreads, table-linen, running fabric are also manufactured. Cotton durries are woven in Jammu.

Spinning is done by the womenfolk of virtually every household and weaving in Kashmir and Ladakh is exclusively a man's work. Rural people wear pattu, a rough tweed-like material produced in a variety of weights and widths. In winter, heavy shawls known as *chadars* serve as blankets. They have a number of different designs, each characteristic of the area where it is made. Quality tweeds, using local wool prepared under commercial conditions have a wide range of designs. Outlets are in Srinagar at Poshish (State Government Handloom Emporium), Pratap Park, Khadi Bhandars and Anjuman-e-Dastakar. Marino-wool shawls and blankets are also found there. Kishtwar has chadars using wool, coloured with local vegetable and mineral dyes in bold checks or natural shades. They are woven in Bhadarwah, Ramnagar, Lati, Dudoo, Basantagarh, Banni, Billawar, Poonch and Rajouri in the Jammu region.

The State Government agencies have revived old colours and designs of classic embroidered pashmina shawls. Bani (Kathua district in the Jammu region) produces affordable and popular pashmina shawls.

Pashmina fabric is referred to as 'Cashmere' in other parts of the world. Main production centres of woollen articles in Kashmir are Gurez, Tillel, Bandipur. Nadihal, Kazipora and Papchal (well known for Kandidar or Bordered chadars), Lolab valley, Badgam, Beerwah, Chadoora, Inder Gadodar, Pulwama, Tral, Shopian, Sophare, Handwara, Magam and Tarzoo.

### Embroidery

Embroidery is a commercial activity, organized professionally under the technical guidance of master craftsmen. Except for zari work, embroidery has been the prerogative of males. Sozani or fine needle-work done by a sozankar is the execution of the darn and herringbone stitch in silk thread on pashmina shawls, high quality raffal shawls, stoles, and furnishings. Satin stitch, chain stitch, buttonhole stitch, slanted darn stitch, stem stitch, herringbone stitch and the knot-stitch are some of the many stitches used in Kashmiri embroidery. Though a popular occupation in all districts, embroidery is mainly concentrated in Srinagar and Badgam. Chain stitch is used on a variety of fabrics from hand-woven cloth made from double-twisted yarn called dosootis to wool, silk and cotton used mostly for upholsteries, curtains, soft-leathers, cushions, garments and floor coverings. It is also known as crewelwork. Excellence in wielding the needle created the dorukha embroidery in which the upper and the under-sides are both embroidered in different sets of colours, repeating the very same design to obtain a reverse mirror image. In the areas surrounding Anantnag in Kashmir, many people are engaged in embroidering raffal and pashmina shawls, pherans (a loose over gown worn by men and women), cotton dosooti fabric, gabbas, namdas. The traditional dogra embroidery of Jammu known as phulkari is rooted in Punjab and Haryana. Unfinsihed, home dyed silk floss is used as the embroidery thread.

### Carpets

Introduced to Kashmir by Sultan Zain-ul-Abedin in the 15th century, the Kashmir carpet ranks amongst the finest in the world today. The weaver takes special pride in his ability to accurately reproduce Persian, Turkish, Turkman, Caucasian, antique Kashmir Moghul and Jaipur Moghul patterns. Amlikar or paisley shawl patterns were introduced in the early 1960s. Carpets are woven in wool or silk and now artificial silk as well, in the districts of Srinagar, Badgam, Kupwara, Pulwama, Baramulla and

Anantnag. In Srinagar there are outlets in Residency Road, Polo View, the Bund, Boulevard and around Dal and Nageen lakes. The Kashmir Government Arts Emporium and its branches all over the country have big carpet sections.

# 5

# Major Sectors of Economic Development and Employment

## Land-use Planning and Employment Generation

Land-use and Agricultural sector of India is providing largest number of employment, i.e. about two-third. It can be increased at par with the developed countries by initiating agro-based industries and will provide number of related economic activities.

In the valley of Kashmir during the field work of villages it was observed that agro-based related spread of economic activities is the poorer as compared to Punjab, Haryana, and Western Uttar Pradesh and North Eastern Hill region of India. It was also observed that seasonal employment for few months are available and for the whole eight to nine months farmers remain unengaged in the farming sector. For this purpose land capability survey is highly needed.

Seasonal rural migration from Kashmir valley is recorded in the absence of local distinguished unemployment is a common feature in the valley while the enormous potential is available. The region is characterized as diversified cropping pattern with highly value added crops such as saffron and its role in socio-economic development. Its spread is only in 4.5 per cent of the cultivated area of the valley. Its demand in National and International market is very high. The valley is rich in major dry fruits cultivation but not in planned and scientific manner as well related economic activities are absent.

Therefore, it is suggested that a proper land capability survey is needed. In the period of specialization in agricultural sector with a suitable example of our neighbouring countries like China is to be adopted. Now we are far behind in agricultural sector and related employment as compared to China. Two decades before, we were a comparable in agricultural sector with China, now we cannot dream the level of China. It is a big question what our scientists are doing in spite of continuous first priority in Five Year Planning from the last six decades? The region or Himalayan region seems to be more neglected as human occupation in the Himalayan region is poorest as compared to other regions of India in spite of diversified rich resources as compared to Indo-Gangetic plain or plateau region.

The land of Kashmir valley is available for variety of uses but proper direction is not seen in the absence of land capability survey, i.e. the land capable for what uses? A brief account is given below of land capability classes of the Kashmir valley.

The land of India is proving inadequate for the burgeoning population that is dependent on it. It is now being realized that all wasteful uses of land should be discouraged and rational land policy should be chalked out to face the challenge. More and more emphasis is now being laid on using land according to its best capability. This is especially significant in view of growing competition between different uses of land, such as residential, recreational, industrial and agricultural. An overemphasis on one use might have a chain reaction on the other. Beside the different competitive uses, the land in the valley is continually menaced by severe erosion and waterlogging, both seriously inhibiting its productive uses. A hopeful feature is that a large chunk of this land is, reclaimable provided a rational strategy is chalked out in this respect.

For all this, and for ensuring rational use of land in the future, a regular survey to establish the capability of different types of land for optimal use is badly needed. An empirical exercise is, however, being attempted here to identity the generalized capability classes based on site, properties of soil, proportion of land under different slope categories, exposure to erosion hazards and dominant land use. Various methods have been developed to categories into capability classes by different authorities. These include some of the most sophisticated techniques, such as the one developed by the US National Resources Planning Board which integrates the whole gamut of physical, economic and institutional factors into a single scheme, as well as most rudimentary ones. The present study is based on a method developed by Bennet which is based on site (altitude, degree of slope and drainage) climate, soil types and major land use. It is suited to such areas as the Kashmir Valley where non-availability of classified information as specific aspects of land inhibits the application of more rigorous methods.

## Factors in Land Capability, Classes and Landuse Planning

According to Bennet, the land capability classification is based on the following criteria:

(i) Soil types;
(ii) Degree of slope;
(iii) Erode ability of surface soil or degree of erosion;
(iv) Drainage; and
(v) Predominant land use pattern.

The soil of Kashmir valley reveals great variation in texture, permeability and fertility status. These typological differences have been used as a variable in the identification of the land capability classes. Areas characterized by steep slopes are liable to erosion the intensity of which will depend on the nature of terrain and vegetal cover.

### *Land Capability Classes*

The land of the Kashmir valley has been classified according to its capability, using Bennet's method based on site peculiarities and physical factors. Primarily, two more categories have been distinguished, land suited to cultivation, and land not suited to cultivation.

The first category can further be grouped into four capability classes. The lands unsuitable for cultivation, on the other hand, lend themselves to a classification into three groups. The general characteristic of these seven land capability classes are described below.

#### *Land Suited to Cultivation*

***Class I***: The soil of class I land is deep, highly fertile and mostly consists of best quality loams and clayey loams. The texture, however, gets heavier with increasing depth. The soil has the high retention capacity and is rich in humus. Class I lands are found in the areas which are either flat or characterized by gentle slope. These lands are by and large free from the hazards of erosion or water-logging and the physical environment favours their maximum utilization.

The area occupied by class I lands although it extends over the entire length of the valley on either side of the Jhelum, has its main expanse in the central part consisting of the parts of Srinagar, Pulwama, Badgam and Sonawari Ganderbal tehsils.

The fertility status of these lands can be further raised if farmers are induced to take to new methods of farming and land management and their capacity to use new inputs enhances.

***Class II***: The Class II lands are characterized by course textured soil. The subsoil is heavy and gets heavier with increasing depth. The surface soil has low to moderate permeability; low at the subsoil and very low at the substratum. These lands are not liable to water-logging or erosion, although lands in the sloping areas suffer from moderate erosion. Substantial areas in Kulgam, Sopore and Handwara Tahsils are dominated by Class II lands. They occur in two compact blocks—the southern one lies in the Kulgam Tahsil while the northern extends over parts of Sopore and Handwara tahsils. Terrace cultivation is a common phenomenon on the periphery of the northern block.

***Class III***: The Class III lands form a narrow belt along the Karewa uplands. The land is dominated by soils with a coarse texture and there is a marked increase in the degree of slopes, the permeability decrease with depth. This class of land is bordered by the extensive marshy tracts in the northern parts of the Valley. Both erosion and water-logging impose serious limitations on its use. The utility of these soils can be improved if erosion is controlled and suitable drainage methods are introduced to combat the problem of water-logging.

The main concentration of the class III land is found in Sonawari, Baramulla, Budgam, Pulwama and parts of Kulgam tahsils.

***Class IV***: The class IV lands are found along the Karewa slopes with their tongue extending higher up in the side Valleys of the Jhelum. The slope increases rapidly with the result that cultivation is possible only on terraces using rigorous measure of soil conservation and drainage. The soil is shallow with variable texture and permeability. The depth of the soil decreases as stoniness increases with increasing altitude.

These four classes of land under cultivation differ vastly in their cropping pattern. Rice is the dominant crop on class I lands and is alternated by maize on higher areas. Among other crops grown are barley and wheat mainly on lands irrigated by wells. Rice continues to be important on class II lands as well with maize as close associate on drier tracts. Wheat and barley sharply decline in importance. Maize emerges as the principal crop on class III land with barley and wheat flourishing on lands provided with ensured water supply. A major proportion of the class IV land is also devoted to maize, although rice is also grown extensively on well-watered terraces.

*Land not suited to Cultivation*

***Class V***: Lands with predominant uses such as grazing and forestry have been categorized as class V. They are characterized by steep slopes and contain shallow, stone-studded soils. The low-lying slopes on rainy aspects are thickly forested. Above the tree line lie grazing lands which are used as summer pastures by transhumant groups. The soil of these *margs* is fairly fertile with a higher moisture-holding capacity.

***Class VI***: This class consists of lands with steeper slopes and poorer soil which has no capability even to support the growth of vegetation. They consist of rocky wastes mainly in the higher precipices of the Pir-panjal and the great Himalayan ranges.

***Class VII***: The higher slopes of the mountain ranges which remain covered with perennial snow have been grouped in this class. These lands have been subjected to rigorous glaciations in the past and are occupied by glaciers even today.

The land capable for what use and land use planning if based on the land of special qualities for special uses; it will generate employment such as:

- Skilled and unskilled workers will be involved at large scale for the survey as it has been done in most of the developed countries and in our neighbouring China.
- Secondly, innovation of new cropping pattern is possible through this type of survey and productivity per unit area will be increased for more employment and better wage rate. Therefore, land resource is still a major sector as compared to other sectors for more employment generation.

## Water Resource Management and Employment Generation

Water in the Kashmir Valley is an extraordinary paradox. Considering the total run-off, area of water bodies and length of water courses, the Valley has no match in the Himalayas. In fact, its water features are the principal components in its scenic beauty. The geomorphic character of the Valley is, however, such that the distribution of water resources is extremely uneven—a situation which renders vast stretches of land totally or partially out of use either due to the excess of water or its deficiency. Water is most plentiful in the low-lying parts of the valley, which remain literally deluged, while the adjoining *Karewa* uplands suffer from aridity imposed by its chronic deficiency. In both these respects the situation seriously constrains the optimal use of the Valley's land potential. The consequence is that the Valley presents the anomalous case of scarcity in the midst of plenty. The rivers carry large volumes of water which they cannot possibly contain as their channels get increasingly choked with silt, making floods a recurrent phenomenon with disastrous consequences on agriculture. Naturally, in the absence of any systematic scheme for water management, the spillover from the ever-rising channels spread all over the low-lying tracts, which have been converted into extensive swamps, called the *Nambal.* The rest of the water flows out practically unharnessed, without being put to any substantial use before it escapes out of the Baramulla gorge. Recent data show that only a tiny fraction of this vast, potential is being utilized for hydroelectric generation, the aggregate annual production from all power houses being about 20,000 kws. The only other use of this enormous resource is in gradient irrigation, through the distribution system of *Kuhls*, in the making of which modern technology has hardly any contribution.

The above remarks are, however, relevant only in the context of the present understanding of the Valley's water potential, which is by no means complete. It is interesting to note that no serious attempt has yet been made to assess this potential, its mode of occurrence, spatial distribution and temporal variations in its availability. Evidently, no comprehensive planning is possible in the absence of such primary data, whether aimed at draining the swamps, augmenting water supply in agriculture or generating hydroelectricity. In fact, the present state of knowledge inhabits even the estimation of the gap between the water potential and the actual amount that is being used productivity.

An attempt will be made here to make an analytical study of the water resources of the valley, both surface and subterranean, temporal variations in its supply as perceived in the incidence of floods or droughts and the current level of its utilization. The Jhelum and its numerous tributaries, a large number of lakes, depressions and springs are the main water bodies of the Valley.

## Hydrological Network and Data

There is a great dearth of consistent hydrological data for Kashmir for any reasonable period of time. This makes a meaningful temporal study of local hydrological phenomena impossible. The meteorological observatory at Srinagar was opened in 1891 and at Gulmarg in 1897. The position has not substantially changed since then. Regular meteorological data are, however, available only for Srinagar, as the Gulmarg observatory functions only during the four summer months—June to September—for reasons best known to the IMD only.

The rainfall is measured at a number of places, though in many cases the records are far from consistent. Other than Srinagar, there are only four places—Wantipore (Pulwama), Anantnag, Uttarmachipura (Handwara), and Sri Partap Singhpura (Badgam)—which have rainfall records for at least seventy-four years. Kulgam and Baramulla have a record for seventy-two years; Langet fifty-eight years; Duru and Sopore fifty-eight years each. Mala Shahibag (Ganderbal) has a record for forty-four years only, beginning with 1924 and with a gap between 1933 and 1940.

Despite its heavy contribution to the valley's moisture supply, snowfall is only casually measured. There are snow gauges at the observatories of Srinagar city and aerodrome, and at Sonamarg, Gulmarg, Pahalgam, Qazigund and Banihal. Of these, the observations at the last five places are highly occasional (Fig. 5.1).

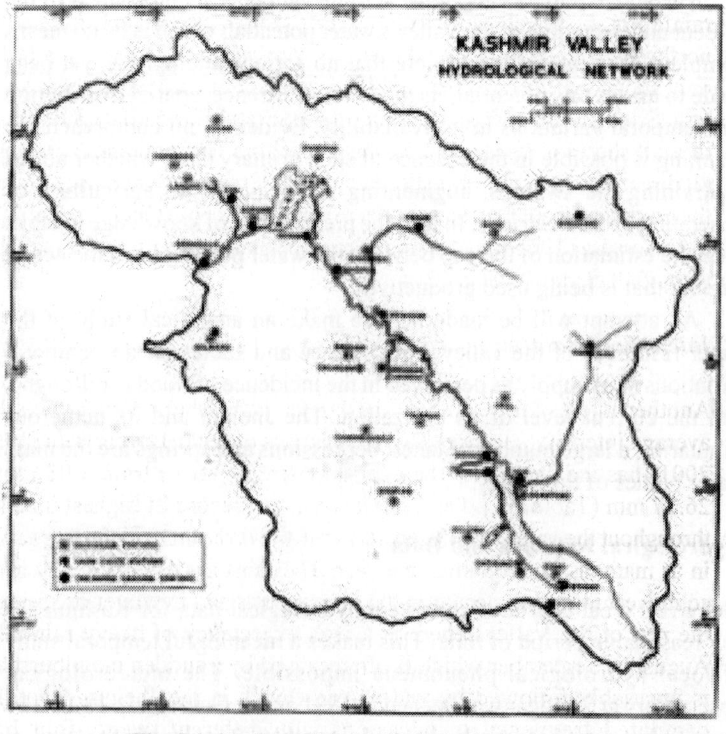


**Fig. 5.1:** Kashmir Valley—Hydrological Network

**Factors in Water Availability**

The availability of water in a region is a function of the whole set of variables which determine the quantum of water inflow, outflow, and storage at a given point of time. While meteorological factors play a fundamental role in these processes, geological strata and topographical setting are decisive in determining the complexion of storage changes. The inflow of water, whether in the form of rainfall, snow or run-off over or through the surface, is of critical importance as later changes in its state or place are only consequential in nature.

***Rainfall***

The Kashmir Valley receives precipitation both in the form of rain and snow. It has been noted that the rainfall has a peculiar distribution pattern through the year. It is overwhelmingly concentrated in the winter and spring months in all parts of the Valley. The share of the winter and spring rainfall is, however, more than three-fourths of the annual total in the northwest (e.g. Handwara, Baramulla, Langet, and Sopore), while it is only about one-third in the central and the southeastern parts of the Valley (e.g. Srinagar, Pulwama, Anantnag, Kulgam and Ganderbal). The annual rainfall shows a regular increasing trend from Badgam and Srinagar in all directions. It is the lowest at Badgam (579mm) and increases towards the northwest from Srinagar (663 mm) through Sopore (756) Langet (873) to Handwara (1005 mm); and towards the southeast from Pulwama (592) through Kulgam (898) to Doru (1195).

***Intensity of Rainfall***

Another interesting feature of the rainfall of Kashmir Valley is its low average intensity per rainy day. An analysis of the fifty-year data (1950-2001) has indicated that the average intensity varies from 5.08 mm to 26.27 mm (Table 5.1). Doru has a consistent record of highest intensity throughout the valley which remains well above the other recording gauges in as many as nine months in a year. The rains are usually heavy in the southwest monsoon period in the central parts and in winter or spring in the rest of the Valley. There is a high expectancy of heavy rainfall in August or September which is often caused by a sudden cloudburst and is invariably followed by widespread floods in the Jhelum. Bhan has computed frequency of occasions with different twenty-four hour

**Table 5.1:** Intensity of Rainfall

*(Millimetres per rainy day, based on average for 1951-2001)*

| Station | Jan. | Feb. | March | April | May | June | July | Aug. | Sep. | Oct. | Nov. | Dec. |
|---|---|---|---|---|---|---|---|---|---|---|---|---|
| Srinagar | 11.00 | 11.71 | 12.47 | 10.76 | 17.08 | 5.08 | 9.53 | 13.81 | 11.48 | 13.44 | 10.71 | 10.80 |
| Pulwama | 12.81 | 18.85 | 17.27 | 13.12 | 12.27 | 15.70 | 14.95 | 14.80 | 14.71 | 14.42 | 14.15 | 14.23 |
| Handwara | 16.11 | 18.93 | 18.86 | 17.71 | 14.83 | 10.58 | 12.13 | 13.55 | 13.35 | 15.87 | 13.16 | 12.09 |
| Anantnag | 13.67 | 14.64 | 12.54 | 7.86 | 12.00 | 11.69 | 13.23 | 13.23 | 19.56 | 15.29 | 10.08 | 12.65 |
| Kulgam | 18.55 | 17.49 | 15.50 | 17.17 | 13.78 | 12.79 | 15.50 | 15.18 | 19.29 | 15.11 | 14.92 | 17.12 |
| Dora | 20.49 | 26.27 | 24.71 | 16.68 | 15.42 | 16.25 | 15.50 | 17.51 | 21.91 | 17.37 | 19.09 | 23.64 |
| Ganderbal | 12.34 | 14.00 | 12.57 | 15.14 | 14.07 | 10.69 | 18.83 | 20.54 | 17.61 | 12.36 | 11.18 | 13.64 |
| Baramula | 14.70 | 16.54 | 17.03 | 15.58 | 13.63 | 11.44 | 12.12 | 12.38 | 12.50 | 13.38 | 12.37 | 13.43 |
| Langet | 13.13 | 10.90 | 18.98 | 17.10 | 13.22 | 11.25 | 10.89 | 11.91 | 11.53 | 14.61 | 11.87 | 11.83 |
| Sopore | 13.32 | 13.66 | 14.97 | 12.69 | 11.90 | 10.25 | 9.37 | 4.66 | 11.76 | 10.58 | 11.13 | 12.95 |
| Gulmarg | — | — | — | — | — | 10.40 | 10.83 | 11.56 | 13.40 | — | — | — |
| Badgam | 10.96 | 15.21 | 12.86 | 12.63 | 11.37 | 9.18 | 12.18 | 11.41 | 17.21 | 14.53 | 11.54 | 10.39 |

*Source*: Based on actually monthly data incents published in Monthly and Annual Rainfall and number of Rainy Day, 1950-2001, India Meteorological Department, New Delhi, 2004.

intensities of rainfall for Srinagar to show that there has been the highest frequency of occasions with an intensity of less than 12.7 millimetres of rain per day. There have been only three occasions in a fifty-year cycle when the intensity of rain exceeded seventy-five millimetres.

## Surface Water Resources

The Surface Water Resources of Kashmir Valley are by any definition very large. The total run-off that escapes down the rivers or accumulates in a large number of lakes and marshes is a powerful indicator of this plentiful supply.

The river systems of the valley are fed both by rain and snow. Naturally, the flow is poor during winter months as most of the precipitation comes in the form of snow. The quantum of surface run-off increases with the onset of summer when the snow melts, and with the rain, generates a higher run-off. Normally, not less than three-fourth of the total annual discharge of the Jhelum flows during the summer in the months of April to August. In winter the discharge falls down substantially—only ten per cent of the annual discharge passes down during November-February, and not more than fifteen per cent during October-February.

As noted earlier, the major streams of the Jhelum system have their sources in the snow fields of the rounding mountains which feed them during summer. The streams rising in the Pir Panjal have a lesser share of the snowmelt and their supplies are augmented by summer rains. The streams of the great Himalayan range, on the other hand, are dependent more on snow than on rain. This produces interesting contrasts between the flow pattern of the Pir Panjal and the Himalayan rivers. The discharge of Pir Panjal rivers is not only low; it is highly variable as the quantity of rainfall is the major component.

While the intensity of snowfall depends on the frequency and intensity of western disturbances which hit the valley during winter, the quantum of summer snowmelt depends on the amount and duration of sunshine and the total intake of solar energy. Summer discharge also depends on monsoon rains, which have a high variability and may be very heavy in the period of high discharge from snowmelt. As a consequence, the run-off in the summer is very high as compared to the discharge during the rest of the year. Thus the discharge in May is ten to twelve times that of December. The discharge rises with the rise in temperature from March onwards when low altitude snow starts melting. The volume of water supply in July and August is also dependent on rainfall and not on snow alone; the contribution of snow to river discharge gradually declines as autumn advances.

A study of the decennial averages (1990-2000) of the monthly discharge of Jhelum at Baramulla (Table 5.2 shows that only 11.65 per cent of the total annual run-off flows during the four winter months (November–February). The five summer months (April-August) accounts for 68.65 per cent of the aggregate discharge. The maximum comes in June although May also does not lag far behind (Fig. 5.2)

**Table 5.2:** Average monthly discharge of Jhelum at Baramulla (1990-2000)

*(Data in Cusecs)*

| *Months* | *Discharge* | *% of the total discharge* | *% of the total discharge in June* |
|---|---|---|---|
| January | 148,985 | 3.48 | 22.16 |
| February | 214,583 | 5.10 | 31.91 |
| March | 368,565 | 8.60 | 54.81 |
| April | 578,480 | 13.70 | 87.37 |
| May | 665,498 | 15.52 | 98.98 |
| June | 672,382 | 15.68 | 100.00 |
| July | 514,356 | 12.00 | 76.50 |
| August | 503,680 | 11.75 | 74.91 |
| September | 286,413 | 6.68 | 42.60 |
| October | 189,565 | 4.32 | 28.19 |
| November | 73,685 | 1.72 | 10.96 |
| December | 62,340 | 1.45 | 9.27 |

*Source:* Based on actually monthly data in cents published in Monthly and Annual Rainfall and number of Rainy Day, 1990-2000, India Meteorological Department, New Delhi, 2004.

## Floods and Nambals – Plenty of Water

Floods have been a recurrent phenomenon in the Kashmir Valley. Their frequency and the devastation caused by them are fairly understandable in the bowl that the Valley is. For one thing, the Jhelum is faced with the predicament of carrying the cumulative discharge of all its streams through a narrow passage down the valley, where silting goes on choking the channels infinitely, incapacitating the river from performing its primary function. The past behaviour of Jhelum shows that it has a maximum capacity of 'safely' carrying only half of a high flood discharges. The other half has but to spill over the banks breaching the embankments that have been constructed to contain floods. Thus, in the photographic

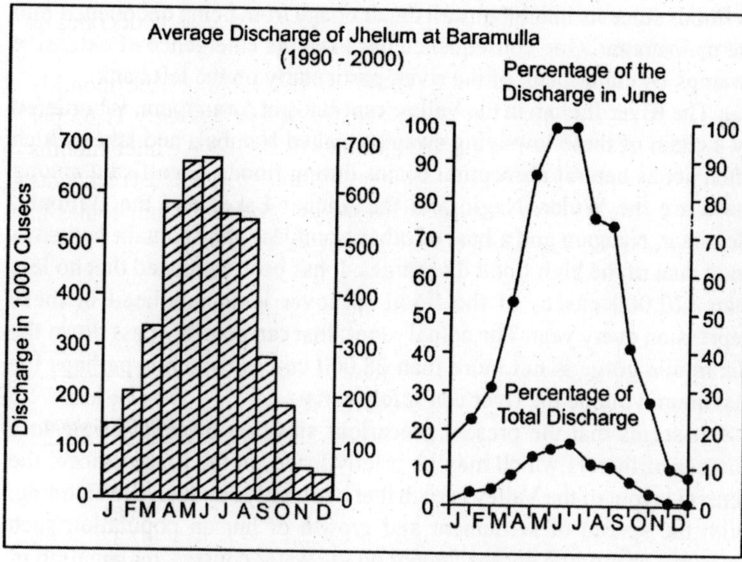


**Fig. 5.2:** Averages Discharge of Jhelum

situation in which the Jhelum is, the floods are but a natural phenomenon.

The magnitude of the flood problem can well be associated in that perspective. Even a casual look at history shows that the frequency of flood problem has been very high ever since the Valley assumed its present form. A heavy precipitation, usually coming during the end month of the summer monsoon and caused by a sudden cloudburst, leads to a severe flood. By now the catchments area of the river is already saturated and the high run-off swells the rivers beyond their capacity, with the result that the river bunds are breached and the whole Valley is converted into a big Nanmal. The spillover from the rivers, particularly the Jhelum but also the Sind and the Pohru, flows to the depressions lying on the fringe of the rivers and inundates the agricultural lands with incalculable losses to the crops, livestock and human settlements. Not all the havoc is created by the nature; man has added to his predicament in a big way. With every increase in population, human settlements have grown and expanded, swallowing up new lands for agriculture and habitation. As cities have grown on the banks of Jhelum, its course has been narrowed and new embankments have been raised to contain its fury. The silting problem being what it is the bed of the river goes on rising to the extent that no embankment can arrest the floods. The *bund* itself acts as a causal factor to floods since its inhabitants all the drainage from being debouched into the mainstream. One consequence has been the emergence of extensive swamps on either bank of the river, particularly on the left bank.

The River Jhelum in the Valley, especially at Awantipura, is bordered by a chain of these low-lying swamps, called Nambals and lakes which often act as natural absorption basins during floods. Significant among these are the Wular, Nagin and the Anchar Lakes and the Batmalu, Hokarsar, Naugam and a host of other Nambles. They contain in them a good deal of the high flood discharges. It has been estimated that no less than 120,000 cusecs of the flood spillover is accumulated in these depression every year. The actual runoff that can possibly pass down the Baramulla gorge is not more than 28,000 cusecs, which is perhaps the maximum volume the river can safely carry.

It seems that the present precarious situation owes its origin to a number of factors which may be briefly listed. In the first instance, the general layout of the Valley is such that it is highly conducive to flooding. With the spread of settlement and growth of human population such measures as gradual encroachment on the water courses, reclamation of low-lying areas for agriculture, channelizing of rivers, creation of bunds along the river banks and construction of transport lines in the flood have further worsened the situation.

Flood control measures have been given top priority since the early stages of history. But effective steps to mitigate the damage caused by floods have all been taken in the 20th century. By 1930 a flood-spill channel, however, rejoins the Jhelum a few kilometres below the city. Other measures that have been adopted from time to time include construction of embankments along the river banks and of diversion channels, along with clearing silt from the river beds. The Irrigation Commission has recommended that the solution to this menace perhaps lies in:

(i) Strengthening and realigning the bunds without raising them;
(ii) Improving the river channel by making cut-offs;
(iii) Providing a supplementary channel or floodway from Dogripura to Wular, and improving the outfall channel by diverting the Ningle (Ningal) and the Pohru rivers into the Wular lake; and
(iv) Stabilizing the torrents below Baramulla and clearing debris from the bed of the outfall channels.

The Commission hoped that if these measures were properly implementing the Wular Lake would be completely sited up and would be "available for cultivation". The Commission's recommendation to silt up the Wular is, however, unrealistic. In the Wular Lake the Jhelum has a vast reservoir which plays a positive role in minimizing the load on the outfall channel during floods. The rise and fall of level in the Wular Lake has a cause-effect relationship with the discharge at the point of outfall. Uppal estimated that during the floods the lake may receive about 60,000 cusecs, although it has the capacity to discharge 30,000-35,000 cusecs only. Understanding, the reclamation of low-lying tracts around the lake is likely to affect adversely its capacity of the lake to act as a moderator of flood in the outfall channel.

## Groundwater Resources

The groundwater resources of Kashmir Valley are only marginally known. No systematic surveys have been conducted to assess the groundwater potential of the valley. There seems to be two main reasons for this lack of concern. First, an abundant supply of moisture from the surface sources, particularly in the floodplain of the Jhelum and other low-lying areas, ruled out the need to depend on underground water. Secondly, the political situation before and after the accession of the state of Jammu and Kashmir never aroused the rulers to care for an integrated development of the valley through optimally managing the land and water resources of the region. For most of the recent history, mounting pressure on land and a subsistence agriculture have been taken for grated, leaving the problem of dry Karewa as something lying out of the ambit of human effort. But it is on the Karewa uplands that the water problem is most acute and where agricultural development is contingent on the feasibility of successfully tapping groundwater reserves.

Lately, the Government of Jammu and Kashmir seems to have become conscious of this problem as the Central Water and Power Commission has been asked to launch a programme to assess the groundwater potential of the Valley.

The present study will, therefore, confine itself to casual observations regarding the availability and utilization of groundwater in certain parts of the Valley. Geologically, the strata that compose the low-lying areas of Kashmir valley are favourable for the occurrence of groundwater. Indirect evidence is provided by the natural springs which seem to draw their supply from the affluent seepage of groundwater to the fringe of the alluvial tract. These springs are known to have sufficient discharge of water which is often put to miscellaneous local uses, though the bulk of it remains unharnessed and unused. The scientists of the Central Groundwater Board have some data pertaining to the processes of recharging of aquifers for the State of Jammu and Kashmir as a whole. The estimates have little relevance to Kashmir Valley.

## Utilization of Water Resources

Water plays a limited though vital role in the economy of Kashmir. Its use is mainly in agriculture and to an average Kashmiri its plentiful supply means prosperity. The main uses are still traditional ones–gradient irrigation, navigation and primitive fishing—reminiscent of Neolithic times. The generation of hydroelectricity is only marginal, and, if compared with the available potential, infinitesimal.

### *Irrigation*

The main use of surface water resources of the valley is in gravity irrigation with the help of primitive technology. There are, however, both political and environmental constraints on the optimal utilization of water potential. The Jhelum is one of the rivers covered by the Indus Waters Treaty which regulates the use of Indus river between India and Pakistan. According to this treaty, while Pakistan is entitled to have a major claim on the waters of the Indus, the Jhelum and the Chenab and their tributaries, India can utilize their waters only to a limited extent. In its use of these waters, notably in the case of the Indus, India is further incapacitated by the difficult nature of terrain and communication problems.

The Kashmiri system of irrigation consists of *Khuls* which take from water courses at convenient points. The *khuls* far surpass the government canals in terms of area covered as well as length of channels. At the beginning of the First Five-Year Plan the area irrigated by *khuls* was as much as sixteen times that of government canals. Although government canals have been consistently expanding their command area since 1950, there is no comparison between them and the *khuls*. The Kashmiri *khuls* irrigation system emerged under the feudal lords who were concerned with the construction and maintenance of these channels. With the abolition of the *Zamindari* system the *khuls* fell into negligence and proved to be a menace to the adjoining agricultural land as the spill-over from these channels caused recurrent floods. The Government has become conscious of this problem only recently and a comprehensive scheme has been chalked out to expedite their restoration and renovation. Initially

**Fig. 5.3:** Kashmir Valley—Drainage Basin

the scheme was designed to cover 2,046 *khuls* only, though it envisaged an eventual takeover of all the remaining *khuls* with a command area of 1,012 hectares. The Government has, however, displayed little interest in the extension of irrigation to drier parts of the Valley, particularly the chronically dry Karewas. Nor will it be possible to extend irrigation to these uplands unless more complex technology is employed which ensures lifting of water to areas tens of metres higher from the river valley floors.

### *Domestic uses of Water*

One of the commonest uses of water is for drinking. Despite a plentiful supply of water in the Valley, there is no systematic distribution except in large urban centres. Among the districts of the Valley, Anantnag seems to the best served. A number of reservoirs have been constructed at different places in the district and tap water is supplied to the public. The towns of Pampore, Shopian, Awantipura and Sedov Tsotopora have water supply schemes. Of the nine urban centres in Baramulla district only four – Baramulla, Sopore, Bandipora and Gulmarg (Tangmarg)—have a regular water supply. So far as rural areas are concerned, only large villages of Wanigam and Bunagam in Baramulla tehsil—Nadihal, Tiyar, Seer and Ajar Aithmulla in Sopore; and Sogam in Handwara tahsil have been provided with a water supply system.

### *Navigation*

Water courses also act as navigation channels. The Jhelum river and most of its tributaries in the floodplain as well as the Dal and the Wular lakes are navigable. Their role as arteries of transport can hardly be overemphasized.

### *Generation of Hydroelectricity*

Although the Valley has a considerable potential for the generation of hydroelectricity, no major attempt has so far been made to exploit it substantively for either industrial or domestic use. There are very few urban areas and fewer villages which are served with electricity.

The Valley has two hydroelectricity stations at Ganderbal and Moharra with an installed generating capacity of 15,000 and 6,000 kws respectively. They cater to the needs of all urban centres besides important tourist resorts and a few villages. The villages so far electrifies are few – 2 per cent of all villages in Anantnag, 1.4 per cent in Baramulla and 8 per cent in Srinagar. Besides these two hydroelectric stations, work on the three projects – Chenani, Upper Sind and Lower Jhelum is in progress. Of the three, Chenani was ready to be commissioned in 1972. A 220 kv transmission line will take the supply to Srinager and will be linked to an inter-regional grid augmenting to Ganderbal supply. It is further proposed that a 33kv line will connect Pattan to Tanmarg, Sopore to Bandipora and Anantnag to Shopian.

One may expect that in the foreseeable future water will be put to more and more varied uses as the economy diversifies and new schemes of resource conservation and utilization receive increased attention. It is, therefore, necessary receive increased attention. It is, therefore, necessary to fix priority at the very outset and chalk out a comprehensive strategy for the optimal utilization of the Valley's water resources.

**Measurement of Scarcity in Plénty of Water Resources**

There are four methods which can be used to measure the scarcity of water amides plenty of water. If resources are not utilized needed for the welfare of the people resources scarcity prevails. There are regions in India where plenty of the water is available. For example, in Brahmaputra Basin comprising an area of 7.1 per cent of India with 3.4 per cent population but water resources of 31.7 per cent of India is available in this basin but all the four parametres needed to meet the requirement of the people are found unfulfilled. These four parametres are as follows:

(1) Irrigated area as percentage of Net Sown area.
(2) Hydroelectricity Production in terms of water availability.
(3) Availability of Potable Water.
(4) Industrial and Urban Water.

These above criteria if applied to measure the scarcity in plenty in the Valley of Kashmir, the result obtained is positively correlated with the situation, i.e. Scarcity in plenty where resources in abundance is available but not utilized as desired and required by the agricultural sector for irrigation.

In the Valley of Kashmir all the cultivated area is not irrigated because of the lack of irrigation. An assured base of irrigation can be achieved but not available for the irrigation especially in the *Karewa* region of the valley occupying about 32 per cent of the cultivated area. Similarly, in many pockets irrigation water is not available for the development of agriculture. It is a matter of great concern for us that amidst plenty of water *Karewa* looks like a desert and when the land above 7000 feet needs water for Maize irrigation but nor available for the development of agriculture.

Secondly, *hydro-electricity* is the major infrastructure for an overall development of the economy as each sector of economy is dependent on availability of water. Our social development as well as economic development is dependent on hydro-electricity and it is used to measure the major indicator of development. In the Valley of Kashmir easiest way is available to produce the hydro-electricity but diesel is still being used to produce the electricity when the region can be on developed at par with the Switzerland which can export hydro-electricity in the summer months if needed can import in the winter.

Lastly, the availability of potable water and industrial water is a serious problem. Almost, all the villages are located on the bank of rivers and water streams. The nature of potable water can well be understood in the total absence of water literacy. Sometimes late snowfall and early melting of snow can be a great source of scarcity of water in the region because it depends on the snowfall frequency.

Such a situation can be characterized as scarcity in plenty because of the availability if plenty of water but for all these four purposes water is not available while there are some countries in the world such as Israel where scarcity in plenty is not located but plenty in scarcity is located.

## Conclusions

- Electricity production should be based on water resources not on diesel.
- Unirrigated *Karewa* land should be tacked through the exploitation of underground water.
- Awareness about Potable water should be developed.
- Nambal Problem should be tackled through constructing the construction of spill channels.

Lastly, snow melt water supply should be regulated so that the large number of villages inhabited at the bank should not be deprived with water.

## Forests/Grazing Land Resource Management and Employment Generation

In response to the peculiarities of habitat, particularly climate and edaphic factors, the biotic type of the Kashmir Valley sharply differ from those of the southern face of the Pir Panjal. The following valley: (i) Absence of oaks as a climax species and of laurels and low level rhododendrons; (ii) a preponderance of fir; and (iii) negligible occurrence of spruce.

The forests are generally composed of a large number of species, although tracts with stands of pure communities are also not uncommon.

## Classification

Botanists employ a number of criteria in classifying the forest of the Kashmir Valley. The different classification system commonly recognized are based on the following criteria: (i) genetic characteristics; (ii) composition; (iii) management; and (iv) economic exportability.

On the basis of their genetic characteristics the forests may be classified into montane, temperate and alpine. The montane and temperate forests are usually found between 1500 and 3200 metres. They have a lower zone in which the broad leaved varieties are preponderant and a higher zone (2100-3200m) in which the conifers predominate. The alpine forest occurs at an average elevation of 3200 metres and above. The birch is the most common tree type, although stunted junipers and rhododendrons are also found.

The Kashmir forest may be classified into coniferous and broad leaved varieties on the basis of their specific composition. As noted above, the broad leaved species are generally found below 2100 metres. For systematic management and better exploitation of forests they are often grouped into reserved, protected, and unclassified types. This distinction is made between first class forest estates meant for better production (these are either reserved or protected) and the inferior stands of forest which are left unprotected and unclassified. The development and exploitation of forests are both dependent on their economic importance and accessibility. A distinction is often made between commercial and non-commercial forests. Forests which are accessible and are capable of yielding good quality timber are considered to be exploitable and classified as commercial. A forest may be considered non commercial if it is inaccessible, or its yield is of such inferior quality that its exploitation would be largely uneconomic.

## Forest Management and Conservation

Forests contribute significantly to the economy of Kashmir. Recent statistics show that they account for about one-fifth of the state income which is slightly more than half the share of agriculture. The importance of forests to the economy of Kashmir may also be judged from the fact that occupies about sixty per cent of the total geographical area of the state. The distribution of area under forests for the tahsils of the Valley is given in Table 5.3.

The proportion of area under forest is the lowest in Srinagar and the highest in Baramulla. There are as many as five tehsils in the Valley in which forests occupy more than three-fifths of the total area.

Forests as ecosystems have a much greater significance for man than is revealed by mere statistics in maintenance, preservation and regeneration of the gamut of land resources. They enrich the soil by providing much needed organic matter and enhance its water holding

**Table 5.3:** Area under Forests by Tehsils

| *Tehsils* | *Geographical area (sq.km)* | *Forest Area (sq.km)* | *Percentage of Forest area* |
|---|---|---|---|
| Ganderbal | 1453.25 | 397.98 | 27.3 |
| Badgam | 1241.90 | 217.69 | 17.5 |
| Srinagar | 469.05 | 302.97 | 71.2 |
| **Total (Srinagar)** | **3121.20** | **918.64** | **29.4** |
| Anantnag | 2688.42 | 1889.59 | 70.1 |
| Kulgam | 1570.83 | 781.43 | 37.7 |
| Pulwama | 1171.72 | 781.43 | 66.7 |
| **Total (Anantnag)** | **5430.97** | **3263.09** | **60.1** |
| Sopore | 2652.42 | 946.07 | 28.8 |
| Karnah | 406.63 | 107.28 | 26.4 |
| Handwara | 1588.45 | 1309.55 | 82.4 |
| Uri | 697.23 | 306.91 | 44.0 |
| Baramulla | 829.32 | 355.56 | 42.6 |
| Sonawari | 394.20 | 222.74 | 56.5 |
| **Total (Baramulla)** | **6568.25** | **3248.11** | **51.0** |

capacity. Equally important is their role in checking soil erosion and excessive run off from bill slopes and other areas susceptible to erosion. In facts, they are a virtually important component in man's environment and are inextricably linked with all other ecosystems. The mutual dependence of air, component may entail a whole series of changes in the rest of the system. It is, therefore, obvious that the problems of exploitation, management and conservation of forest resources cannot be considered in isolation since a policy regarding these would have a direct impact on the entire environment expressing itself in soil and water regimes and all living organisms, including man, dependent on them. Forest conservation can only be a component of a larger conservation policy encompassing all of them.

Happily a further exploitation of the forest wealth of Kashmir Valley is constrained by the occurrence of forest on difficult terrain in areas which are highly inaccessible. The forest cover in such areas is still wholly or partly untouched. The accessible tracts of forest, on the other hand, have been subjected to indiscriminate destruction for timber. A carelessly liberal policy towards grazing and felling of trees seems to have been another major factor contributing to the widespread devastation of floral wealth.

The degradation of Kashmir forest has been a cause of general concern. More and more emphasis is now being laid on improved methods of forest conservation. The measures that have been adopted in different

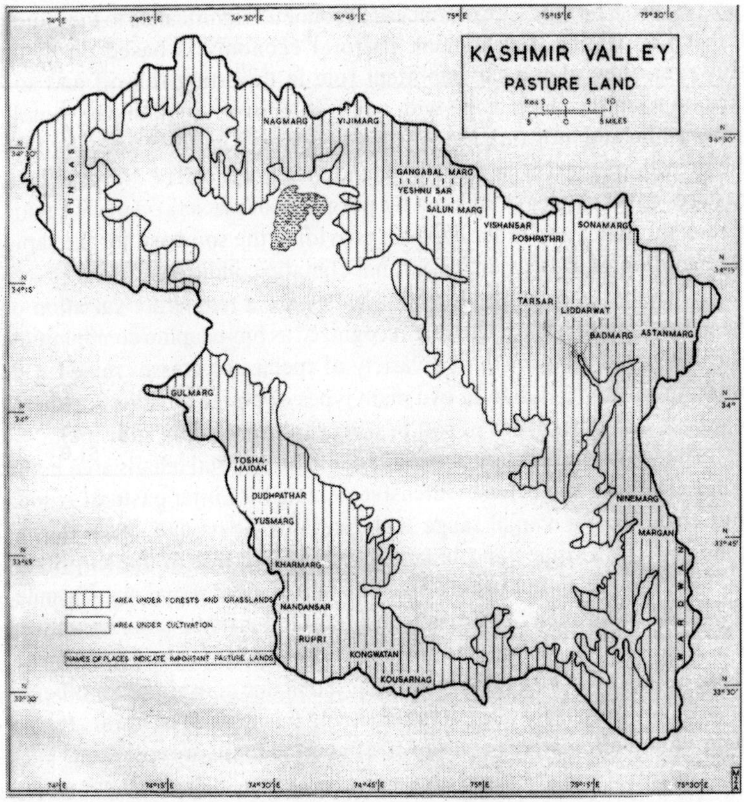


**Fig. 5.4:** Kashmir Valley—Pasture Land

parts of the valley include: raising the area under "stock" forests; improving the promotion of valuable species; bringing new areas under forests, particular in tracts exposed to severe erosion; rehabilitating degraded forests by fencing them; regulating nomadic grazing in forested areas; planting suitable species in open space within forests; and providing substitutes for wood fuel. Suitable species have been suggested for different habitats in different soil regimes and altitude zones.

## Grasslands

Climatic and edaphic conditions, particularly in the surrounding highlands, favours the growth of a variety of temperature and alpine species of grasses, these pastures are of immense economic significance to the Gujjar Bakarwals whose transhumant, pastoral economy is based on them. However, they play a far important role in thwarting run-off and soil erosion from the steep slope with a thin soil cover. An abundant supply of sunshine and moisture are the only necessary conditions required for the growth of grasses in these highland meadows, called *Margs*. These pastures cover extensive areas on the periphery of glaciers on tracts having glacial moraines and other deposits providing the soil base for the rapid regeneration of grasses under optimal climatic conditions.

The grasslands of the Kashmir Valley are a temperate variation of the mesophiclons group. They are recognized as bio-edaphic communities. Puri has noted the growth of a variety of species of grasses mixed with other forms of vegetation in two main types of alpine meadows: general moraines and other types of soil *in situ* or transported by snowmelt.

The grass land occupy about one-tenth of the total tehsils area in the valley. They are subjected to intensive grazing by Gujjar pastoral groups who cross the Pir Panjal range with herds of Goats and sheep during summers. The Gujjar transhumant economy, like that of the Kirghiz in the Tien Shan, is an interesting phenomenon of great social significance. The forest department, however, considers Gujjar transhumant practices as a great erosion hazard and imposes restrictions on their movement. There is, however, no evidence to suggest that due consideration is being given to any proposal aimed at rationalizing this form of pastoral grazing or providing alternative means of livelihood to these groups.

The forest and grassland area and its coverage in the Kashmir valley is so large that its exploitation will boost the economy of the valley as well as will help the Gujjar and Bakarwals in the socio-economic development as they are the most vulnerable economically deprived groups of the region. Various types of economic activities can be generated on this neglected and primitive use of this resource.

## Potential of Employment Generation in Horticulture Sector of Jammu and Kashmir

Horticultural crops play a unique role in India's economy by improving the income of the rural people. Cultivation of these crops is labour intensive and as such they generate lot of employment opportunities for the rural population. Fruits and vegetables are also rich source of vitamins, minerals, proteins, and carbohydrates which are essential in human nutrition. Hence, these are referred to as protective foods and assumed great importance as nutritional security of the people. Thus, cultivation of horticultural crops plays a vital role in the prosperity of a nation and is directly linked with the health and happiness of the people. Fruits and vegetables are not only used for domestic consumption and processing into various products (pickles, preserves, sauces, jam, and jelly) but also substantial quantities are exported in fresh and processed form, bringing much-needed foreign exchange for the country. These groups of crops also provide ample scope for achieving bio-diversity and diversification to maintain ecological balance and to create sustainable agriculture and can make an impact on the national economy in the years to come.

Horticulture forms the major chunk of the economy of the Jammu and Kashmir State, it generates about 120,000 million rupees annually and provides employments to about 0.25 million people both directly and indirectly. The total earning includes a foreign exchange component of Rupees 140 crore (US $ 31.1 million). The State has the largest area under horticulture production and a variety of fruits are grown which ideally suit for the cultivation of almost all kind of temperate and some varieties of subtropical and tropical fruits.

At present about 8.1 lakh hectares of area is under horticulture in the State. There are sufficient amount of orchards in all the districts of the states, but in the districts of Srinagar, Baramula, Pulwama and Kupwara the area and production of horticultural crops is on top. The other districts of the state also have variable amount of orchards. The State has a great potential of fruits cultivation and to become a major hub of fruit growers because of its favourable climate, soil, drainage and relief features.

Horticulture sector has a pivotal role in the socio-economic development and transformation of the area by providing employment opportunities increasing income, developing infrastructure facilities by generating educational facilities, better housing conditions, health and hygiene. Therefore, modernization of horticulture will promote higher productivity and better quality agro-produce and in turn higher economic return, income and employment to the people. There is a phenomenally increase noted in fruits production from just over 1.56 lakh tonnes in 1971-72 to a record figure of more then 11 lakh tonnes (1100,000 tonnes) at present, like wide area under orchards was 0.50 lakh hectares in 1971-72 which now increase to 20 lakh hectares in 2007-08. The Department of Horticulture Planning and Marketing has now proposed plan to provide opportunities to maximize land under horticulture and its production as well as opportunities to the perspective buyers for buying the fruits at various places in the state by establishing the markets and helping to improve the socio-economic conditions of the people in the state.

During the first few Five Year Plans priority was assigned to achieve self-sufficiency in foodgrains production, over the year's horticulture emerged as an indispensable and growing part of agriculture, offering a wide range of choices to the farmers for crop diversification. It also provides ample opportunities for sustaining large number of agro-industries which generate substantial employment opportunities. With agriculture and allied sectors finding alternative ways of increasing productivity of crops, horticulture as a sub-sector is a revelation showing remarkable signs of progress in the State.

Jammu and Kashmir is well-known of its horticultural produce both in India and abroad. The State offers good scope for cultivation of all types of horticultural crop covering a variety of temperate fruits like apple, pear, peach, plum, apricot, almond, cherry and sub-tropical fruits like mango, guava, citrus, litchi, phalsa, berete. Besides, medicinal and aromatic plants, floriculture, mushroom plantation crops and all types of vegetables are cultivated in the State. Apart from this, well-known spices like saffron and black Zeera are cultivated in some pockets of the State. Horticulture is gaining momentum in the State as revealed by its contribution to the State Gross Domestic Product and to its relative share in the agriculture sector as well. Almost 45 per cent of economic returns in agriculture sector are accounted for by horticulture showing its growing importance in the state economy. Its contribution to Gross State Domestic Product has been estimated to be 7-8 per cent. For the year 2008-09, an amount of Rs. 5796.49 lakh was earmarked on horticulture sector both under Plan and Non-plan budget. The projected amount being spent on this sector during 2009-10 works out to Rs.7929.18 lakh both under Plan and Non-plan budget. The horticulture sector provides remunerative means for diversification of land use for improving productivity and returns. It increases employment opportunities and earns foreign exchange. It also provides nutritional security and raw material for growing agro-processing industries.

As a result there is a perceptible change in the concept of horticulture development in the State. In this activity around 5 lakh families comprising about 30 lakh people in one way or the other way are involved. Horticulture development is one of the thrust areas in the agriculture and numbers of programmes were implemented in the past resulting in the generation of higher incomes in the rural areas thereby improving the quality of life in villages. As per the data made available by the

Horticulture Department, income of Rs. 2000.00 crore has been generated from fruit production during 2008-09 which includes an amount of Rs. 300.00 crore from dry fruits.

The growth of horticulture sector can be attributed to the various initiatives towards market interventions like establishment of fruit mandies provision for support price, technological support, awareness options, extension and research and exploitive market structures. Specifically speaking Apple is by far the most important fruit. As per last horticulture Census 1999-2000 about 55 per cent of the area is covered under this fruit. It is also important in terms of production and has the maximum marketable surplus.

Food processing industry offers tremendous opportunity for commercial exploitation for the State. The State is blessed with vast potential for growing all kinds of fruits. The State has four distinct Agro-climatic zones, i.e. Sub-tropical, Intermediate (Sub-temperate), Temperate and Cold Arid Zone. Growing of high value cash crops on large scale will not only conserve the natural resources, but will also make our farmers prosperous, which will ultimately result in employment generation. Such an orientation of fruit growing to this varied type of climate formed the corner stone of the strategy for development of horticulture in the State during Tenth Five Year Plan. The strategy adopted for development of horticulture in the State, therefore, stresses the need for zonalisation of the fruit cultivation.

### Area under Fruits in Jammu and Kashmir

The area under fruit has increased over the years and during 2008-09 an area of about 3.06 lakh hectares was under fruit cultivation with production of 16.91 lakh tonnes, recording an increase of 3.55 per cent and 3.36 per cent respectively in area and production figures over previous year. Increase in area and production of fruits during last seven years in Jammu and Kashmir State is given in Table 5.4.

### Production of Fruits, Export and Foreign Exchange

The over all production of fruit has been recorded to be 16.36 lakh tonnes for the year 2007-08 recording net addition of 1.32 lakh tonnes over the production figures of previous year measuring 8.79 per cent rate of growth. In the production figures share of fresh and dry fruit is 90.33 per cent and 9.67 per cent with 14.78 lakh metric tonnes and 1.58 lakh tonnes

**Table 5.4:** Area and Production of Fruits

| Year | Area (Ha) | Production (MT) |
|---|---|---|
| 2000-01 | 2 | 3 |
| 2002-03 | 231727 | 1146587 |
| 2003-04 | 242545 | 1273815 |
| 2004-05 | 258311 | 1331861 |
| 2005-06 | 267411 | 1403226 |
| 2006-07 | 283085 | 1504011 |
| 2007-08 | 295141 | 1636203 |
| 2008-09 | 305621 (3.55)* | 1691000 (3.35)* |

*Figures in brackets indicate percentage increase over previous year.

*Source:* Directorate of Horticulture (P&M), J&K.

respectively. Apple ranks first with a share of 80.18 per cent followed by walnut with 8.98 per cent. District-wise fruit production figures reveal that Baramulla emerges as the major district with 28.70 per cent, the next major district is Shopian claiming 14.09 per cent placing Kupwara to occupy 3rd rank with 10.92 per cent. Reasi and Kargil are the lowest districts with 0.30 per cent and 0.34 per cent contribution respectively. While specie-wise production of fruit is given hereunder in Table 5.5.

The production of fruit for 2008-09 was 16.91 lakh tonnes with 15.31 lakh metric tonnes fresh and 1.60 lakh tonnes dry fruit over an area of 3.06 lakh hectares including over one lakh hectare under dry fruit.

**Table 5.5:** Production of Fruit during 2004-05 to 2007-08 ('000 MTs)

| Years | Fresh fruits | | | | Dry fruits | | | | Total fruits |
|---|---|---|---|---|---|---|---|---|---|
| | Apple | Pear | Others | Total | Walnuts | Almonds | Others | Total | |
| 2004-05 | 1093.33 | 40.25 | 84.02 | 1217.60 | 100.60 | 13.47 | 0.19 | 114.26 | 1331.86 |
| 2005-06 | 1151.34 | 42.36 | 86.73 | 1280.43 | 108.27 | 14.33 | 0.20 | 122.80 | 1403.23 |
| 2006-07 | 1222.18 | 43.09 | 108.41 | 1373.68 | 114.93 | 15.18 | 0.22 | 130.33 | 1504.01 |
| 2007-08 | 1311.85 | 45.86 | 120.31 | 1477.92 | 146.78 | 11.26 | 0.24 | 158.28 | 1636.20 |
| 2008-09 | 1332.81 | 47.38 | 150.74 | 1530.94 | 147.64 | 12.17 | 0.25 | 160.06 | 1691.00 |

P: Provisional

*Source:* Directorate of Horticulture.

### *Export of Fruit Outside the State*

Horticulture product is not only used for domestic consumption and processing into various products but also substantial quantities are exported in fresh and processed form bringing much needed foreign exchange for the State.

Export of fruit outside Jammu and Kashmir has occupied a prominent place in trade of the State. Export of fruit has shown considerable progress. The total quantity exported has gone up to about nine lakh tonnes during 2005-06, while as it has decreased by 14 per cent in 2007-08 as compared to previous year (2005-06). During 2003-04, 60.83 per cent of the total fruit production was exported outside the State which increased to 62.61 per cent during 2004-05. While as in the year 2005-06 proportion of exports has fallen to 62.01 per cent and in the year 2007-08, it has again recorded a fall to 45.84 per cent.

For the last one decade, the exports outside the State are almost stagnant and there is no sizeable growth in the volume exported over the years. The total fruit exported during 1999-2000 stood at 7.85 lakh tonnes while as during 2007-08 the figure stands at 7.50 lakh tonnes. The total production of the horticulture is increasing in volume year by year while as there is no significant growth in the export of horticulture produce outside the State.

**Table 5.6:** Export of fruit outside the State

*(Lakh tonnes)*

| Years | Production | | | Exports | | |
|---|---|---|---|---|---|---|
| | Fresh | Dry | Total | Fresh | Dry | Total |
| 2003-04 | 11.65 | 1.08 | 12.74 | 7.63 | 0.13 | 7.76 |
| 2004-05 | 12.18 | 1.14 | 13.32 | 8.20 | 0.14 | 8.34 |
| 2005-06 | 12.80 | 1.23 | 14.03 | 8.58 | 0.12 | 8.70 |
| 2006-07 | 13.74 | 1.30 | 15.04 | 7.35 | 0.15 | 7.50 |
| 2007-08 | 14.78 | 1.58 | 16.36 | 7.34 | 0.16 | 7.50 |
| 2008-09 | 15.26 | 1.65 | 16.91 | 11.01 | 0.16 | 11.17 |

*Note*: Figures in brackets indicate per centage of total production.
*Source:* Department of Horticulture

During the year 2008-09, export of fruit outside the state is provisionally recorded as 11.17 lakh tonnes of which 11.01 lakh tonnes (98.57%) were fresh fruit. Export of fruit outside has recorded growth rate of 48.93 per cent during 2008-09 over 2007-08 figures.

***Foreign Exchange Earnings***

The Jammu and Kashmir State fruit especially dry fruit goes also to the other countries and in turn earns substantial foreign exchange. The export of dry fruit, viz. Almond and Walnut (in shell and kernel) during the year 2007-08 was 6889.11 tonnes comprising 197.11 tonnes Almond, 6692 tonnes Walnut. The foreign exchange earnings were Rs.115.95 crore during 2005-06 and Rs. 161.44 crore during 2007-08.

**Table 5.7:** Foreign Exchange earned on Horticulture Produce

| *Kind* | *Quantity Exported (MTs)* | | | *Foreign Exchange earned (Rs. In crores)* | | |
|---|---|---|---|---|---|---|
| | *2005-06* | *2006-07* | *2007-08* | *2005-06* | *2006-07* | *2007-08* |
| (a) Almond | 296.45 | 260.88 | 197.11 | 1.48 | 1.82 | 0.91 |
| (b) Total Walnut | 5256.00 | 5437.00 | 6692.00 | 114.47 | 118.02 | 160.53 |
| (i) In Shell | 179.00 | 376.00 | 161.00 | NA | NA | NA |
| (ii) In Kernal | 5077.00 | 5061.00 | 6531.00 | NA | NA | NA |
| **Total Dry (a+b)** | **5552.45** | **5697.88** | **6889.11** | **115.95** | **119.84** | **161.44** |

*Source:* Directorate of Horticulture (P&M), J&K.

**Employment Opportunities in the Horticulture Sector**

One hectare of land planted with fruit trees provides additional employment for one thousand mandays, thereby generating employment for approximately 9 crore of mandays or over 6 crore mandays additional employment for the 65000 hectares. Some hands assist the farmers in marketing their produce; others help in providing the seeds, the plant material and insecticides and chemicals to the farmers so as to ensure that the plants are protected from disease and pests; others assist in the picking/harvesting of fruit. The cultivation of fruits is labour intensive and requires a significantly higher labour force, starting from the stage of planting the trees, to the point of its marketing. The manpower requirement in the cultivation and marketing of apples as well as field crops is met by employing paid workers and even the support of family members.

As per the trade, around 5 lakh farm families comprising of 30 lakh people in one or the other way are involved in this sector. Each hectare of orchard generates 400 mandays per year (1.30 lakh man per year).

## Future Strategies for Employment Generation

### *Apple Insurance Scheme*

As a significant measure to reform and promote Horticulture Sector, the Jammu and Kashmir Bank Limited has decided to launch Apple Insurance Scheme. The initiative is first of its kind. For introducing modern pre- and post-harvest technologies in the Horticulture Sector, the Government under public-private tie up with Jammu and Kashmir Bank Ltd. has decided to construct a chain of compressed AIR (CA) stores in each district of the State to withstand stiff market competition in the liberal trade regime. The Government have devised a well thought strategy to increase productivity from 10 tonnes to 20 tonnes per hectare during the Tenth Five Year Plan by way of encouraging public private participation.

### *Development of Olive Cultivation*

Production of Olive is the most extensively cultivated fruit crop in the world. Its cultivation areas have tripled in the past 44 years, passing from 2.6 to 8.5 million hectares. In India, Jammu and Kashmir alone can earmark 30,000 hectares of area for Olive production. In Jammu and Kashmir, olives can be grown in Poonch, Rajouri, Doda, Udhampur, Ramban, Reasi and in Kathua districts. If we only take Jammu and Kashmir into account and make an effort to have a yield of about 20 to 25 q/ha from these pockets of Olive cultivation areas, we can produce minimum 600,000 quintals of olives. Roughly 96,000 quintals of Olive oil can be produced from the State of Jammu and Kashmir. During the period 1997-98 to 2005-06, 88919 olive plants at horticulture farm Ramban have been distributed among the beneficiaries for expansion of area under olive cultivation.

### *Walnut Cultivation in Jammu*

Walnut cultivation plays a significant role in the economic profile of the farmers living in hilly and backward areas, where economic condition of the people is extremely fragile.

In order to improve the production and productivity of walnut, one Walnut Nursery is under establishment with the financial assistance from APEDA at Siot Rajouri where all the facilities are being created including installation of Hi-Tech Green Houses for production of quality plant material. This will help the department to produce sufficient budded/ grafted planting material for distribution to the farmers of the Division.

### *Provision of Cold Storage in Valley*

Lack of cold storage in Valley forces growers to sell produce at peanuts. The main reason of mismatch in supply and demand is the lack of cold and conditional atmospheric storages in the valley. Government is trying to provide cold storage facilities to growers. Apple from valley has rich taste and contains high nutrient contents compared to those coming from other States, but the valley does not possess a single cold storage facility for apple preservation. According to the figures available, 400,000 tonnes of apple are ruined by the scab every year. Other diseases like alternaria, red might and powdery mildew also spoil the crop. Cold storage facilities are to be created in all the districts of the State where the fruit could be stored for a longer period.

## Major Issues and Constraints in the Development of Horticulture

The major constraints for development of horticulture include:

- Fragmented, small and marginal holdings with little or no irrigation facilities.
- Non-existence of organized and planned irrigation infrastructure for the orchards when 70 per cent orchards are un-irrigated.
- Lack of mobility facilities for supervision of field activities.
- Less market accessibility due to poor communication/road links.
- Hilly terrain and small holding size hinders mechanization.
- Lack of organized market and marketing.
- Lack of value addition and processing facilities.
- Poor or no public private partnership.

## Major Benchmarks in the Development of Horticulture

- Area under fruits by the end of 2008-09 is 3.06 lakh hectares in Jammu and Kashmir State as compared to 2.95 lakh hectares in 2007-08.
- Production of fruit during 2007-08 recorded as 16.36 lakh tonnes as against 11.47 lakh tonnes for 2002-03. Production of fruit during 2008-09 was of the order of 16.91 lakh tonnes.

- The Annual turnover of fruit Industry is around Rs. 2000 crore in case of Apple and other Fresh fruits and Rs. 300 crore in case of dry fruits.
- Five lakh families are involved in horticulture activity directly or indirectly involving 30 lakh farmers.
- Export of dry fruit during 2008-09 recorded 0.16 lakh tonnes earned income of Rs. 300 crore.
- Revenue earned on account of export of cherry has reached to a level of Rs. 120 crore during 2008-09 and is expected to scale the level of Rs. 150 crore by 2012.
- Potential for production of fruit in the State is about Rs. 3000 crore. This can be achieved through vertical and horizontal expansion.
- Zonalization of fruit crops has been planned for future plantation under area expansion programmes.
- There is scope to increase production of fruits from the current level of 16.91 lakh tonnes of fresh and dry fruits to 20 lakh tonnes by 2012.
- Creation of irrigation infrastructure for Horticulture crops is top priority with the department to increase the productivity.

**Horticulture Potential**

- The diverse Agro-climatic conditions of the State offer great potential for growing a variety of fruits like Apple, Almond, Mango, Litchi, Cherry, Apricot, Plum, Kiwi, Olive, Citrus etc.
- Potential for production of Apple fruit from present level of 10.27 tonnes to 14.00 tonnes per hectare through introduction of advanced technologies.
- Potential for production of fruits from present level of 16.91 lakh tonnes to 20 lakh tonnes.
- Potential for bringing additional area under Walnut is enormous. As per preliminary estimates about 0.50 lakh hectares are available on which walnut cultivation can be undertaken successfully. This will help to create green cover in hill areas and conserve soil from erosion, besides, providing high value wood for wood carving industry, as well as walnuts for export purposes.

**Thrust Areas for Development**

- Promotion of dry land horticulture in hilly and backward areas.
- Area expansion related to economical and consumer oriented diversification, to meet the market challenges for earning better returns.
- Increase in per unit production of fruit crops (productivity) by scientific management of orchards and by introduction of improved cultivation.
- Human Resource Development in private as well as public sector.
- Developing market linkages and value addition.
- Creation of adequate irrigation infrastructure like Deep Bore Wells.
- Shallow Wells, Tube Wells, Water storage/Harvesting Tanks in rain fed areas.
- Encouragement, introduction and cultivation of rare fruit crops, viz. olive, peanut, strawberry, grapes, pomegranate and kiwi (diversification and zonalisation).
- Rejuvenation of old and senile orchards.
- Standardization of existing root stocks of apple under normal density plantation.
- Survey/selection/identification of true to type cultivars of apple for further multiplication.
- Standardization of vegetative propagation techniques of walnuts.

**Potential of Employment Generation in Tourism Sector of Kashmir**

Tourism has no doubt remained an instrument of economic growth in the State of Jammu and Kashmir and has contributed a lot in developing the economy, particularly in the valley of Kashmir. Tourism is the most important industry of 21st century. This sector has given jobs to a large number of people and generated economic activities especially in the tertiary sectors. Its impact is visible in the service sector of the State such as transport, hospitality, horticulture and other small scale industrial sectors. Tourism open up a new window for resources, both investment and generation leading to employment generation as well as socio-economic development of the local population at large.

The State of Jammu and Kashmir has three distinct regions, viz. Jammu, Kashmir and Ladakh and all three have immense potential for employment generation in tourism both from domestic as well as international tourists. There are number of locations which are untapped and can be developed as major tourists destinations, having all the natural as well as cultural resources for attracting tourists. Some of the important natural resources are excellent climate, beautiful lakes, locations for adventure sports, wild life, pastures, natural and manmade parks like Shalimar, Nishat and Chashma-e-shahi of the Mughal period, flora and fauna, alpine forest, natural water falls and streams. As far as the cultural resources, the state has some of the most important religious shrines of Hindus, Muslims, historical monuments, plethora of local festivals, distinct cuisine, craftsmanship skills for intricate and fine woodwork, woollens, textiles, paper mache, inlay works etc.

But the ground reality is that tourism has been directly hit at least in the region of Kashmir Valley. There is a state of despondency in all support service in the state tourism industry. Within the Kashmir Valley the level of unemployment amongst youth is high and assuming dangerous proportion. Because of the violence prone environment in the valley no well-known financial institutions are willing to invest in the State.

Tourism is one of the states major industries. It has played an important role for developing the economy and employment particularly in the valley of Kashmir. The industry has given jobs to large number of people, particularly of the younger generation and generated economic activities in the primary, secondary and tertiary sectors of the State which owes dependence to a large extent to this industry. Some of the key attributes of the tourism industry in Jammu and Kashmir are as virgin areas, different geographical locations, climate, landscape, architecture, pilgrimage, culture, handicraft, hospitality and historical heritage.

Jammu and Kashmir has a huge potentiality of employment generation and economic development because; it has many untapped tourist areas which are yet to be developed. The State is full of colourful Rocky Mountains, valley trekking trail, several high rising chortons, snowy mountains, meadow of flowers, lakes, gardens and orchards, monuments and temples, forts and palaces. Ladakh is famous for its caves and monasteries, while Jammu is famous for its temples and religious tourism. The region of Ladakh is the major choice of foreign tourists; Jammu attracts pilgrim tourists, while the valley attracts a large number of domestic tourists and a fair sprinkling of foreign tourists.

Tourism in the state has led to the development of the whole service industry including transport, hospitality, camping retail shops, horticulture and in the small scale sectors by generating employment but it has remain quite susceptible to even minor changes in the law and order situation in the state. This is evident in the year 2000-01 when the international tension of the border affected the tourist traffic in both foreign and domestic sectors in the region. It results in a severe recession in the whole service industry.

Growth of this industry for developing income and employment has remained an unpredictable feature. Growth in the tourist traffic also continues to vary from year to year in direct relation to the threat perception. To develop the infrastructure for the visitors advance planning in each sector of the industry for the opening of the new facilities is a must.

## Historical Perspective of Tourism in Employment Generation

Kashmir is an important tourist destination and has been a place of attraction since centuries. Tourism in Kashmir remains a major source of employment since ancient time. History remains glorious for tourism by generating jobs to the people of Kashmir both directly and indirectly. In spite of Geographical isolation, political issues, insurgency, insecurity and remoteness from other parts of India, Kashmir Valley has experienced an influx of invaders, traders and kings rule due to its strategic location since the ancient times. History of tourism in Kashmir Valley, its growth, development and employment generation is closely associated with all our ancient civilization. Travellers from far and wide have visited the 'Kashmir Valley' for centuries past. It has been the main route of cultural and commercial intercourse between India and rest of the eastern World including Middle East and Central Asia. Tourism in Jammu and Kashmir was badly hit ever since insurgency intensified in 1989. Ever since, a bitter enmity has developed between India and Pakistan. The two countries have been at war twice over Kashmir (1947-1949, 1965), and clashed there again during the Kargil Conflict of 1999. The region remains one of the most heavily militarized zones in the world. Due to insurgency and militancy in some spots tourist visit decreases to very low level while, some tourist spots either shrink or totally disappear, e.g. there were 700 tourist spots around the Dal Lake in the past but there number steeply fall to less than 200.

However, there is a huge potential of tourism development and employment generation. In the year 1951 the potential of domestic and foreign tourists was 20500 and 5000 while only 9933 domestic and 1246 foreign tourists visit Kashmir due to the problems prevailing in Kashmir. The number of domestic tourist recorded highest in 1981 with potential

**Table 5.8:** Year-wise Breakup of Domestic and Foreign Tourist Arrivals in Kashmir Valley (1951-2005)

| *Year* | *Domestic* | *Potential* | *Foreign* | *Potential* | *Total* |
|---|---|---|---|---|---|
| 1951 | 9933 | 25500 | 1246 | 5000 | 10579 |
| 1956 | 57341 | 82000 | 7012 | 10645 | 64353 |
| 1961 | 79241 | 95240 | 13214 | 18300 | 92455 |
| 1966 | 112127 | 120550 | 7149 | 12550 | 119276 |
| 1971 | 76612 | 100125 | 15240 | 20240 | 94855 |
| 1976 | 286412 | 290800 | 38078 | 45480 | 324490 |
| 1981 | 598555 | 620556 | 43745 | 50780 | 642300 |
| 1986 | 536598 | 640000 | 53118 | 56000 | 589716 |
| 1991 | 1400 | 50000 | 4887 | 6550 | 6287 |
| 1996 | 375 | 40000 | 9592 | 11000 | 9967 |
| 2001 | 66732 | 90730 | 5859 | 8500 | 72591 |
| 2002 | 24670 | 60540 | 2686 | 4550 | 27356 |
| 2003 | 182205 | 200760 | 8959 | 12890 | 191164 |
| 2004 | 358095 | 390000 | 18634 | 27500 | 376729 |
| 2005 | 585702 | 680635 | 19680 | 30790 | 605382 |
| 2006 | 412879 | 530000 | 20002 | 32000 | 432888 |
| 2007 | 417264 | 580000 | 24576 | 35000 | 441840 |
| 2008 | 550100 | 600000 | 22000 | 35000 | 572100 |

*Source:* Department of Tourism, Jammu and Kashmir, 2007.

of 620500 tourists while highest figure of foreign tourist was recorded in 1986 with 53118 tourists while potential of foreign tourist was 56000. The lowest number of domestic tourist was recorded in 1991 and 1996 with 1400 and 375 tourist respectively with potential of 50000 and 40000. The fall in the number of foreign tourists was also recorded during the same period. Again the number of domestic as well as foreign tourist gain momentum for the proceeding years.

It is a stalk reality that till late 1980s the State of Jammu and Kashmir attracts huge number of national as well as foreign tourists, but the tourism sector received a serious jolt with the out-breaking of militancy in the year 1989. The tourist influx declined considerably up to 2002 during which period the State heavily suffered in this sector due to effect of militancy and insurgency. The tourist rush in 1986-88 was recorded as the highest. The infrastructure created over the years suffered colossal damage besides the destruction to the tourist spots, gardens and parks. With the improvement in the security scenario the state made all possible efforts for the revival of tourism sector by raising the requisite infrastructure for restoration of the pristine glory of the places of tourist attraction. The average flow of tourists between 1990 and 1996 was just around 10000 per annum.

However, tourism in Kashmir declined during the late 1980s and 1990s, due to the terror perpetrated by separatist militants and self-styled freedom fighters. Victimized by Islamic fundamentalists and mercenaries, thousands of innocent Kashmiri lives have been lost. However, the proportionate share of foreign tourists increased abruptly to 96.23 per cent and the proportionate share of domestic tourists was only 3.76, ever lowest, in 1996. In recent years tourist flow shows that the share of Asia, in the tourist flow of the Valley is gradually increasing. The leading countries, which constitute the major chunk of Asia tourists, are Hong Kong, China, Japan and Taiwan. However, the contribution of USA and Australia is also increasing (Hasan).

Today the situation has comparatively improved with both countries agreeing to come to the negotiating table and discuss all outstanding issues with an open mind. All this augurs well for the state of Jammu and Kashmir and hopefully, peace will return to Kashmir — followed by tourists, who remember its beautiful parks, Rolling Meadows, spectacular mountains and scenic destinations with nostalgia Kashmir has often been described as a Paradise on Earth, and with scenic snow capped mountains, verdant valleys, beautiful streams dotted with houseboats, and acres of pine and deodar forests. Kashmir is indeed stunningly enchanting. Kashmir is that part of the State of Jammu and Kashmir, India that comprises the Jammu region, the Kashmir Valley, and Ladakh. Surrounded on both sides by River Jhelum the Valley of Kashmir comprises Kishtwar, Ladakh & Zanskar ranges. One of the most alluring aspects of a Kashmir Tour is the chance to experience a charming stay aboard a houseboat while floating on Dal Lake.

**Potentials of Tourism in Employment Generation**

Tourism plays a crucial role in employment generation from ancient times with a great potential of further opportunities for the generation to come. Regional physical complex of the Valley has given birth to the various tourism potentials ranging from natural to artificial attractiveness. The rich tourism potential in terms of both physical and cultural dimensions of the region which are being harnessed for the tourism development and employment generation will further be utilized for their purpose. Kashmir Valley extending from Qazigund to Baramullah and Sonmarg to Aharbal is a land of interests. A combination of hilly and plain areas, region varies in its climate, culture and custom from place to place. Pleasant climate, Glacier, pilgrimages, scenic splendours, charming culture, history, art

**Table 5.9:** Classified (Types) Tourist Destinations

| S. No. | Tourism Types | Destinations |
|---|---|---|
| 1. | Leisure | Dal Lake, Wular Lake, Phalgam, Kokernag, Sheerbag, Tulip Garden. |
| 2. | Adventure | Gulamrg, Wular Lake, Lidder Valley, Sonmarg, Phalgam. |
| 3. | Heritage | Mughal Gradens, Pari Mahal, Dargah, Masjid, Kheerbhawani Temple, Hari Parbat, Charar-e-sharif, Jamia Masjid. |
| 4. | Health | Gulmarg, Pahalgam, Sonmarg, Wadi-lolab, Aharbal, Tarsinag, Tatta Pani. |
| 5. | Conventional | Srinagar, Dal Lake. |
| 6. | Border | Baramullah, Pattan, Kupwara, Kargil. |
| 7. | Wildlife | Dachigam Wildlife Sanctuary, Gulmarg Biosphere Reserve, Tulip Garden. |
| 8. | Pilgrimage Tourism | Hazratbal Shrine, Khanqah of Shah Hamadan, Kheer Bhawani, Amarnath Cave, Hari Parbat, Charar-e-sharif, Hazratbal mosque, Khanqah-e-moulah, Kheer Bhawani, Shankaracharya temple, Martand. |
| 9. | Ecotourism | Vermul, Aru, Pahalgam, Veinag, Kokernag, Achhabal, Tangmarg, Kilanmarg, Gulmarg, Sonmarg. |
| 10. | Rural Tourism | Kheer Bhawani, Martand, Shesnag, Aru, Aharbal, Watlab, Athwatoo. |

*Source:* Based on Field Survey (2007-2008).

and unexplored and untouched places are the wealth of the region. Generally, physical, socio-economic and historical factors become important in the process of spatial interaction. Physical aspects provide the basic tourism potentials of the region. Basically, there are three elements of tourism, i.e. locale, transport and accommodation. Identification of the existing attraction is the first priority for tourism development, subsequently comes infrastructure, market, profit, loss etc. though all the components of tourism are important for the growth but attractions provide the energizing power. It may be also called as stimulator and motivator for tourists. It thus becomes important to find out the tourism potentials of the region in various terms.

The multiplicity of tourist attractions in the region is in the form of leisure, adventure heritage, convention, border, and ecotourism and pilgrimage tourism. The tourism resource of the region has vast potential and can transform the whole economy as a tourism driven economy by providing jobs with all its concomitant trickling affect. The Kashmir Valley of the State of Jammu and Kashmir is endowed with the natural resources which are required to encourage the various forms of tourism like pilgrimage tourism, ecotourism, border tourism, cultural tourism and adventure tourism. The province has some rich potential that are as shown in Table 5.9.

## Development of Major Tourist Nodes and Circuits

The Kashmir Valley has identified some major tourist nodes and tourist circuits, which are popular tourist destinations and are playing an important role in the economy and employment generation for the local peoples to which they belongs. The Kashmir Valley has the fortune of being endowed by prominent circuits belonging to different religious ideologies. Above all, a circuit route has been established all along the places related to natural beauty.

These tourist circuits and nodes are the important sources of income and employment for the people of Kashmir in general and the local people in particular. These tourist nodes and circuits have huge potential for further development by connecting them with proper road network. It is seen that the tourists visiting to the Amarnath covers a long distance through Pahalgam. If these tourists want to visit Sonmarg, they firstly return to Srinagar from where they visit Sonmarg through another route. They are not able to visit this tourist spot directly from Amarnath because of the lack of proper connectivity. Thus there is a dire need to develop and connect Srinagar, Pahalgam and Sonmarg circuit. It becomes easy for the tourists to visit these tourist spots without returning to the base by developing these tourist circuits.

## Tourist Potentials—Measurements—Efficiency

The Valley of Kashmir being described "Paradise on the Earth". Both domestic as well as foreign tourists visit the Valley since time immemorial. Tourism remains a major source of employment and income for the people of the valley from ancient times. The domestic tourists are confined to the Pilgrimage centres like Amarnath, Kheer-Bhawani and other shrines. Besides this, the Valley has enormous tourist potential due to its scenic beauty, climatic conditions, and adventurous sports, ruins and relics of pre-historical and cultural has a great attraction for domestic as well as foreign tourists. It has been observed that all tourist spots of the Valley are dominated by domestic tourists. These tourists are coming from the rich parts of the country. However, the number of foreign tourists is very dismal which is given in Table 5.8. Since 1975, there has been a tremendous increase in foreign as well as domestic tourists. Table 5.8 as well as Fig. 5.6 reveals that the proportionate share of domestic and foreign tourists in 1975 was 88.98 per cent and 12.01 per cent respectively.

In 1985 the proportionate share of domestic tourists increased further to 92.45 per cent and proportionate share of foreign tourists decreased to 7.54 per cent. In 1990 the proportionate share of domestic tourists have declined and reached 0.00 per cent in 1993 while the foreign tourist's arrivals get increased in the same period. The starting 1990s were reverse

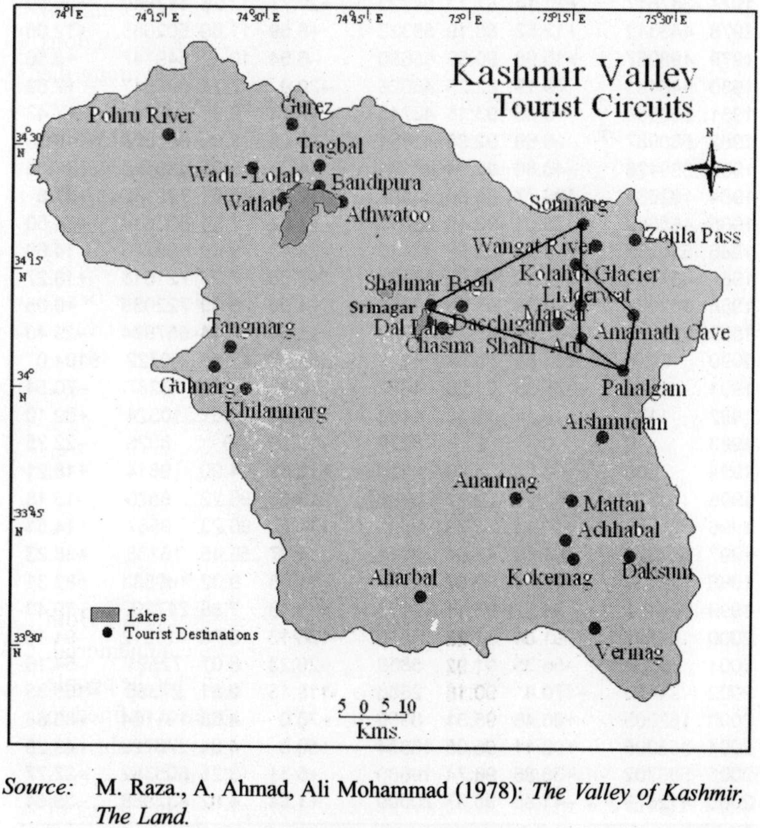


*Source:* M. Raza., A. Ahmad, Ali Mohammad (1978): *The Valley of Kashmir, The Land.*

**Fig. 5.5:** Kashmir Valley—Tourist Circuit

trend in the domestic as well as in foreign tourist arrivals in the Valley of Kashmir where as the later years recover from this as in given Table 5.8. In starting 1990s due to infiltration and other political issues the Kashmir was in turmoil. So, no one domestic tourist was interested to take the risk

**Table 5.10:** Year-wise Breakup of Domestic and Foreign Tourist Arrivals in Kashmir Valley (1975-2005)

| *Year* | *Domestic* | *Fluctuation %* | *% share* | *Foreign* | *Fluctuation %* | *% share* | *Total* | *Fluctuation %* |
|---|---|---|---|---|---|---|---|---|
| 1975 | 162676 | – | 87.98 | 22214 | – | 12.01 | 184890 | – |
| 1976 | 286412 | +43.20 | 88.26 | 38078 | +41.06 | 11.73 | 324490 | +43.02 |
| 1977 | 387817 | +26.14 | 87.73 | 54223 | +29.77 | 12.26 | 442040 | +26.59 |
| 1978 | 443342 | +12.52 | 88.19 | 59323 | +8.59 | 11.80 | 502665 | +12.06 |
| 1979 | 498067 | +10.98 | 90.59 | 55680 | –6.54 | 10.12 | 549747 | +8.56 |
| 1980 | 548491 | +9.19 | 92.25 | 46026 | –20.9 | 7.74 | 594517 | +7.53 |
| 1981 | 598555 | +8.36 | 93.18 | 43745 | –5.21 | 6.81 | 642300 | +7.43 |
| 1982 | 560987 | –6.69 | 92.90 | 42851 | –2.08 | 7.09 | 603838 | –6.36 |
| 1983 | 398428 | –40.80 | 90.64 | 41101 | –4.25 | 9.35 | 439529 | –37.38 |
| 1984 | 192684 | –106.77 | 84.08 | 36458 | –12.73 | 15.91 | 229142 | –91.8 |
| 1985 | 465599 | +58.61 | 92.45 | 38015 | +4.09 | 7.54 | 503614 | +54.50 |
| 1986 | 536598 | +13.23 | 90.99 | 53118 | +28.43 | 9.00 | 589716 | +14.60 |
| 1987 | 664081 | +19.19 | 92.02 | 57537 | +7.68 | 7.97 | 721618 | +18.27 |
| 1988 | 662097 | –0.29 | 91.69 | 59938 | +4.00 | 8.30 | 722035 | +0.05 |
| 1989 | 490212 | –35.06 | 87.85 | 67762 | +11.54 | 12.14 | 557974 | –29.40 |
| 1990 | 6095 | –7942.85 | 56.84 | 4627 | –1364.49 | 43.15 | 10722 | -5104.0 |
| 1991 | 1400 | –335.35 | 22.26 | 4887 | +5.32 | 77.73 | 6287 | –70.54 |
| 1992 | 1175 | –19.14 | 11.38 | 9149 | +46.58 | 88.61 | 10324 | +39.10 |
| 1993 | 0 | 0 | 0 | 8026 | –13.99 | 100 | 8026 | –22.25 |
| 1994 | 500 | +100 | 5.09 | 9314 | +13.82 | 94.90 | 9814 | +18.21 |
| 1995 | 322 | –55.27 | 3.77 | 8198 | –13.61 | 96.22 | 8520 | –15.18 |
| 1996 | 375 | +14.13 | 3.76 | 9592 | +14.53 | 96.23 | 9967 | +14.51 |
| 1997 | 7027 | +94.66 | 43.54 | 9111 | –5.27 | 56.45 | 16138 | +38.23 |
| 1998 | 99636 | +92.94 | 90.67 | 10247 | +11.08 | 9.32 | 109883 | +83.31 |
| 1999 | 200162 | +50.22 | 92.11 | 17130 | +40.18 | 7.88 | 217292 | +49.43 |
| 2000 | 104337 | –91.84 | 93.23 | 7575 | –126.13 | 6.76 | 111912 | –94.16 |
| 2001 | 66732 | –56.35 | 91.92 | 5859 | –29.23 | 8.07 | 72591 | –54.16 |
| 2002 | 24670 | –170.4 | 90.18 | 2686 | -118.13 | 9.81 | 27356 | –165.35 |
| 2003 | 182205 | +86.46 | 95.31 | 8959 | +70.0 | 4.68 | 191164 | +85.68 |
| 2004 | 358095 | +93.11 | 95.05 | 18634 | +50.9 | 4.94 | 376729 | +49.25 |
| 2005 | 585702 | +38.86 | 96.74 | 19680 | +5.31 | 3.25 | 605382 | +37.77 |
| 2006 | 412879 | –41.85 | 95.37 | 20009 | +1.64 | 4.62 | 432888 | –39.84 |

*Source:* Department of Tourism, Jammu and Kashmir.

and visit the Valley. This period was also known as "Dark Age" in tourism sector in Kashmir Valley. Only 8026 foreign tourists visit the Valley in 1993 and make 100 per cent foreign arrivals in the Valley.

But after 1996 the normalcy prevails in the Valley and the proportionate share of domestic tourists began to increase again and share of foreign tourists decreased continuously and the respective share of domestic tourists was 96.74 per cent and foreign tourists was only 3.25 per cent in 2005.

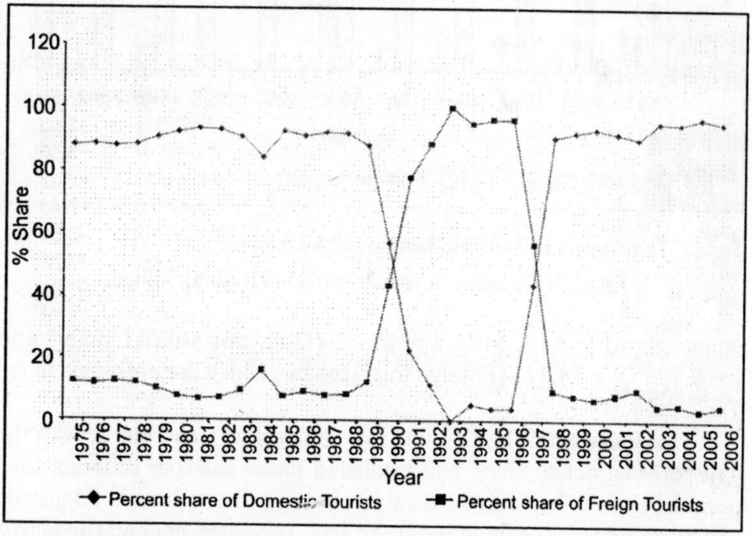


**Fig. 5.6:** Projected Share of Domestic and Foreign Tourists in Kashmir Valley

Annual tourist flow shows a threefold increase in the decade 2002-2005 (Table 5.8). During 1998 tourist flow was little bit affected by nuclear tests conducted by India and Pakistan. Many package tours involving foreign tourists were cancelled. The Kargil crisis following in 1999 caused a decline in tourist visits between domestic as well as foreigners alike during the summer as well as spring seasons. During September 2001 similar declines in domestic as well as the foreign tourists recorded in autumn season.

Figure 5.8 reveals the domestic and foreign share of tourists in Kashmir Valley. It is revealed through the actual trend line and estimated linear trend line for the time period 1975-2006. The estimated linear value of tourist share for each time point has been find out based on the

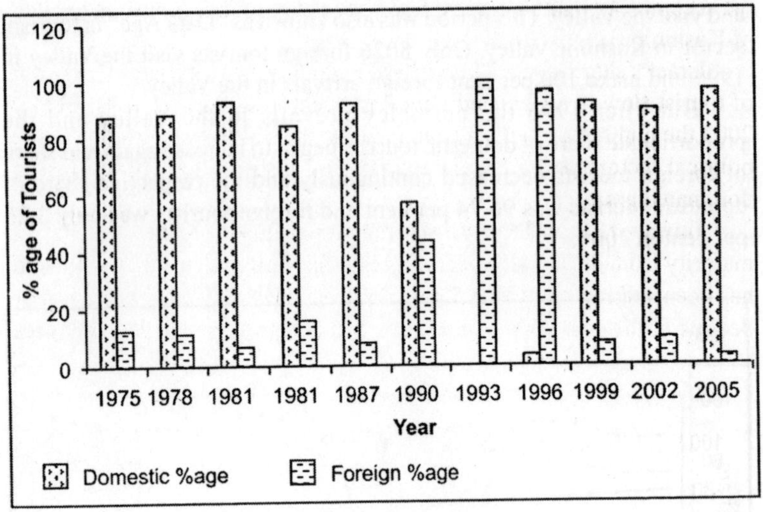


*Source:* Department of Tourism, Jammu and Kashmir

**Fig. 5.7:** Variation in Tourist Arrival in Kashmir Valley

equations of $y = -0.5125X + 81.52$ (Domestic tourist share) and $y = 0.5095X + 18.543$ (Foreign tourist share) which are presented in the Table 5.10.

The deviation of linear trend line from actual trend line reveals the gap between actual share and estimated linear share in different time period. Figure 5.7 reveals the contrast characteristics of trend of domestic and foreign tourist share in the study area. However, in domestic tourist share it is exhibited the splendid (drastic) downfall of domestic share 1989-1991. The declining trend remains continued till 1997. The share of foreign tourist drastically increased from 1989-1991 and remain continued till 1997. Another contrasting figure is that while the linear trend of domestic share shows declining but the share of foreign tourists shows increasing trend.

Table 5.12 shows the number and percentage of tourists visiting from different parts of the world to the valley of Kashmir annually. Honkong ranks first during 2000, 2001 and 2004. In 2000, Honkong shares 16.89 per cent tourists, 18.14 per cent in 2001, and 11.14 per cent in 2004. But in 2003 Honkong ranks second sharing 9.69 per cent of tourists to the Valley. In 2005, it shares 7.43 per cent of tourist flow to the Valley. From 2003 the trend of tourist arrivals in the Valley changes and Israel become the second leading country and ranks second in tourist flow to the Valley of Kashmir.

Israel's sharing was 12.24 in 2003 while in 2004 it shares 9 per cent of tourist flow to Valley and only 8 per cent in 2005 (Fig. 5.9). Before 2003 the number of tourists from Israel to the Valley was low due to the political factors as the Israel's tourists feel insecure to visit to Muslim dominated area.

Taiwan, U.K. and U.S.A. sharing tourist flow to Kashmir Valley in majority from the last five years and also through out the history. Taiwan has been sharing more than 5 per cent from 2000 onwards with a minor decline in the year 2005. But U.S.A. and U.K. are the leading countries

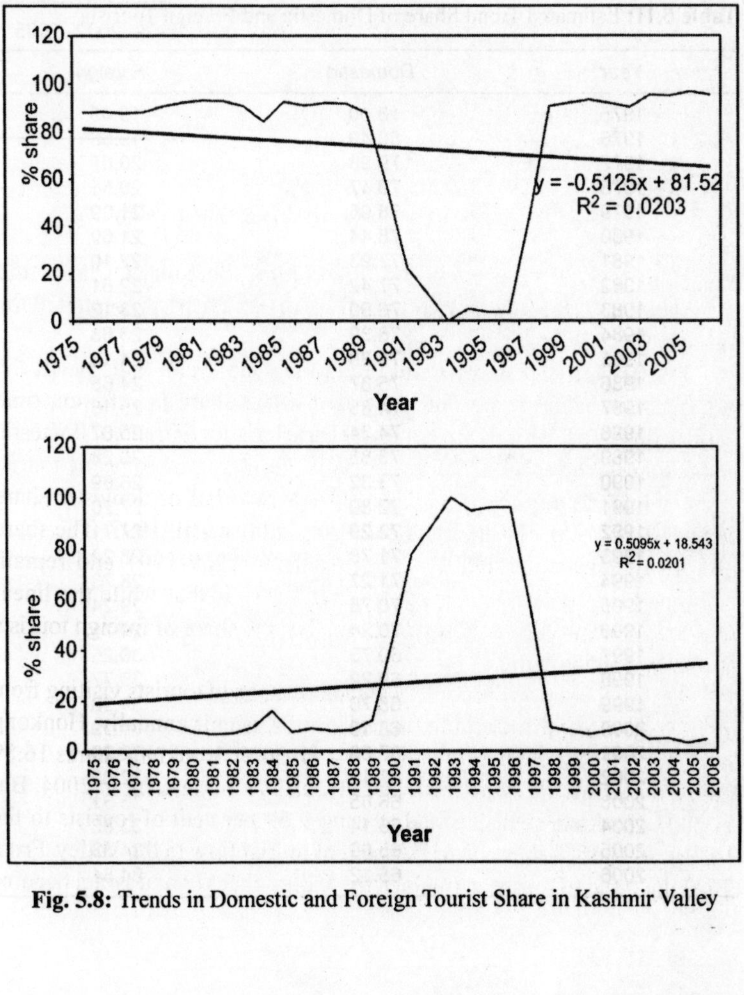


**Fig. 5.8:** Trends in Domestic and Foreign Tourist Share in Kashmir Valley

from where the tourists visit the Valley of Kashmir from time immemorial. Besides other countries, which contribute the major portion of tourists' arrival in Kashmir Valley, are Malaysia, China, Germany, Italy and Singapore. Other countries, which contribute tourist arrivals in the Valley in minor proportion, are South Africa, Japan, Australia, Argentina, Brazil, and Korea. There is a great temporal variation in international tourist arrivals to the Kashmir Valley. During 2000, seven thousand seventy five tourists arrived in the Valley while their number increases year by year because of the political stability, as well as declined insurgency. In 2002 only 2686 foreign tourists visited Kashmir Valley, this declination is because of the attack of 11th September, 2001. Again after 2002 foreign

**Table 5.11:** Estimated Trend Share of Domestic and Foreign Tourists

| *Year* | *Domestic* | *Foreign* |
|---|---|---|
| 1975 | 18.00 | 19.05 |
| 1976 | 80.49 | 19.56 |
| 1977 | 79.98 | 20.07 |
| 1978 | 79.47 | 20.58 |
| 1979 | 78.95 | 21.09 |
| 1980 | 78.44 | 21.60 |
| 1981 | 77.93 | 22.10 |
| 1982 | 77.42 | 22.61 |
| 1983 | 76.90 | 23.12 |
| 1984 | 76.39 | 23.63 |
| 1985 | 75.88 | 24.14 |
| 1986 | 75.37 | 24.65 |
| 1987 | 74.85 | 25.16 |
| 1988 | 74.34 | 25.67 |
| 1989 | 73.83 | 26.28 |
| 1990 | 73.32 | 26.69 |
| 1991 | 72.80 | 27.20 |
| 1992 | 72.29 | 27.71 |
| 1993 | 71.78 | 28.22 |
| 1994 | 71.27 | 28.73 |
| 1995 | 70.75 | 29.24 |
| 1996 | 70.24 | 29.75 |
| 1997 | 69.73 | 30.26 |
| 1998 | 69.22 | 30.77 |
| 1999 | 68.70 | 31.28 |
| 2000 | 68.19 | 31.79 |
| 2001 | 67.68 | 32.29 |
| 2002 | 67.17 | 32.80 |
| 2003 | 66.65 | 33.31 |
| 2004 | 66.14 | 33.82 |
| 2005 | 65.69 | 34.33 |
| 2006 | 65.12 | 34.84 |

tourist arrivals increases to the Valley but in 2006 it again declines because of the attack on tourists on 29th May, 2006. Besides throwing of hand-garnets and other attacks on tourists the other factors, which are responsible for declination of tourist arrivals in Valley are political issues.

**Rise of Domestic Tourism and Employment Generation in Kashmir**

In spite of the fact that during the period of 1948 and 1950, Kashmir was in crises, this area did not attract the people of other parts of the subcontinent to visit. In 1988 the Valley has been visited by record number of over 722,000 lakh tourists. But, because of the uncertain law and order situation affecting the State, this ever increasing tourist's traffic dramatically fell to an unbelievingly low of 6600 tourists visiting the

**Table 5.12:** Country-wise Tourist Arrivals in Kashmir Valley (in %age as well as in Number) 2000-2005

| *Name of the country* | *2000* | *2001* | *2002* | *2003* | *2004* | *2005* |
|---|---|---|---|---|---|---|
| Honkong | 1280<br>(16.89) | 1063<br>(18.14) | 101<br>(3.76) | 869<br>(9.69) | 2077<br>(11.14) | 1464<br>(7.43) |
| U.K. | 431<br>(5.68) | 422<br>(7.02) | 363<br>(13.5) | 849<br>(9.47) | 1296<br>(6.95) | 1400<br>(7.11) |
| U.S.A. | 495<br>(6.53) | 506<br>(8.56) | 394<br>(14.66) | 562<br>(6.27) | 1088<br>(5.83) | 1318<br>(6.69) |
| Israel | 220<br>(2.9) | 93<br>(1.58) | 57<br>(2.12) | 1097<br>(12.24) | 1862<br>(9.99) | 1592<br>(8.08) |
| Malaysia | 122<br>(1.6) | 113<br>(1.92) | 7<br>(0.26) | 248<br>(2.76) | 1496<br>(8.02) | 1671<br>(8.49) |
| Taiwan | 537<br>(7.08) | 471<br>(8.03) | 221<br>(8.22) | 641<br>(7.15) | 1020<br>(5.47) | 528<br>(2.68) |
| Singapore | 401<br>(5.29) | 291<br>(4.96) | 38<br>(1.41) | 474<br>(5.29) | 1020<br>(547) | 1238<br>(6.29) |
| China | 443<br>(5.84) | 300<br>(5.12) | 20<br>(0.74) | 321<br>(3.58) | 2049<br>(10.99) | 1121<br>(5.69) |
| Germany | 461<br>(6.08) | 288<br>(4.9) | 183<br>(6.81) | 374<br>(4.17) | 666<br>(3.57) | 679<br>(3.45) |
| Italy | 224<br>(2.95) | 221<br>(3.77) | 49<br>(1.82) | 341<br>(3.80) | 486<br>(2.60) | 781<br>(3.96) |
| Others | 2961<br>(39.08) | 2091<br>(35.68) | 1253<br>(46.64) | 3183<br>(35.52) | 5574<br>(29.91) | 7888<br>(40.08) |
| **Total** | **7575** | **5859** | **2686** | **8959** | **18634** | **19680** |

*Note*: Figures in Parentheses related to percentage.

*Sources:* Department of Tourism, Jammu and Kashmir, 2006.

valley in the year 1993. Due to this dramatic fall in tourism the economy and employment situation were deteriorated and people suffers a lot.

It is between these two statistical extremes, efforts have been made to work out a way through to develop a new plan of revival of tourism for the State and contemplate a scenario for the next 20 years. Almost a regular growth pattern can be seen in the tourists arrival in Jammu and Kashmir State (Table 5.13). But this regular growth pattern is generally because of the tourist coming to the religious places like Amarnath and Vaishno Devi. These tourists are considered to be domestic tourists and the duration of their stay is limited from 3-4 days to one month. There is limited diversion to other tourist places.

It has been seen that the percentage growth of tourists remain negative for the year 1990, 1993 and 2001 which is –26.65, –4.46 and –2.67 respectively due to increasing insurgency and militancy in the region as a whole. However, for the remaining years the percentage growth of tourists

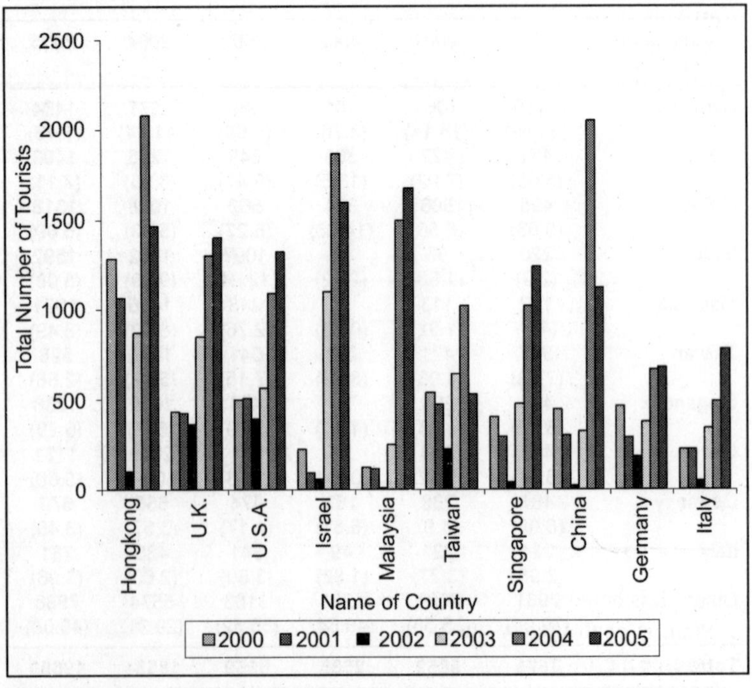


*Source*: Department of Tourism, Jammu and Kashmir

**Fig. 5.9:** Country-wise Flow of Tourists, 2000-2005.

**Table 5.13:** Tourist Growth in Jammu and Kashmir

| *Year* | *Tourists in J&K* | *Growth %* |
|---|---|---|
| 1989 | 2987964 | – |
| 1990 | 2191486 | –26.65 |
| 1991 | 3182251 | 45.20 |
| 1992 | 3608269 | 13.38 |
| 1993 | 3447162 | –4.46 |
| 1994 | 3770208 | 9.37 |
| 1995 | 4118632 | 9.24 |
| 1996 | 4482072 | 8.82 |
| 1997 | 4546200 | 1.43 |
| 1998 | 4903930 | 7.86 |
| 1999 | 5013571 | 2.23 |
| 2000 | 5412863 | 7.96 |
| 2001 | 5268246 | –2.67 |

in the State remains favourable. Analysis of the break-up of the tourists in the decade shows that almost 90 per cent to 95 per cent of the tourist arrivals in Jammu and Kashmir are because of the Vaishno Devi and Amarnath shrines. It is being projected that by the end of 2011 the tourist arrival in Jammu and Kashmir would be around 1,18,91,251, considering the fact that normalcy will occur in the next 2-3 years which will rise to 2,27,08,506 by the end of 2020.

**Table 5.14:** Projected Number of tourists in Jammu and Kashmir

| *Year* | *Number of Tourists* |
|---|---|
| 2011 | 11891251 |
| 2012 | 12770613 |
| 2013 | 13716589 |
| 2014 | 14734445 |
| 2015 | 15829895 |
| 2016 | 17009148 |
| 2017 | 18278954 |
| 2018 | 19646661 |
| 2019 | 21120269 |
| 2020 | 22708506 |

It is believed that if everything goes normal and the militancy in the State is controlled in the coming 2-3 years time Jammu and Kashmir foresee a growth of tourism and the number of tourists soaring to above 20 million, enough to give a kick start to the economy and employment of Jammu and Kashmir and bringing it back on track.

## Infrastructure Development for Tourism Development and Employment Generation

The tourism activities at a particular place are directly related to the arrival of tourists at that place. The more arrival, the more economic activities get generated and making impact on the related sector accordingly. Accommodation and infrastructure development is basic requirement for the tourists. Infrastructure development is a major sign of development of any region. When there is better infrastructure development, food and facilities the tourist attraction to visit the area increase which directly and indirectly helps the area to enhance its economy through tourism by generating employment. To handle such a traffic flow, the development of infrastructure has to match these projections. The infrastructure requirement in terms of accommodation, transport etc. is as under.

**Projection of Infrastructure Development/Requirement**

**Hotels**

| | *2011* | | *2015* | | *2020* | |
|---|---|---|---|---|---|---|
| | *Hotels* | *Beds* | *Hotels* | *Beds* | *Hotels* | *Beds* |
| Total | 1028 | 43039 | 1715 | 63653 | 3018 | 97600 |

**Guest Houses**

| | *2011* | | *2015* | | *2020* | |
|---|---|---|---|---|---|---|
| | *Hotels* | *Beds* | *Hotels* | *Beds* | *Hotels* | *Beds* |
| Total | 896 | 58052 | 1607 | 40108 | 3023 | 65663 |

**Transport**

| *Type of transport infrastructure* | *2010* | *2015* | *2020* |
|---|---|---|---|
| Buses | 27659 | 38178 | 60462 |
| Taxis | 11755 | 16226 | 25697 |

To cater the tourist flow for economic development and employment generation apart from infrastructure, the development of the sites and the tourist places in the state is also essential. The development of the towns and enhancing the available facilities is also an essential part of the perspective plan. The tourists are attracted to the destination not only because of the natural resources or the natural beauty of the place, but also because of the return they get on the expenditure they do in the tourist place. These could be satisfaction of the psychological needs like proper, safe, hassle free and affordable accommodation, good transport facilities in and around the tourist place, good water, hygienic and sanitation facilities. The other could be related to the attributes of the destination or the tourist places in terms of various sites to visit in and around the tourist places. Some other could be satisfying his personal tastes like adventure sports, music, cultural shows. The tourists also come to tourists places to buy the traditional things like handicrafts, handloom, and jewellery. In a nutshell the tourists destination should have all the things where the tourists can spent the time and money in a satisfied and justifiable manner. There are thousands of tourist places from which the potential tourist has to choose his destination. So the destination has to be world class if the foreign tourist is being targeted and also from this point of view the facilities should be better and comparable to other best of places in India.

## Economic Benefits and Employment Generation in Tourism

Tourism industry has played an important role in the development of the economy of the state as a whole. The economic activities are generated in the primary, secondary and tertiary sectors of the Valley of Kashmir. Hence, tourism generated employment which may be classified into three major heads, one is direct employment that shall provide goods and services directly, e.g. hotels, restaurants, shops etc. second one is indirect employment, which generally supply goods, services to the tourism business and thirdly investment related employment in construction and other goods industries. It is clear from Table 5.15 that total employment generation would be 34.062 lakh till 2020 for a tourist inflow of 227.08 lakh.

In 2002 the number of employed persons was 9.4245 lakh, which increase to 10.1145 lakh in 2003 and 16.6095 lakh in 2010. At the end of 2011 the number of projected employ is 17.8365 lakh. Tourism has major economic significance for the people of Jammu and Kashmir. The visits from domestic and international tourist provide a valuable source of earning. Visitors spending generates income for both public and private sectors besides affecting wages and employment opportunities.

**Table 5.15:** Employment generation on Implementation of Tourism Development Plan

| *Year* | *Additional tourist inflow (in lakhs)* | *Direct Employment (in lakhs)* | *Indirect Employment (in lakhs)* | *Total Employment Column (2)+(3)* |
|---|---|---|---|---|
| *1* | *2* | *3* | *4* | *5* |
| 2002 | 62.83 | 1.57075 | 7.85375 | 9.4245 |
| 2003 | 67.43 | 1.68575 | 8.42875 | 10.1145 |
| 2004 | 72.36 | 1.809 | 9.045 | 10.854 |
| 2005 | 77.66 | 1.9415 | 9.7075 | 11.649 |
| 2006 | 83.36 | 2.084 | 10.42 | 12.504 |
| 2007 | 89.48 | 2.237 | 11.185 | 13.422 |
| 2008 | 96.06 | 2.4015 | 12.0075 | 14.409 |
| 2009 | 103.13 | 2.57825 | 12.89125 | 15.4695 |
| 2010 | 110.73 | 2.76825 | 13.84125 | 16.6095 |
| 2011 | 118.91 | 2.97275 | 14.86375 | 17.8365 |
| 2012 | 127.70 | 3.1925 | 15.9625 | 19.155 |
| 2013 | 137.16 | 3.429 | 17.145 | 20.574 |
| 2014 | 147.34 | 3.6835 | 18.86375 | 22.101 |
| 2015 | 158.29 | 3.95725 | 19.78625 | 23.7435 |
| 2016 | 170.09 | 4.25225 | 21.26125 | 25.5135 |
| 2017 | 182.78 | 4.5695 | 22.8475 | 27.417 |
| 2018 | 196.46 | 4.9115 | 24.5575 | 29.469 |
| 2019 | 211.20 | 5.28 | 26.4 | 31.68 |
| 2020 | 227.08 | 5.677 | 28.385 | 34.062 |

According to the economic survey there were 6318 in 2000 hotels and restaurants enterprise in Jammu and Kashmir of which 4307 were "Own Account Enterprise", 1790 were 'Non Directory Establishment' and 221 were Directory Establishment. Out of the total hotels and restaurants enterprise in Jammu and Kashmir, 2432 hotels were in rural area whereas 3886 were in urban areas.

The "Own Account Enterprise" is that enterprise which are owned and operated with the help of household labor and the establishments are those which employ hired workers. In the Jammu and Kashmir state employment in hotel and restaurant enterprise were 13,785 of which 6524 were in own account enterprise, 4497 were in non directory establishment and 2764 persons are employed in directory establishment sector. Out of the total employment in hotel and restaurant sector 9869 people were employed in urban areas while 3916 were employed in rural areas.

Tourism is highly labour intensive in comparison to the other sectors of economy. WTTC and PHDCC study indicates that Rs. 10 lakh spent on Hotel and Tourism industry generate 89 jobs while in agriculture it generates 45 jobs and manufacturing 13 jobs. The labour-capital ratio was calculated at 1985-86 prices. In 1994-95, the direct employment in the tourism sector was 2.4 per cent of the total labour force. The tourism industry as a whole, taking all segments together, and ratio is 47.5 jobs, still higher than other sectors. According to the industry source 1.2 international tourists provide employment to one person while 17 domestic tourists generate employment to one person.

Tourism definitely generates employment though it is difficult to measure and calculate the number of employment as these jobs are scattered across many sectors and cannot be easily identified. The greatest number of tourism jobs is found in the major central areas but it can be said that most of the jobs would be created in service sector like hotels and restaurants and travel and transportation.

Mainly three areas of employment in Tourism are:

- Hotels and similar establishments and restaurants
- Passenger transport
- Distributions of the tourists' product, i.e. travel agency, tour operator, guides and reception staff.

Consideration are given to all the above mentioned sectors for projecting the employment estimation in the next ten years and it is projected that nearly 25 people would get direct employment per 1000 tourist and 125 persons would get indirect employment per 1000 tourists, on that basis total 34.062 lakh person would get employment in the end of 2020 in the Jammu and Kashmir as indicated in Table 5.15.

**Future Prospects of Tourism and Employment in Kashmir Valley**

Tourism in Kashmir Valley is still in a discovering stage. Many sites are still lying untapped. Not only the natural or historical sites, but also huge reservoirs of traditional and cultural heritages still remain to be unearthed. People are fully keen to explore it all, for the development of whole State. But the political factors create problems for development of tourism in the Kashmir Valley. Tourist flow to Kashmir Valley has shown remarkable increasing trend for last several decades. A positive growth in tourist flow has been recorded in case of both domestic and foreign tourists till present times. The number of tourists increased from 10,579 in 1951 to 7,00,000 in 1986. However, since 1988, the tourism of Kashmir

Valley received great set-back resulted almost negligible tourist flow up to 1996, but since then tourist flow has been increasing again rapidly. Another aspect of tourism in Kashmir Valley which has shown an upward trend is the development of pilgrim tourism. Every year the Valley has been receiving about 50,000 to 1,00,000 *yatries* (Tourists) to Holy Amarnath Cave though for a shorter duration. Apart from that tourists also visited the Muslim Shrines Charar-e-Sharief, Khanqah-i-Mualla and Hazratbal mosque.

The tourism potential of the Kashmir Valley has not been fully exploited. The region is known as 'paradise unexplored'. Global tourism has been booming and future projections show that this trend will continue. The new generations of travellers who are 'money rich and time poor' are increasingly looking for unique experiences. More and more people are looking at tourism as less of a journey and more of an experience – a phenomenon being called the emergence of the 'experience economy'. For these new and growing breed of tourists the Kashmir Valley with its variety and uniqueness holds immense attraction. The rich natural beauty and its diversity, exotic cultural and ethnic mosaic, flora and fauna and the serenity of the virgin, unexplored ecosystems provide possibilities of a totally different experience for the tourists.

This region has enough potentiality for tourism development due to the presence of carpeted meadows, lush green forests, sprinkling water running from glaciers and mild climate during summers. The surrounding mountains of these side valleys provide the excellent potential for sport tourism especially trout fishing, mountaineering, trekking and hunting. Among the side valleys the important tourist potential valleys are Aru, Sind, Lidder. The Sind valley is one of the most fascinating and charming from scenic point of view. The area possesses the natural beauty like forests, glaciers, flowing water, pastures, meadows, high altitude lakes, trekking routes, sports like trout fishing and game bird sanctuaries. Hence, the region has the largest potential and attraction from the tourist point of view. The presence of pastures and meadows have ramified the beauty of the Valley more in the sense that they provide camping sites to the tourists within these meadows are situated normally 2800 mts., surrounding by the forests, carpeted with green grass and area subjected to grazing by cattle during summers and under snow cover during winters. Besides high altitude lakes, springs and glaciers have played a vital role in attracting the tourists to Kashmir Valley. Glaciers have helped in the expansion of Himalayan tourism, ice skiing provides the tourists an entertainment, sports and an experience.

**Suggestions for Development of Tourism in the Kashmir Valley**

For the development of tourism to enhance its potentiality for employment generation following are some of the suitable suggestions:

1. Building the capacity of tourist site management to deal with Tourism.
2. Training local community members in tourism related activities to participate in the industry and receive tourism's benefits.
3. Aiding communities around the sites to market their products.
4. Raising public awareness of Tourism development and building pride with local communities and visitors through conservation education.
5. Using tourism generated funds to supplement site conservation and protection costs.
6. Spreading the lessons learned to other sites and protected areas.
7. Building increased awareness of Tourism and its activities and policies for tourism industry officials and their clients.
8. It is very important to raise awareness of handicraft and tourism development to village people in a simple way.
9. Developing a detailed master plan is very important.

# 6
# Peace Process and Prospects of Peace in Kashmir

## Introduction

Kashmir as a major source of conflict in Indo-Pak relations is now passing through a process of transformation. From a bilateral issue the conflict of Kashmir is now changing its shape and witnessing the gradual involvement of people of Jammu and Kashmir (J&K) in a process of conflict management and resolution. The Kashmir conflict is the outcome of a process of neglect, discrimination, suppression of Kashmiri identity and the pre-eminence of power centric approach held by the successive regimes of India and Pakistan. Regretfully, the end of the cold war at the superpower level couldn't bring any qualitative change in the mindset of people at the helm of affairs in New Delhi and Islamabad. On the contrary, Indo-Pak tension over Kashmir reached new levels after the outbreak of an uprising in the Indian controlled Valley of Kashmir in the late 1980s. The question is not the failure of the past initiatives for conflict de-escalation, management and resolution in Indo-Pak relations but how an alternate structure of peace and conflict resolution could be created and what can be done at the state and society level to fill the gaps in the approaches and perceptions of parties involved in the Kashmir conflict? Can such a structure for peace be acceptable to New Delhi, Islamabad and the Kashmiri leaders or will the contradictions which exist among them further delay the process of conflict resolution in the region? Conceiving a plausible solution of the Kashmir conflict within the parametres of maintaining the state structures, order, fairness and justice is an uphill task. For around 57 years, the people of Jammu and Kashmir (J&K) have been suffering from a set of issues: injustices, insecurity, violence, terrorism and identity crisis. For the people of J&K this is compounded by a longer term threat to their survival because of an uncertain future, the region of South Asia, particularly India and Pakistan is also a victim of "conflict process" and "violence process" in Kashmir. These two processes are primarily the outcome of the failure of New Delhi and Islamabad, the two major players in the Kashmir conflict, to create conditions for peace and providing people of J&K relief from years of bloodshed and killings. Conceptually, the conflict in Kashmir has four important dimensions impacting on Indo-Pak relations and the future of South Asia as a whole. First, the role of state actors, second centrifugal forces who at the present are out of the power structure, third the question of security and insecurity engulfing the people of Jammu and Kashmir and fourth the broad question of religion and ethnicity. If all the four dimensions are analyzed the process of conflict resolution in Kashmir could be understood in a better manner. As far as the state actors are concerned, to a large extent, the position taken by Pakistan and India on the issue of Jammu and Kashmir has remained intransigent and devoid of much flexibility. After the offering of a hand of friendship by the then Indian Prime Minister, Atal Bihari Vajpayee to Pakistan on April 18, 2003 and Islamabad's positive response, one can see some change in the positions taken by India and Pakistan on the Kashmir conflict. The meeting which took place in the sidelines of 12th SAARC Summit held in Islamabad on January 6, 2004 between Vajpayee and President Pervez Musharraf resulted in the holding of a composite dialogue so as to resolve various issues, including the one related to Jammu and Kashmir, through negotiations. With the unleashing of the Indo-Pak normalization process from early 2004, one can see some progress as far as the resolution of Kashmir conflict is concerned.

### *The India-Pakistan War of 1947*

The India-Pakistan War of 1947-48, sometimes known as the First Kashmir War, was fought between India and Pakistan over the region of Kashmir from 1947 to 1948. The result of the war still affects the geopolitics of both the countries.

The war was fought within the borders of the former princely state of Kashmir and Jammu by Indian Army, paramilitary and the erstwhile princely state forces opposed by Pakistan Army, paramilitary and local militias from the North-West Frontier Province (NWFP) and Federally Administered Tribal Areas (FATA). The princely state forces were unprepared for the initial assault of the Pakistani forces, having been deployed thinly on the borders of the princely state for purposes of maintaining border security and deterring militant activity. The state defences quickly collapsed in the face of the assault, some individuals and units joining the tribal forces.

### *The Tribal Invasion of 1947*

In 1947 two related incidents turned the Kashmir issue into an Indo-Pak conflict. The first was a localized revolt in the pre-dominantly Muslim Poonch area, focused against the administrative neglect of the Maharaja Hari Singh's rule. This strategic border region had long been a recruiting base for the Indian Army, and since the end of Second World War, the home of thousands of demobilized Muslim soldiers of British Indian Army. The second incident was the initiation of an economic blockade of Kashmir by Pakistan. To this effect, Pakistan began to apply an economic squeeze on Kashmir, stalling food supplies to the valley this was done on the land routes from Pakistan into Kashmir even the Sialkot Jammu rail service was suspended. Simultaneously, certain small arm groups of Pakistani have been probing the military defensibility of Kashmir, and they drew conclusions that favoured the Pakistani idea of large scale invasion of Kashmir.

### *The Indo-Pakistan War of 1965*

The Indo-Pakistan War of 1965 was a culmination of skirmishes that took place between April 1965 and September 1965 between India and Pakistan. This conflict became known as the Second Kashmir War fought by India and Pakistan over the disputed region of Kashmir, the first having been fought in 1947. The war began following Pakistan's Operation Gibraltar, which was designed to infiltrate forces into Jammu and Kashmir to precipitate an insurgency against rule by India. The five-week war caused thousands of casualties on both sides. It ended in a United Nations (UN) mandated ceasefire and the subsequent issuance of the Tashkent Declaration. Much of the war was fought by the countries' land forces in Kashmir and along the International Border between India and Pakistan.

### *The Indo-Pakistan War of 1971*

The Indo-Pakistan War of 1971 was a military conflict between India and Pakistan. Indian, Bangladeshi and international sources consider the beginning of the war to be Operation Chengiz Khan. During the course of the war, Indian and Pakistani forces clashed on the eastern and western fronts. The war effectively came to an end after the Eastern Command of the Pakistani Armed Forces signed the Instrument of Surrender, the first and perhaps the only public surrender to date on December 16, 1971 following which East Pakistan seceded as the independent state of Bangladesh.

### *Shimla Agreement-1972*

In 1972 the Shimla Agreement was signed between India and Pakistan. It followed from the war between the two nations in 1971 that had led to the independence of East Pakistan as Bangladesh. The agreement laid down the principles that should govern their future relations. It also conceived steps to be taken for further normalization of mutual relations. Most importantly, it bound the two countries "to settle their differences by peaceful means through bilateral negotiations. The Kashmir dispute again came to the core-issue when India and Pakistan signed the controversial Shimla Accord in July 1972 in the wake of the Indo-Pak War on 1971. The accord converted the 1949 UN "Cease-fire Line" into the Line of Control (LOC) between Pakistan and India.

The then Pakistani Prime Minister, Zulfiqar Ali Bhutto, also promised the then Indian Prime Minister, Mrs. Indira Gandhi that his country would accept the Line of Control (LOC) in the state of J&K as the *de facto* border and would not try to destabilize it. This was not formally entered in the agreement because Bhutto said it would cause domestic problems for him at this juncture. Mrs. Gandhi magnanimously accepted his promise and did not formalize that part of the agreement.

The Government of India and the Government of Pakistan are resolved that the two countries put an end to the conflict and confrontation that have hitherto marred their relations and work for the promotion of a friendly and harmonious relationship and the establishment of durable peace in the subcontinent, so that both countries may henceforth devote their resources and energies to the pressing task of advancing the welfare of their peoples.

### Issues Pertaining to Population Displacement and Resettlement

1. The State of Jammu and Kashmir became an integral part of India after signing an Instrument of Accession in favour of Indian Union on 20th October, 1947.

2. With the accession of the State of Jammu and Kashmir to India jurisdiction in matters of External Affairs, Defence and communications was transferred to the Government of India and the Union Parliament was given power to make laws for the state for the purpose of these matters only.
3. The special position to Jammu and Kashmir was accorded through Article 370 of the Constitution of India.
4. Right after the British withdrawal, Pakistan claimed the state of Jammu and Kashmir on the basis of Muslim majority character of its population and its contiguity to Pakistan.
5. Muslim Separatists displaced approximately 2,50,000 Kashmiri Pundits from J & K between 1989 and 1996.
6. There are compelling explanations for the departure of most Kashmiri Pundits from the Kashmir Valley.
7. The Kashmiri Pundits are minority Hindus in the Kashmir valley.
8. The displacement of the Kashmiri Pundits started in December 1989 when they started leaving their homes in response to separatist's and fundamentalist's threats and attacks on their homes, business and temples, imposition of direct central rule between 1990 and 1996 and terrorist violence should be enquired properly for such a statement, not like propaganda.
9. The Jammu and Kashmir Liberation Front (JKLF) launched an armed campaign for independence on July 31st, 1988.
10. In 1989 Civil Disobedience and political violence by Kashmiri Muslims had gathered pace.
11. By February and March 1990 about 1,50,000 Kashmiri Pundits had fled the Valley.

**Plight of Pundits (Hindus)**

The Pundits, who are the Hindu community of Kashmir and have an ancient and a proud culture, have been amongst the most afflicted victims of the Pakistani-supported campaign of terrorism in Jammu and Kashmir. Their roots in the Kashmir Valley run very deep. They are the original inhabitants of this beautiful valley. Their number being small and peace-loving by nature, they have been the soft targets of terrorists. Virtually the populations of 250,000 Kashmiri Pundits have faced the trouble and large number of them left ancestral home and property. Armour of threat and violence from Muslim fundamentalists, they have been turned into refugees in their own country leaving behind their shops, farms, cattle and age-old memories. Not only Hindus Muslims also felt the terror and decent living was not possible, therefore, a large number of them also left the area for safety and education. Fundamentalists and terrorists have also targeted and assassinated Muslim intellectuals and liberal Muslim leaders too, who spoke of Hindu-Muslim unity and brotherhood. Terrorist acts by Kashmiri militant groups have also taken place outside Jammu and Kashmir.

India claims most of the separatist militant groups are based in Pakistan and Pakistan-administered Kashmir (also known as Azad Kashmir). Some like the All Parties Hurriyat Conference and the Jammu and Kashmir Liberation Front (JKLF) demand an independent Kashmir.

India is unwilling to lose even one additional inch of her land. New Delhi is also concerned that Kashmiri autonomy would set a precedent for breakaway movements in other Indian states (e.g. Punjab or Assam). To Pakistan, Kashmir is symbolic of its national ethos and commitment to protect Muslim interests against Indian encroachment. It believes that the creation of a separate, strongly sectarian nation is incomplete without contiguous Kashmir. In brief, Kashmir is a target of externally sponsored religion-based terrorism. Local terrosim does not exist at all and Muslim *versus* Hindu Pundits divisiveness is totally abstent (our survey findings).

The aim is to divide people on the basis of sectarian affiliation and undermine/weaken the secular fabric and territorial integrity of India.

However, as and now with the passage of time, the passion of the *Jihad*/movement which once had the mass public support has started declining since it has turned out to be a movement run by those who are more interested in their own personal gains. Confusion within the separatist groups too has weakened the movement. The hard liners led by Jamat-e-Islami advocate total merger of Jammu and Kashmir with Pakistan whereas the soft liners led by JKLF (Jammu and Kashmir Liberation Front) stands for total independence of Jammu and Kashmir. This has given rise to a totally confusing and conflicting situation resulting in disillusionment, disarray and disinterest of the common man in Kashmir who (Hindu & Muslims) has suffered a lot for the past 2 decades and is not prepared to suffer any more. On the basis of various surveys (during the period 2009-2011) it is resulted that now not more than 2 per cent Kashmiri population want to merge with Pakistan.

## Details of Refugee Camps in Jammu

**Table 6.1:** Statement Showing Numbers of Registered Migrant Families of Kashmiri Pundits in 2001

| *Place* | *Total No. of families* | *% of total families* |
|---|---|---|
| Jammu | 33618 | 60.36 |
| Delhi | 19338 | 34.72 |
| Others | 2743 | 4.92 |
| **Total** | **55699** | **100.00** |

**Table 6.2:** Distribution and Amenities Available in Different Migrant Camps

| *S. No.* | *Camps* | *No. of public stand post* | *Dispen-saries* | *Bath room* | *No. of families* | *Family size* | *Total population* |
|---|---|---|---|---|---|---|---|
| 1. | Muthi I | 3 | 1 | 84 | 493 | 5 | 2455 |
| 2. | Muthi II | 3 | 1 | 80 | 492 | 5 | 2706 |
| 3. | Purkho I | 1 | 1 | 60 | 419 | 6 | 2514 |
| 4. | Purkho II | 3 | 1 | 30 | 230 | 5 | 1150 |
| 5. | Purkho III | 4 | 1 | 120 | 920 | 5 | 5060 |
| 6. | Mishriwala I | 4 | 1 | 120 | 804 | 5 | 4020 |
| 7. | Mishriwala II | 4 | 1 | 30 | 144 | 5 | 720 |
| 8. | Mishriwala III | 5 | 1 | 90 | 130 | 5 | 726 |
| 9. | Nagarota | 2 | 1 | 30 | 796 | 6 | 4776 |
| 10. | Battal Ballian | 2 | 1 | 30 | 385 | 4 | 1540 |
| 11. | M.A.M. Stadium | 1 | 0 | 6 | 209 | 5 | 1045 |
| 12. | Railhead Complex | 1 | 0 | 0 | 36 | 6 | 216 |
| 13. | Transport Nagar | 1 | 0 | 0 | 15 | 5 | 75 |
| | **Total** | **34** | **10** | **680** | | **5.25** | **26287** |

**Table 6.3:** Magnitudes of Kashmiri Migrants from the Place of Origin (Families)

| *Districts* | *Total* | *%* | *Urban* | *%* | *Rural* | *%* |
|---|---|---|---|---|---|---|
| Srinagar | 12788 | 38.0 | 10441 | 51.67 | 347 | 3.57 |
| Badgam | 3935 | 11.7 | 1704 | 8.43 | 2231 | 22.98 |
| Pulwama | 2884 | 8.6 | 1196 | 5.92 | 1688 | 17.39 |
| Anantnag | 7636 | 22.7 | 3769 | 18.65 | 2667 | 29.53 |
| Baramulla | 3928 | 11.7 | 2146 | 10.62 | 1762 | 18.36 |
| Kupwara | 2447 | 7.3 | 950 | 4.90 | 793 | 8.17 |
| **Total** | **33618** | **100.00** | **22206** | | **11412** | |

**Table 6.4:** Statement Showing Number of Registered Migrant Families in Jammu

| Place | Dec.91 | Pop. | Dec.95 | Pop. | Dec.2001 | Pop. |
|---|---|---|---|---|---|---|
| Jammu | 44423 | 214471 | 25187 | 121041 | 33618 | 168090 |
| Udhampur | 4480 | 17842 | 4292 | 19314 | 4136 | 20680 |
| Kathua | 313 | 1420 | 322 | 1492 | 1582 | 7910 |
| **Total** | **49216** | **233733** | **29914** | **143587** | **39336** | **196680** |

## Civilian Unrest and Kashmir Peace

There emerged a number of political parties to solve the Kashmir issue but moderate Hurriyat leader Abdul Ghani Bhat is ready to talk to India and Pakistan to solve the issue. He says we offer talk to both India and Pakistan. He says we are willing to talk what is the other option to solve the Kashmir issue? It is not possible to solve the issue through war because both countries are nuclear power and they cannot go to war. He said the Kashmir issue cannot be settled without a dialogue. He said that J&K government should not be afraid of dialogue. Bhat invited the ruling National Conference and oppositions, Peoples Democratic Party to join hand with Hurriyat for a final settlement of the issue, they should come forward and talk about aspirants of Kashmiris if NC and PDP say that Kashmir is a dispute and needs a solution. Kashmiris have given enough sacrifices to solve the problem. Moderate Hurriyat chairman Mirwaiz Umar Farooq earlier called for a joint India, Pakistan and Kashmiri effort to solve the Kashmir dispute. He said that separatists were willing to "walk two steps New Delhi walks one". There is need for joint effort and a round table conference should be called in which leadership of India, Pakistan and Kashmir can sit and solve the dispute. He said neither New Delhi nor Pakistan shows any interest and has not taken any concrete steps to solve the dispute. The issues cannot be solved at the level of interlocutors but at the leadership level of India, Pakistan and Kashmiris.

The flow of army inside the Kashmir (except of border), stone pelting by Kashmiri, bullets killing and terrorist flow from across the border can never bring peace neither prosperity in this region. One should be very sincere (India, Pakistan and Kashmiri) to solve the problem for a decent and prosperous way of living in Kashmir. Enough sacrifices by the people of India, Pakistan and Kashmiris have been given.

There have been no major positive developments in the efforts to move towards delineating a framework for resolving the Kashmir issue except a change that choice between India and Pakistan, Kashmiris has changed their mind neither towards India nor towards Pakistan but want to achieve freedom. Therefore, its impact is positive that there will be no situation of war over Kashmir issue between India and Pakistan. It should be treated as the best indicator of peace process and, hence, there is no hurry to decide the case of freedom "*azadi*" demanded by Kashmiris as some other better situation may occur if we start the strategy to give the proper social and economic status to Kashmiri outside the territory of Kashmir by increasing the accessibility with Kashmiri Land and the People. This is the proper way to minimize the hostile attitude from both the sides. A free access towards the main land will minimize the hostile attitude of the people. The youth has no life in Kashmir, nowhere to go, nothing to do after 5 p.m. and no economic activities during the day hours and living in deep depression. Most of them come to Delhi and other cities for work and find that they cannot get a house; they cannot get a job, and are looked upon as terrorist. They return to hopelessness. Even they are treated like this in most of the Muslim educational institutions also where they prefer to study. An intensive survey of these academic institutions reveals that they don't feel homely there also. Girls feel insecure even in Kashmir Valley and their parents are very shaky.

### *New Norms to Handle Civilian Unrest and Peace Prospect*

A new set of guideline have been framed for the security forces deployed in Jammu and Kashmir to handle civilian protest by using non-lethal weapons as it is the general feeling in Kashmir that we are fighting with stones and forces are using lethal arms. They quote the various incidences happening in New Delhi that lethal arms are not being used in any agitation as frequently as in Kashmir. Home Minister P. Chidambaram said the new standard operating procedures have been formulated for use of non-lethal weapons to handle civilian protests (press conference). The group of interlocutors had completed its seventh visit to state. The interlocutors have prepared the report. We are shorting out 700 applications from those who have embraced the militancy want to return for a peaceful and decent living. A soft corner with Kashmiris has to be adopted in the process of peace in Kashmir.

Various attempts have been made to solve the Kashmir issue even after the changed objectives to bring peace in the region.

"Finding out an amicable solution to the issue of Kashmir lasting peace and economic prosperity in the whole region is absolutely interlinked". "Line of Control (LoC) should be transferred into "Line of

Trade". "Union Government India has responded on the issue of Youth Unemployment. However, the appointment of interlocutors to take the dialogue to the Kashmiris is a positive step. It will work but only if key actors in New Delhi and Srinagar have the will to make it work."

New Delhi's interlocutor will have the unenviable task of negotiating a way through the maze that has claimed so many peace efforts. Various Prime Ministers from Atal Bihari Vajpayee to Manmohan Singh have launched serious effort at making peace. Both Mr. Vajpayee and Dr. Singh have had direct meetings with key secessionist leader. Dr. Singh's latest effort included two round-tables which threw up key recommendations to institutionalize the peace process in the troubled states.

Prime Minister Singh and President Parvez Musharaf came close to such a deal in 2006. Since then crisis ridden Pakistan has shown little interest in moving forward. Each talk failed peace effort has left behind a trail of betrayed hopes, engendering frustration and cynicism. But the overwhelming of national solidarity with Kashmiris suffering as demonstrated by the visit of the all party delegation should ensure that this time, the peace process does not fail.

After years of terrorism in Kashmir, Kashmiri youth is not going into blind *jihad.* Renovation of temples is being done by Muslims.

On 23 June, 2010, in Srinagar 57th Sacrifice day of Dr. Shayama Prasad Mukharjee, on this eve, former General Ved Prakash Malik organized a seminar on the topic "Rising India and Challenges of Neighbouring Countries."

Kashmir needs development, prosperity and peace. This can be fulfilled if all Kashmiri youth are not only considered as the means of terrorism but they should be treated as our brother and they should be provided with all the facilities which are given in other region of the country. (*Amar Ujala*, 24 June 2010)

On 5th December, 2010, President Musharraf has reiterated his willingness to withdraw the Kashmir dispute from the UN Security Council if talks with India over dispute show tangible progress. In an interview to NDTV, he offered a four staged interim solution, but warned "My view is that it is easier said than done. I mean it is not as simple as put in across four stages of it. This could be left for trial for five years, 10 years, and 15 years and then we can get together again to see its efficacy, if it is functional, well if there are some modifications required, again."

According to NDTV, Gen. Musharraf's four stages involve the following: (i) Kashmir will have the same borders but people will be allowed to move freely back and forth in the region; (ii) The region will have self-governance or autonomy, but not independence; (iii) troops will be withdrawn from the region in a staggered manner; and (iv) a joint supervision mechanism will be set up, with India, Pakistan and Kashmir represented on it.

Reacting to Gen. Musharraf's comment, former BJP president Venkaiah Naidu said Pakistan had to stop terrorist attacks on India before any progress could be made on other issues.

## Present Peace Status of Jammu and Kashmir

Broadly speaking, when justice and right are denied to a person over a longer period of time, the person is left with two options: bear the situation patiently, or the reaction is anguish, and that reaction, in the process culminates into terrorism. Besides other things, spreading of communal hatred, religious frenzy, separatist tendency, etc. are the tools which terrorists generally use. Guns too are used to achieve the so-called specified mission. Fanaticism, extremism, radicalism, separatism, militancy, activism, etc. are its other names or manifestations. This is one side of the picture of terrorism. (Terrorists fighting for a genuine cause, i.e. liberating themselves, their society/country from the oppressor/ perpetrator). Another side of the picture is disgusting and questionable. Over the years terrorism has emerged as a systematic use or threatened use of violence to intimidate a population, community or government and thereby effect political, religious or ideological change just to achieve personal gains.

Modern terrorism has resorted to other option of intimidation, i.e. influence the mass media, in an effort to amplify and broadcast feelings of intense fear and anger among the people. Needless to mention here that acts of terror are carried out by people who are indoctrinated to the extent of following a strategy of dying to kill. They are the ones who have become pawns in the hands of their masters who direct their paths, sitting in the comforts of far off places with all the facilities available to them. Masters have their vested political interests while as pawns seemingly have nothing to gain except suffer for a cause about which they themselves don't know or know very little.

Terrorism in Kashmir is almost two decades old now and has likeness to the second side of the picture. It has a history long enough to be traced from the date when partition was forced resulting in the emergence of two nations—India and Pakistan—after the subcontinent freed itself from the colonial rule of the British Empire. It may not be out of context here to probe into the consequences in detail that gave rise to terrorism in Kashmir. But again, before that, giving a brief introduction of this widely known beautiful valley would be too apt.

Kashmir-Paradise on Earth (Switzerland of Asia) Nature's grand finale of beauty is a masterpiece of earth's creation of charm and loveliness. Famous for its beauty and natural scenery throughout the world and for its high snow-clad mountains, scenic spots, beautiful valleys, rivers with ice-cold water, attractive lakes and springs and ever-green fields, dense forests and beautiful health resorts, enhance its grandeur and are a source of great attraction for tourists. It is also widely known for its different kinds of agricultural products, fruit, vegetables, saffron, herbs, and minerals, precious stones handicrafts like woollen carpets, shawls and finest kind of embroidery on clothes. During summer, one can enjoy the beauty of nature, trout fishing, big and small game hunting, etc.; during winter climbing mountain peaks and sports like skating and skiing on snow slopes are commonly enjoyed. In addition to the above, Pilgrimage to famous religious shrines of the Hindus and the Muslims make Kashmir a great tourist attraction. About Kashmir Sheikh Sadie a great Persian poet is believed to have said, "If there is any heaven on earth, it is here in Kashmir, in Kashmir, in Kashmir only."

Apart from natural beauty, Jammu and Kashmir has a unique cultural blend which makes it different from the rest of the country (India). It is not only distinct in cultural forms and heritage, but in geographical, demographical, ethnical, social entities, forming a distinct spectrum of diversity. The people of Kashmir, Jammu and Ladakh, all follow diverse religion, language and culture, but continuously intermingling which symbolizes Indian Unity amidst diversity. Its different cultural forms like art and architecture, fair and festivals, rites and rituals, seers and sagas, languages and literatures, embedded in ageless period of history, speak of endless unity and diversity with unparalleled cultural cohesion and amicability. Kashmir has been a great centre of learning. A treasure of rich Sanskrit literature is to be found here. Early Indo-Aryan civilization has originated and flourished in this land. It has also been embracing point of advent of Islam bringing its traditions of Persian civilization, tolerance, brotherhood and sacrifice.

After the British withdrew from the Indian subcontinent in 1947 and India and Pakistan emerged as two separate countries, princely states were given an option to choose the country they wanted to stay on. Obviously, the states falling geographically within had no other option but to merge with the country they were situated. Border states like

Kashmir, Jodhpur, etc. took time to come out with their firm decisions probably because they wanted to enjoy the status of an independent Statehood. In the case of Kashmir, where Maharaja (King) Hari Singh was the ruler, situation worsened considerably. Territorial disputes over Kashmir had already started brewing—Pakistan claiming that Kashmir should go to his side since Muslims were in majority there. Apprehending that Maharaja might opt for an accession to India, Pakistan prepared for an aggression in a bid to capture the State forcibly hoping that masses, mainly Muslims, would support its mission but that didn't happen. Secular forces headed by the then popular mass leader Sheikh Mohammad Abdullah fondly known as Sher-i-Kashmir motivated the Kashmiri people (Hindus, Muslims and Sikhs) to rise to the occasion and stand united to counter and frustrate the evil designs of the enemy who was marching to the capital city Srinagar indulging in bloodshed and mayhem. A new slogan echoed the entire Valley: "*Hamlavar khabardaar, hum Kashmiri hai tayaar—Hindu Muslim Sikh Ithaad, Naya Kashmir Zindabaad*"—Beware you attackers! We Kashmiris are ready to counter you—Long live the Unity of Hindus, Muslims and Sikhs !!—At Hazuri Bagh, Srinagar before a large crowd on October 1, 1947, Sher-i-Kashmir proclaimed: "Till the last drop of my blood, I will not believe in two-nation theory." It was a rebuff to Mr. Jinnah—father of the nation of Pakistan—who was watching the developments so closely from his country side. Finding their designs on Kashmir not fructifying, Pakistan rulers launched an armed attack on Jammu and Kashmir to annex it. Tribes in thousands along with Pak regular troops entered the State on October 22, 1947 from several points and indulged in loot, arson, rape, bloodshed and mayhem. Bowing before the wishes of the people and seeing his own regular army being out-numbered and to push back the invaders, the Maharaja signed the Instrument of Accession in favour of India on October 26, 1947 on the prescribed terms and conditions. This was accepted by the Governor General of India, Lord Mountbatten the next day. The Instrument of Accession executed by Maharaja Hari Singh was the same which was signed by other rulers of the other princely States. Similarly, the acceptance of the Instrument of Accession by the Governor General was also identical in respect of all such instruments.

With J&K becoming legal and constitutional part of Union of India, Indian army rushed to the State to push back the invaders and vacate aggression from the territory of the State. The first batch of Indian Army troops arrived at Srinagar airport immediately after the Accession was signed. On October 30, 1947 an Emergency Government was formed in the State with Sheikh Mohammad Abdullah as its head. The Army fought sustained battle with the tribals/Kabayilies and after several sacrifices pushed them out of the Valley and other areas in the Jammu region. (Earlier Brigadier Rajendra Singh Chief of State Forces with a small number of soldiers at his disposal fought valiantly with the enemy and laid down his life in the process.) Meanwhile, the people of Kashmir under the towering leadership of Sher-i-Kashmir were mobilized and they resisted the marching columns of the enemy. Till the arrival of Indian troops, it was mainly the Muslim volunteers under the command of Sheikh Mohammad Abdullah who braved death to push back invaders. While the army pushed back the invaders, there were several instances where people put up a gallant resistance and stopped the advancing invaders. The most glaring examples of people's resistance were the martyrdom of Mohammad Maqbool Sherwani and Master Abdul Aziz both staunch followers of Sher-i-Kashmir Sheikh Abdullah. Sherwani did not oblige the invaders when they enquired from him the route to Srinagar. Instead, he put them on a wrong track gaining time for troops to reach Srinagar from New Delhi. Somehow, the tribesmen came to know about his tactics and nailed him at a Baramulla crossing and asked him to raise pro-Pakistan slogans. He did raise slogans but these were different. These were pro-Hindu-Muslim unity and in favour of Sher-i-Kashmir. Enraged by this, the ruthless tribesmen emptied their guns on him. The sacrifice of Master Abdul Aziz too was exemplary. The invaders who raped the nuns and wanted other non-Muslim women to be handed over to them, Master Abdul Aziz, a tailor by profession, held the holy *Quran* in his hand and said that they can touch the women only after they pass over his dead body and the holy *Quran*. The brutal killers did not spare him either.

On January 1, 1948 India took up the issue of Pak aggression in Jammu and Kashmir to UNO under Article 35 of its Charter. The Government of India in its letter to the Security Council said, "... Such a situation now exists between India and Pakistan owing to the aid which invaders, consisting of nationals of Pakistan and tribesmen... are drawing from Pakistan for operations against Jammu and Kashmir, a State which has acceded legally to the Dominion of India and is part of India. The Government of India requests the Security Council to call upon Pakistan to put an end immediately to the giving of such assistance which is an act of aggression against India. If Pakistan does not do so, the Government of India may be compelled, in self-defence, to enter into Pakistan territory to take military action against the invaders." After long debates, cease-fire came into operation on the midnight of January 1, 1949. Eventually,

India filed a complaint with the UN Security Council, which established the United Nations Commission for India and Pakistan (UNCIP). Pakistan was accused of invading the region, and was asked to withdraw its forces from Jammu & Kashmir. The UNCIP also passed a resolution stating: "The question of accession of the State of Jammu & Kashmir to India or Pakistan will be decided through the democratic method of free and impartial plebiscite". However, this could not take place because Pakistan did not comply with the UN resolution and refused to withdraw from the State. The international community failed to play a decisive role in the matter saying that Jammu & Kashmir is a "disputed territory".

In 1949, with the intervention of the United Nations, India and Pakistan defined a ceasefire line (Line of Control) that divided the two countries. This has left Kashmir a divided and disturbed territory up till now.

In September 1951, free and fair elections, as per the Constitutional modalities, were held in Jammu & Kashmir, and National Conference party under the leadership of Sheikh Abdullah came into power. With the advent of the Constituent Assembly of the State of Jammu & Kashmir representing the aspirations of the people of Jammu and Kashmir, the State became an integral part of India constitutionally. After Sheikh Abdullah; Bakshi Gulam Mohammad, G.M. Sadiq, Mir Qasim, Gul Shah, Mufti Sayed and Dr. Farooq Abdullah ruled the State as Chief Ministers. Mr. Gulam Nabi Azad and Mr. Omar Abdullah are the current Chief Minister of the J&K State.

Though the governments ran smoothly over the years, continued instigations and arousing religious frenzy by Pakistan did not stop. The year 1965 saw a war between India and Pakistan claiming so many lives on either side. A cease-fire was established and the two countries signed an agreement at Tashkent (Uzbekistan) in 1966, pledging to end the dispute by peaceful means. Five years later, the two again went to war that resulted in the creation of Bangladesh. Another accord was signed in 1972 between the two Prime Ministers—Indira Gandhi and Zulfiqar Ali Bhutto—in Simla. After Bhutto was executed in 1979, the Kashmir issue once again flared up.

During the 1980s, massive infiltrations from Pakistan were detected in the region, and India has since then maintained a strong military presence in Jammu & Kashmir to check these movements along the cease-fire line. India says that Pakistan has been stirring up violence in its part of Kashmir by training and funding "Islamic guerrillas" that have waged a separatist war since 1989 killing tens of thousands of people. Pakistan has always denied the charge, calling it an indigenous "freedom struggle".

In 1999, intense fighting ensued between the infiltrators and the Indian army in the Kargil area of the western part of the state, which lasted for more than two months. The battle ended with India managing to reclaim most of the area on its side that had been seized by the infiltrators.

In 2001, Pakistan-backed terrorists waged violent attacks on the Kashmir Assembly and the Indian Parliament in New Delhi. This has resulted in a war-like situation between the two countries, with Pakistani President General Pervez Musharraf asking his army to be "fully prepared and capable of defeating all challenges," and the then Indian Prime Minister Atal Behari Vajpayee saying, "We don't want war but war is being thrust upon us, and we will have to face it."

### Issues of Possible Solutions and Peace

1. Hamid Gul's warning—Beware of Clinton, Beware of Clive. No intervention by America.
2. Bhutto Doctrine—opening up of all borders and free but monitored movement of population.
3. Vajpayee's initiatives—open Dialogues or "*Sidhi baat*" and end the cross border terrorism.
4. All party Referendum in Kashmir.
5. Initiatives by K.C. Pant, N.N. Vohra to induce APHC to participate in elections.
6. Prime minister Dr. Man Mohan Singh's initiatives by setting up of working groups to monitor bilateral issues.
7. Gilani's 5 demands: (i) India should accept Kashmir as disputed territory; (ii) demilitarized Kashmir; (iii) release political prisoners; (iv) bring to book all armed forces personnel responsible for the recent killings of 112 people; and (v) revoke the Armed Forces Special Power Act.
8. Interlocutors. Not needed in Peace dialogue.
9. Amenities, Facilities, Relief Funds should be equal to other states.
10. Remove army from inside the valley, post it at border.
11. A special status to be given.

### Common Man's View over Kashmir Peace

- Any possible solution to the problems in Kashmir would come through negotiations only. Now that the government has rolled out its plans and has appointed interlocutors, it is expected from the people of Kashmir to grab the opportunity with both hands. Youths should come ahead and discuss their problems and expectations with the government agents at full stretch. People of Kashmir have already shown signs to accept peace process initiatives by the government, by allowing their children to go to schools defying secessionists' call of complete blockade.

- Every political party in India and the UPA government itself are concerned about the growing unrest in Kashmir and the recent visit of leaders of various parties to Kashmir and their amiable interaction with separatist leaders are indications of this. Those who have been closely watching the worsening situation in that unfortunate State are genuinely worried that the situation might spin out of control. However, the response of the political parties seem to be half-baked and drawn up in haste. For example, how can a group of interlocutors engage with the State's people? In any case are the people protesting only against their economic plight? Are they also not agitating to drive home a political point? When the government and the separatist leaders have taken up firm positions on political issues with apparently no negotiating margin, can economic largesse satisfy the agitating people sufficiently as to make them withdraw from the streets? The grey cells of the policy-makers in New Delhi need some rejuvenation. Why is the media silent on these matters?
- How can you solve a problem when you do not understand what is the problem?

The problem should be viewed keeping in mind: (1) Minorities—Kashmiri Pundits, Sikhs and other Hindus were driven out from the valley. (2) Officially 72 Temples have been destroyed. (3) The properties/ancestral houses were burned down in the Kashmir valley, so that they do not return to their homes. (4) There are numerous pro-India agitations by People of Jammu and Ladakh which are Hindus and Buddhist. From the backdrop of above facts how can you say that this is an agitation for freedom? Why this false propaganda from media and political parties? Why you see the agitation in valley and surrounding areas only? Why not in Ladakh and Jammu? If this is a freedom agitation then Ladakh and Jimmies also wants a freedom from J&K state itself. So how many partitions we are talking about? Clearly this is not agitation for freedom but is a *jihad* driven by a religion in the garb of a freedom movement.

This is same as what happened during 1947. We have already given a country to Muslims of United India of 1947. We should ask them to leave India if they wish to, but no more portion of the country.

- Let us hope that peace talks will be successful. It is in the interest of Kashmiris and India that the bloodshed is stopped. The youth must have a future in Kashmir (jobs and security and equal rights). The Government of India should create a peaceful environment in Kashmir in order to lure investors and tourists coming back to Kashmir. Brutal suppression of Kashmiris must be stopped only deeds which improve the standard of living of Kashmiris will win the hearts of the people. 60 years of unrest, despair and bloodshed should come to an end as soon as possible. And there shall be hope that this time the peace process will work (Annex I).

## Interlocutors and Peace Prospect

India's group of interlocutors appointed for the Jammu and Kashmir in October 2010, with the mandate of holding a sustained dialogue with the people in order to ascertain their views on what could comprise a solution to the vexed 64 years old conflict. Their first task was to hear the grievances and aspirations across the state. In the past few months or one year (till July 2011), interlocutors surveyed and organized discussions in 18 districts out of total 22 districts of Jammu and Kashmir State. They consulted political and civil society representatives, they consulted the leaders and local branches of political parties of all the political parties, MLAs, policy analysts, editors and journalists, bar associations, community organizations, clerics, traders associations, youth and minority groups, the parents and relatives of those who tragically died during the troubles, parents of the disappeared, political prisoners in jail, stone-pelters, former militants and their victims, and most recent newly elected, local representatives (Panchayats Head). The member of the interlocutors met with the Hurriyat M and G, JKLF and other allied groups (Annexure I).

The results achieved not very useful and satisfactory, but distressing but still with some hope. The group recorded the pain and suffering of each group in each region (Ladakh, Kashmir Valley, and Jammu Region). The situation observed is related to decline in armed conflicts and Hurriyat stressed on need for the peaceful negotiations. People began to hope for lives free from the gun and free from the yoke of an unresolved political status. Secondly, my survey is related to the situation that Kashmiris have given enough sacrifices and they have forgotten the merging with Pakistan, i.e. only 5 per cent of upland (*pahari*) people they innocently talk and favours about Pakistan. These situations are most favourable for India, and now it is right moments to negotiate and decide and end the Kashmir issue with effort to introduce the economic development in a sustainable manner.

But recent movement (2006-07) turned the situation because of the fresh conflict. Violence, stone-pelting etc. In this year 120 youth died tragically in clashes with the police which cannot be forgotten and forgiven and cannot be allowed to happen again. This highly tragic incident has turned the direction of Kashmir issue and has given a new turn to Kashmir politics and crisis.

But interlocutors despite these terrible events have found in this 10 month of dialogue yearning for a peaceful and lasting resolution. The interlocutors in a public meeting at Langate observed the pledge for peace. In Jammu region despite the communal and multi-ethnic characteristics the stress was on peace. In Kargil region the Buddhist member of hill council and in Ladakh they expected their views for the end of the conflict and bring peace. Academic Radha Kumar one of the 3 interlocuters told media persons that "the biggest commonality that has been found across the state is that the people want a permanent and irreversible solution to the Kashmir crisis". It seems to me that there is no record in the history of Kashmir crisis that these three regions ever discarded the peace, therefore, the findings of interlocuters are not very laudable and cannot be appreciated and should not be recorded in the history of Kashmir crisis. This finding shows the repetition of many previous suggestions, therefore it is a delaying tactics in achieving the permanent and irreversible solution for peace. Instead of suggesting how the peace should be maintained by granting some of the demands of the Kashmir people or if, the Kashmiri surrender totally without fulfilling any demand without this permanent solution of the peace cannot be achieved.

The suggestions and recommendations by the interlocutors must be reviewed as it is very much laudable but not applicable at large scale, if it is made applicable it will be just like to bring moon on the surface of Kashmir land.

# Conclusion and Suggestions

There is a general tendency in the ruling circles of the country to blame others for things that go wrong as a result of our own short-sighted approach in dealing with religious minorities and regional aspirations of the people. It is, therefore, not surprising that the developments in Kashmir are being viewed from the same point of view. The entire blame for the present turmoil is being put on Pakistan and the only solution at the moment seems to be in adopting a hard line and in handling over the Valley to army and para-military forces. Pakistani designs in Kashmir are well-known. Certain misguided but highly motivated youngmen who have been talking about the liberation of Kashmir have been getting training and encouragement from across border. The majority of the Kashmiris are not pro-Pakistani but they are not happy with India either. This growing disenchantment with the India has encouraged the anti-Indian forces to operate more freely in the valley. Needless to say that the success of Pakistan in misleading the Kashmiri youth is largely due to our own failures. Regional aspirations of the people, if not taken care of, are bound to result in violence and instability as we have seen in the case of AASU agitation, the Gorkha movement, the Bodo demands for autonomy and the Jharkhand and Maoist movement. Happily for us these regions do not have common borders with an unfriendly neighbour ever willing to fish in troubled waters.

It must be found out as to what has gone wrong and why is it so that a people who had rejected the two-nation theory and opted to be a part of the Indian Union have developed an anti-Indian feeling. Kashmir Valley is a unique region of India in many respects. It is of great strategic significance owing to its location in high Central Asia, close to Central Asian Nation, China and Afghanistan; it is a region of exceptional scenic beauty inhabited by people who were made to suffer and exploited for centuries by conquerors after conquerors – Muslims, Sikhs, Hindus—making a talented people a spiritless, evasive lot, easily overawed and very different from their rulers. Incidentally, Kashmir is the only state of India with a Muslim majority population.

The framers of our Constitution had taken these realities into consideration. For them the emotional integration of Kashmir with India was the primary consideration and so the state was given a special status under Article 370 of the Constitution. The Kashmiris who were fighting Dogra oppression in the state were being helped by the leadership of the national movement. They rejected the two-nation theory and after Indian independence, opted to be a part of secular and democratic India rather than to go with a theocratic Pakistan.

One basic reason for the present discontent in Kashmir is due to the fact that once the state became a part of India, we had to face a hostile Pakistan staking claim over Indian Territory. And in our effort to keep the territory under control so that it continues to remain an integral part of India, somewhere on the way, we forgot that the integration of Kashmiri population should have been an equally important consideration.

Two groups of people were involved by the Central Government in our policy formulations on Kashmir. First was the leadership of the National Conference which over the years has alienated itself from the mainstream Kashmiri population because while remaining in power it did little to stop the gradual erosion of the special status guaranteed to Kashmir under the Constitution. In order to rule the state the National Conference tried to be more loyal than the King and gave the Indian Government the impression that they are the only nationalists and but for them, Kashmir would go to Pakistan. And hence it was to ensure their rule in Kashmir through means fair or foul.

The second group of advisers consisted of those people who had flourished during the Dogra regime, specially the Kashmiri Pundits who were well-educated and articulate but happened to be a minority. Just after independence whereas no Kashmiri Muslim was qualified and trained enough to take up responsible positions in the State and Central administration. This group got easily absorbed at different levels in the administrative hierarchy and was able to influence government policy. Needless to mention that there has been no love lost between this group and the majority of Kashmiri population.

The national conference gradually lost its following and credibility with the people because it failed to project their real feelings and aspirations. The masses began to look towards the post-independence generation of educated Kashmiri Muslims who like young men elsewhere in the country were fearless, conscious of their right and willing to fight for a just social order. These youngmen wanted to get rid of the one family rule which was inefficient and corrupt. They failed in their efforts because whereas in other states of the country the people were having a government of their choice, successive elections in Kashmir have been hardly free and fair, to put it mildly. The people, thus, were greatly disappointed.

Another factor which could have reassured them and helped the Kashmiris to come closer to India was secularism. There was a time, not long ago, when Kashmiri was considered a model of communal peace and harmony. But it could not remain unaffected from what was happening in different parts of country. Not only Kashmiris but the people in India are rather apprehensive about the future of secularism in the country. The growing frequency and intensity of communal violence and the talk of taking over the Muslim place of worship by force in the name of correcting the wrong done to the Hindus in the distant past, are things that have shaken the faith of Kashmiris in secularism.

Pakistan has rightly been told in no uncertain terms that the developments in Kashmir are purely an internal matter of India and any outside interference will not be allowed. At the same time, it must be made abundantly clear to the extremists in the valley that they cannot be allowed to have their way and the state apparatus will put down any talk of secession from India with a firm hand.

Much water has flown down the Jhelum since Kashmir decided to join India. The new generation of Kashmiris is restive and wants to be assured that justice will be done to them. There is an urgent need to review our Kashmir policy, for it would be unwise to treat the present developments as a simple law and order problem. History is replete with instances where people of a territory who have been put under control by force have revolted against the central authority. This has been specially so in the case of religious and ethic minorities who are willing to lay down their lives for the preservation of their identity. In a country like India which has a multiplicity of languages, religion and culture, any attempt to impose a majority decision on the unwilling minorities will be counter-productive in the long run.

Taking into consideration a long-range perspective it is essential that certain steps be taken after the present phase of turmoil in the Valley is over, in order to isolate and marginalize that small but misguided section of population which thinks that the interest of Kashmir will be best served in Pakistan. Firstly, the Kashmiris should be reassured that their special status under Article 370 will be maintained and necessary steps will be taken to restore to them what has been taken away in the name of bringing Kashmiris closer to India.

Secondly, Kashmiris should be given full freedom to elect their own representatives and form their own government in the state. There should be no apprehension and misgiving, if as a result of free and fair elections a state government which is opposed to the centre comes to power, as long as its activities do not in any way challenge or question the finality of Kashmir's accession to India.

Thirdly, it should be made clear to all that no section of the population, whether in Kashmir or elsewhere in country, will be allowed to undermine our secular fabric and that the religious and linguistic minorities will be provided full protection under the law of land.

Finally, effective measures must be undertaken for the speedy economic development of Kashmir which is bound to generate employment, increase the economic level and improve the living standard of the population. Kashmiri Muslims have hardly any representation in the various Central Government agencies and administrative set-up. The deserving Kashmiris should be encouraged to move out and take up challenge assignments outside the Valley.

It is only when we are able to assure the Kashmiris that their genuine interest are fully protected in India, can we stop them from looking across the border and make them understand that they had taken a right decision in opting to put their faith in a democratic and secular India rather than going to a theocratic Pakistan which is still stricken with internal strife and sectarian violence and has little to offer except the empty slogan of religious brotherhood.

Now it is a much cherished aim of the people of J&K for a long lasting peace sustainable peace, in various regions of J&K State. Therefore, it is necessary to organize together at regional level and at party level either in power or not. The public opinion at various constituency level should be canvassed for this peace purpose convincing them that we have given all possible sacrifices, not only a major chunk of Kashmiri Pundits left their homes but even Muslims more in number than Kashmiri Pundits are suffering, their daughter and sons are scared after leaving valley for higher education and after finishing their education not even ready to return to their home in Kashmir Valley and in Indian side they are not being treated properly as mentioned above, i.e. ill treatment of the local people not renting the house slogan against Kashmiri in M.P. (Bhopal), discriminated in various job opportunities. The university like Barakatullah University in Madhya Pradesh and Aligarh Muslim University are the main attraction for them because of the Muslim names and identity. Even the Muslims they doubt about their Kashmiri identity in academic institutions. A new generation of different thinking is emerging those who born 20 years before have seen the militancy terror and fear, their role seems to be towards peace and prosperity, a society without conflicts, a society with decent living. Therefore, a sudden involvement of the government agencies in developmental activities in rural and urban areas is the need of hour for the sustainable peace.

Lastly, the role of interlocuters seems to be very significant appointed in October 2010. the have given the acivements on 14th July in the *Hindustan Times* that all three regions (Kashmir Valley, Jammu & Ladakh) they are on common platform of peace, a sustainable and long lasting peace. The interlocuters have to go a long way only though outdated and well-known suggestions that these three regions are commonly willing for peace. The troubled Kashmiri before and even after militancy (1989) they opted for peace but we the people and Government of mainland India were not sensitive enough to understand the level of situation and never given the weightage that we have done the political and economic injustice both to Kashmir as we have never realized deeply that we have given the gross economic injustice with Jharkhand, Chhattisgarh etc. (Maoist troubled area).

Lastly, an intensive and comprehensive socio-economic resource survey and potential employment survey is needed to distribute and locate the diversified economic activities.

# ANNEXURES

*ANNEXURE-I*

## Peace and Processes of Violence

**An observation on situation in Jammu and Kashmir from 2002 to 2009***

### Introduction

The data about killings, disappearances, suicides, fratricides, etc. in Jammu & Kashmir collected by JKCCS from 2002 to 2009 is based on the daily reportage in newspapers published from Jammu and Kashmir. All these newspapers are primarily fed by the reports of daily killing by the Jammu and Kashmir Police department.

The data presents a deeply disturbing pattern of impunity in Jammu and Kashmir and contains only reported killings. There might be killings which are not shared with journalists in official records and may have remained unreported.

Inferences can be drawn from the data collected on selective forms of violence that have resulted in killings, disappearances, suicides and fratricide, etc. But it excludes other equally painful types of brutality like torture, injuries, arrests, rapes, human shields, molestations and forced labour, etc. along with the humiliations and their lasting traumatic consequences as the data available for such crimes is difficult to obtain.

Just a cursory glance at the graph of killings demonstrates a real quantitative decline that registers the fact that an attempt at creating an enabling atmosphere was made that could have carried forward the media-hyped processes of peace.

---

* *Source:* A report by Jammu & Kashmir Coalition of Civil Society, The Bund Amira Kadal, Srinagar, 190001, Email: css@jkccs.org.

However, the impression generated by the rhetoric of peace-process between India and Pakistan that reached its peak during April 2005 with the opening of Srinagar-Muzaffarabad bus service, does not seem to correlate with the factual details of violence on ground zero in Jammu and Kashmir.

From January 2002 to December 2009 more than 14,000 people lost their lives which depict Jammu and Kashmir more as a war zone. These people include militants, troopers, civilians, political activists and others.

The data also throws up a picture of Kashmir wherein the residents look perennially besieged within the uncertainties of long-drawn conflict, an image that runs contrary to impressions of normalcy created by the superficial discourses of peace.

Unfortunately, 6588 people were killed from January 2004 to November 2008 (till the attacks in Mumbai), the period during which both the states trumpeted peace process. The number of killings looks colossal in times of war let alone in a time of peace.

The initiation of the peace process should have with time factored in the ground itself with the cessation of hostilities from all sides coupled with respectful and meaningful engagement with the people of Jammu and Kashmir.

Moreover, the decline in the number of killings should have been inversely proportional to the concrete peace building measures taken in the context of conflict resolution. But the pattern that emerges from 2002, where in the graph experienced a relative decline; the peace process appears to have been initiated in the paradigm of management rather than resolution.

Rhetoric of peace process has unfortunately been used to cover the sustained patterns of impunity over the years in Jammu and Kashmir. Killing of people in response to people's resistance has continued unabated, irrespective of the forms of resistance.

People of Jammu and Kashmir have been responsive to the larger global and regional geo-political realties in their modes of resistance. In the changed global scenario mass protests in Kashmir emerged as the dominant expression against Indian oppression but these peaceful unarmed demonstrations were responded to by disproportionate use of state force, resulting in loss of life, injuries and continued trauma.

The state of India has shown indiscriminate mercilessness in its responses to both violent and non-violent forms of people's resistance, choking all the spaces for expressions of dissent.

Transition to non-violence, as the data of civilian killings (and bullet injuries) of last two years suggests, has been disregarded by the Indian state and met with brutal response, which is also reflective of the state's approach towards conflict transformation. This state violence was intended to choke the limited available space of dissent.

Such a huge loss was inflicted on humanity despite claims made by the then Indian Prime Minister, Mr. Atal Bihari Vajpayee in 2002 that the free and fair elections held for the first time would usher in an era of peace. However, daily life in Jammu and Kashmir continues to be marked by killings, torture, indignities, humiliations and other brutalities inflicted by the state.

The media bought and sold vociferously the state-induced rhetoric that free and fair elections are a remedy that can cure the conflict of its causes as well as consequences in Jammu and Kashmir.

But the killings of 14033 people from January 2002 to December 2009 is indicative of the fact that free and fair elections don't translate into bringing peace unless the deeper public yearning for political justice is addressed.

Despite holding many elections and changing many regimes peace, security and resolution remain elusive for the actual stakeholders—the citizens of Jammu and Kashmir.

**Lives lost from 2002 to 2009***

The conflict from 2002 to 2009 has resulted in the loss of life of 3404 civilians, 7504 militants (claimed by government), 2451 troopers and 674 others.

A huge majority of those killed are Kashmiris which burdens the lives of survivors in the society. The state of affairs continues. Notwithstanding many PR exercises, there seems to be no genuine effort in place from the states to stop further bloodshed and other forms of suffering.

The insecurity at present, coupled with past anxieties, continues to darken the future of the majority of people here. The reason for this insecurity and the subsequent loss of lives merits immediate redress to arrive at peaceful resolution of the conflict.

**Custodial Killings and Enforced Disappearance**

According to media reports there were 225 custodial killings and 360 persons were subjected to enforced disappearances from 2002 to 2009.

---

* *Source:* A report by Jammu & Kashmir Coalition of Civil Society, The Bund Amira Kadal, Srinagar, 190001, Email: css@jkccs.org.

**Suicides and Fratricides**

From 2004 to 2009, 157 troopers committed suicide while as 55 personnel were killed in fratricidal incidents. The data suggests high level of stress on the soldiers in the current conditions. The magnitude of stress on the civilian population as a result of existing besieged and insecure conditions can only be guessed.

**Probes**

According to the available data, from 2002 to 2009 the government ordered 140 probes on different human rights abuses, out of which only 16 enquiries have been concluded. In just one case an army personnel who was accused of rape has been punished for misbehaviour and sent to 1 year rigorous imprisonment.

**Killings by Unidentified Gunmen**

From the available data for the years 2008 and 2009, mysterious killings by unidentified gunmen have resulted in the killings of 47 persons in 2008 and 26 people in 2009.

**Children Killed**

January 2002 to December 2009, the conflict has consumed the lives of 258 children (under the age of 18). In the first two months of 2010, 3 boys, Inayat Khan of Dalgate, Wamiq Farooq of Rainawari and Zahid Farooq of Brein Nishat have become prey to the indiscriminate use of violence.

The year 2008 witnessed mass uprising in response to a perception of Amarnath land grab and the subsequent economic blockade of an entire landlocked region. The year 2009 witnessed mass protests in response to rape and murder of Aasiya Jan and Neelofar Jan of Shopian.

The means of protests that were civil in both the cases evoked violent and indiscriminate response from the state.

Despite the repeated pledges of zero tolerance to rights violations by Indian Prime Minister Mr. Manmohan Singh and the ex-Chief Minister Mr. G.N. Azad and present Chief Minister Mr. Omar Abdullah, people witnessed 152 civilians killings in 2008, while as in 2009, 84 civilians lost their lives besides 13 custodial killings were reported during the two-year period.

According to media reports available, between June 2008 and December of the same year, 1876 people including women and children were injured in state violence and as per the hospital reports out of them 640 were operated upon and 6 were amputated.

Similarly, year 2009 witnessed indiscriminate use of force by the state forces as a response to people's protests injuring 1600 civilians, which includes women and children.

In 2007, 2 political activists of National Conference and one each from Congress and PDP were killed. In 2008 two political activists of PDP and Congress were killed while as 5 political activists of National Conference were killed in the year 2009.

## Recommendations by JKCCS

Often the world media in general, and Indian media in particular, presents the killings and other acts of wanton violence as something unconnected and as an aberration whereas the analysis of facts shows that these atrocities are intrinsic to the military suppression of a democratic demand for exercising the right of self-determination. It also convinces us of the need for creating an environment free from fear for necessary conditions, the absence of which primarily contribute to commission of war crimes in the disputed territory.

In order to create proper ambience for resolution, an immediate end to the hostilities against the people of Kashmir is a must created by forces and Kashmiris facing outside the Kashmir in education, business and attitude of the maintained people.

Process of resolution cannot be used as an excuse for denial of rights today. So the human rights must be protected, promoted and respected now. While doing this, the sense of urgency should be quite visible and meaningful in people's assessment.

Any processes initiated by the stakeholders for the final resolution of Jammu and Kashmir needs to acknowledge the inalienable civil and political rights including right to life of the principal party, i.e. people of Jammu and Kashmir.

Contrary to the claims by the states that the aspirations of the people of Jammu and Kashmir will be respected in the final resolution, Indian government continues to hold hostage the right to life and security of people presently.

An essential confidence building measure in this regard by the Indian state would be to put a complete end to its present belligerent policies towards people including the constriction of public dissent.

Based on the above observations and conclusions (by the JKCCS), we appeal the international conscience represented by various institutions like UN, EU, OIC and other humanitarian organizations to intervene for effective lobbying and persuade Indian state to commit itself to protect civil and political rights of Jammu and Kashmir people today. This in our view will facilitate the initiation of a genuine process for peaceful resolution of the long pending Kashmir problem.

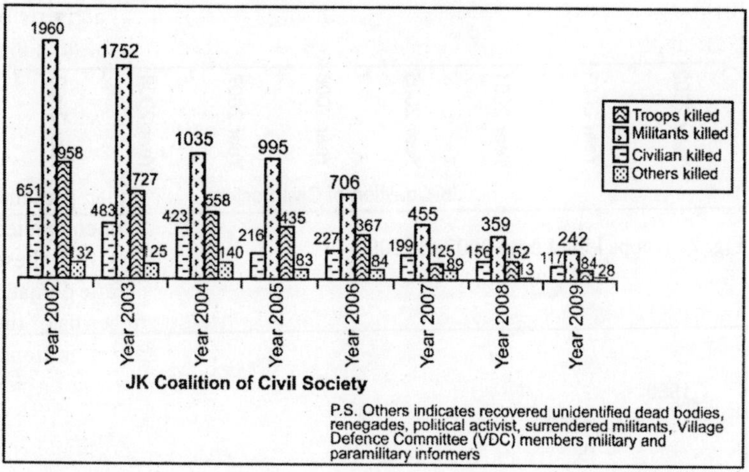


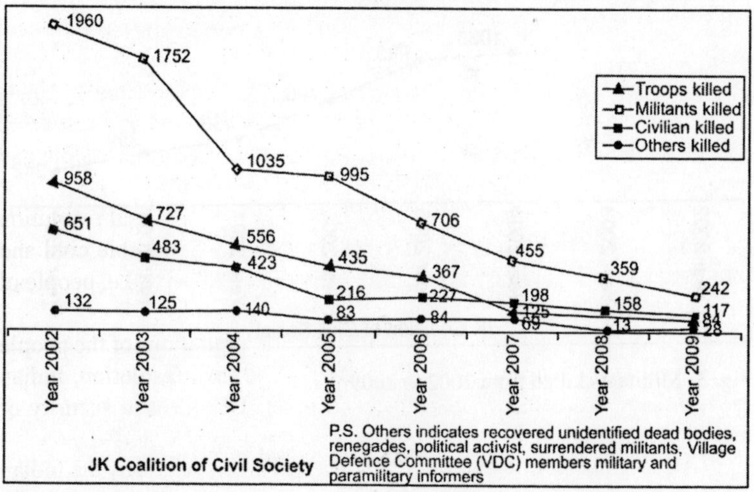


**Fig. 1:** Graphical Representation of people killed from 2002 to 2009

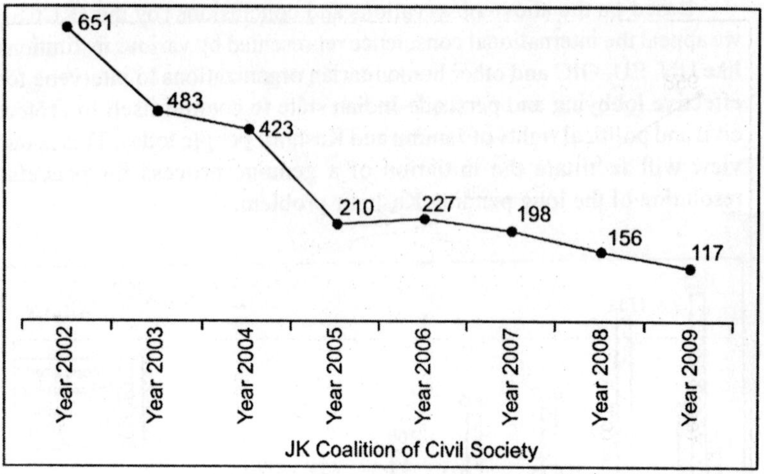


**Fig. 2:** Troops killed from 2002 to 2009

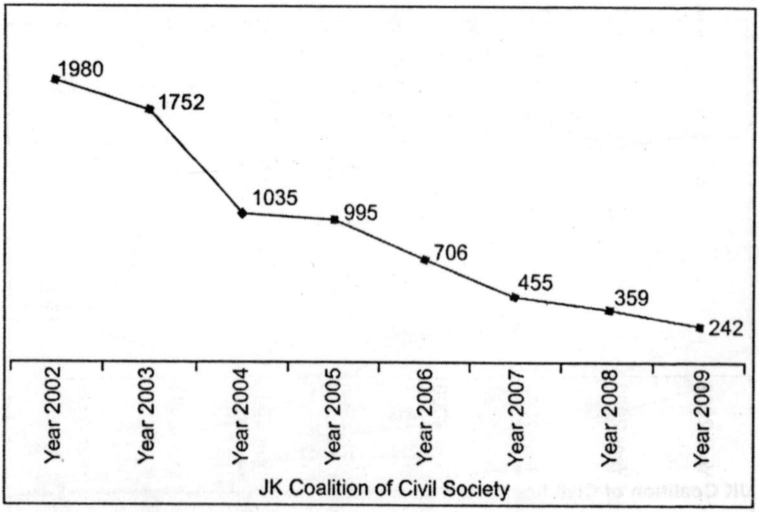


**Fig. 3:** Millitants killed from 2002 to 2009

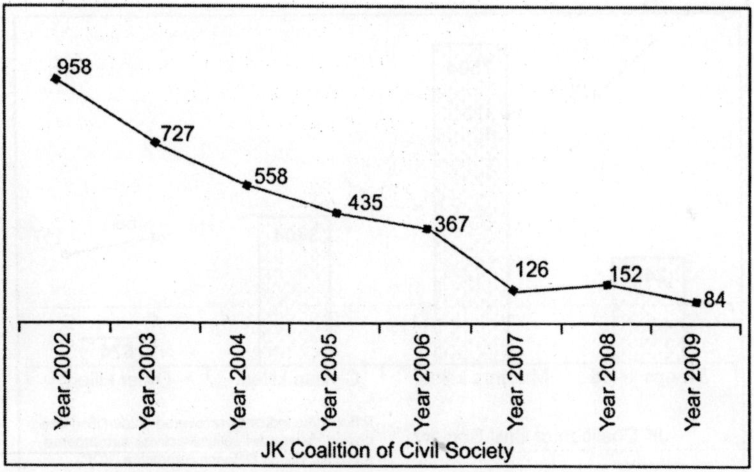


**Fig. 4:** Civilians killed from 2002 to 2009

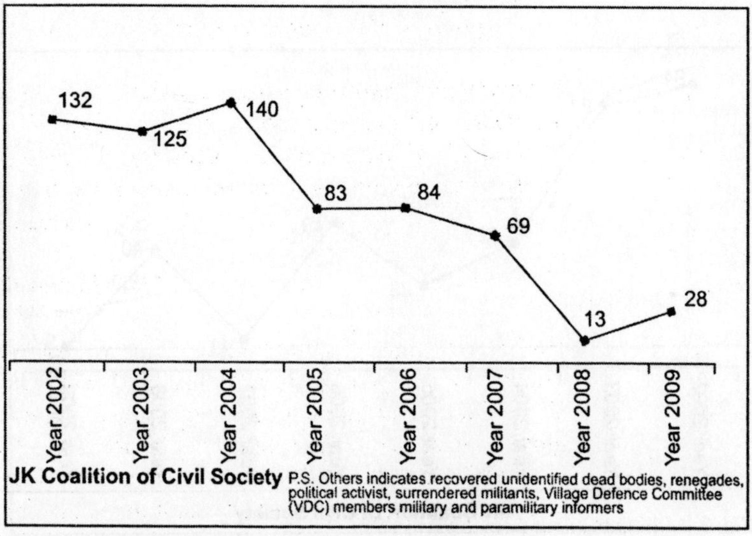


**Fig. 5:** Others killed from the year 2002 to 2009

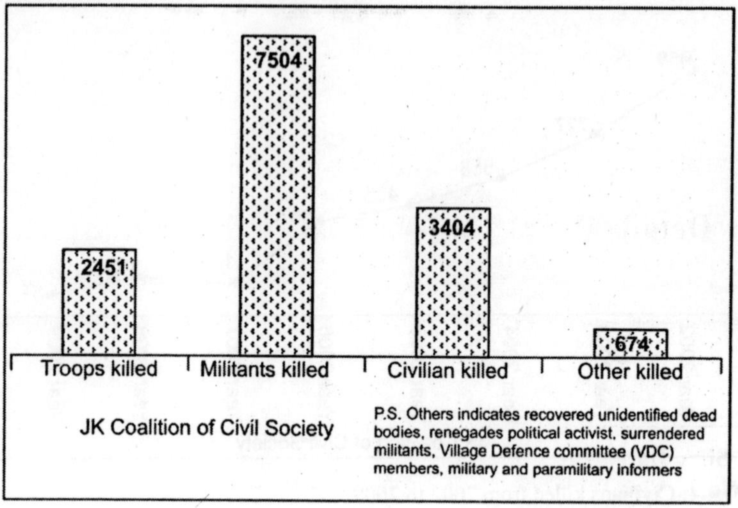


**Fig. 6:** Total killing from 2002 to 2009

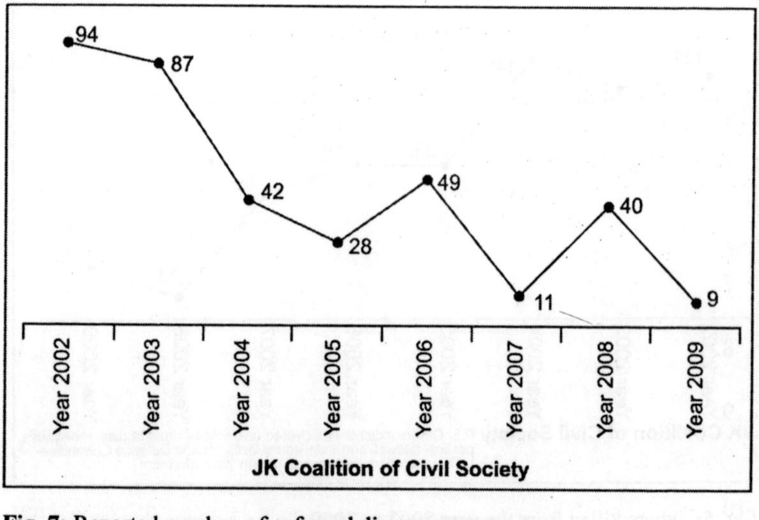


**Fig. 7:** Reported number of enforced disappearance cases

*ANNEXURE-II*

# Details Regarding Number of Delegations Met at Places Visited by the Interlocutors

| Sl. No. | Date(s) of Visit | Place(s) | Name of Delegation/Individual |
|---|---|---|---|
| 1. | October 2010 | Jammu, Srinagar | Delegation from S.O.S. International, an Organization for PoK Refugees |
| 2. | | | Meeting with Yusuf Tarigami, MLA, Kulgam |
| 3. | | | Meeting with Ab. Rashid, MLA, Handwara |
| 4. | | | Meeting with Mufti Md. Syed, Ms. Mehbooba Mufti |
| 5. | | | Visit to Srinagar Jail, Meeting with Naeem Khan, a youth |
| 6. | | | Meeting with Balraj Puri |
| 7. | | | Shri Teja Singh, former Addl. Chief Secretary and Chairman, J&K PSC |
| 8. | | | Members of Shia Federation, Jammu Province |
| 9. | | | Delegation of Hindu-Muslim Ekta Peace Foundation, led by Chairman, Mr. Umar |
| 10. | | | Delegation of Jammu Kashmir Vichar Manch |
| 11. | | | Delegation of Kashmir Minority Front |

*Source*: Interlocutors Report, 2012, A New compact with the people of Jammu & Kashmir.

| Sl. No. | Date(s) of Visit | Place(s) | Name of Delegation/Individual |
|---|---|---|---|
| 12. | | | State Organizer, Congress Seva Dal |
| 13. | | | Members of SAWERA. NGO |
| 14. | | | Member of the Coordination Committee, Centaur Lake View Hotel |
| 15. | | | Delegation from Panun Kashmir |
| 16. | | | Delegation from Kashmir Minority Forum |
| 17. | | | Delegation of the Displaced Welfare Committee, Muthi Camp, Phase I Jammu |
| 18. | | | Delegation of the All Parties Sikh Coordination Committee |
| 19. | November 2010 | Ladakh | Delegation of Monks |
| 20. | | | Round-table with Autonomous Hill Development Council |
| 21. | | Leh | Delegation of Ladakh Buddhist Association |
| 22. | | | Delegation of Manila Congress |
| 23. | | | Delegation of PDP |
| 24. | | | Delegaton of NC |
| 25. | | | Delegation of BJP |
| 26. | | | Delegation of Muslim Minority |
| 27. | | | Visit to new housing blocks for flood affected |
| 28. | | Kargil | Round-table with KAHDC |
| 29. | | | Delegation of Congress |
| 30. | | | Delegation of National Conference |
| 31. | | | Delegation of PDP |
| 32. | | Baramulla | Delegation of Journalists |
| 33. | | | Delegation of Nambardars |
| 34. | | | Delegation of Transport Association |
| 35. | | | Delegation of Sikhs |
| 36. | | | Delegation of Sangrama |
| 37. | | Anantnag | Round-table with members of the Bar Association, Political Parties, Community Organizations, Youth Associations (@ 100 people) |

| Sl. No. | Date(s) of Visit | Place(s) | Name of Delegation/Individual |
|---|---|---|---|
| 38. | | Bandipora | Round-table with Intellegentia (@ 100 people) chaired by MLA Nizamuddin Bhat |
| 39. | | Handwara (Langate) | Public meeting with Langate organized by MLA Ab. Rashid ( @ 3000 people) |
| 40. | | | Delegation of NC, PDP, Congress |
| 41. | | Uri | Town Hall meeting organized by Minister Taj Mohiuddin ( @150 people including Lawyers, media, youth, intelligentsia, Political parties members) |
| 42. | November 2010 | Jammu, Srinagar | Mohammad Rafique Bhatt, Media Adviser and Columnist |
| 43. | | | Delegation of People for Education Research Scholarship Outward Nutrition |
| 44. | | | Meeting with students of Srinagar University |
| 45. | | | Delegation of the Pahari Forum |
| 46. | | | Delegation of the Jammu & Kashmir Youth Forum |
| 47. | December 2010 | Jammu, Srinagar | Meeting with State Women's Commission |
| | | | Meeting with Women's Development Corporation |
| | | | Meeting with State Human Rights Commision |
| | | | Delegation led by Mr. Sunil Dimple, President, Jammu West Assembly Movement |
| 48. | | | Members of J&K Pahari Speaking People |
| 49. | | | Delegation of the J&K Awami National Conference |
| 50. | | | Interactive meeting with Vice-Chancellor, Academicians and Students at Kashmir University |
| 51. | | | Meeting with Shri Saifuddin Soz, President, J&K Pradesh Congress Committee |

| Sl. No. | Date(s) of Visit | Place(s) | Name of Delegation/Individual |
|---|---|---|---|
| 52. | | | Meeting at Langate with MLA and other groups |
| 53. | | | Interaction with Vice-Chancellor, SKUAST, Islamic University and Central University |
| 54. | | | Delegation of the Displaced Kashmiri Pandits, Udhampur |
| 55. | | | J&K PoK Rufugee Front-1947, 1965, 1971 — Delegation |
| 56. | | | Delegation of the Khalsa Democratic Front |
| 57. | | | Delegation of the Shiromani Akali Dal (Badal), Kashmir |
| 58. | | | Delegation of J&K Gujjar & Bakerwal Tahreek-e-Insaaf, led by Mohd. Aslam Kohli |
| 59. | | | Delegation led by Shri Anam Choudhary, President, All J&K Gujjars Conference |
| 60. | | | Delegation of All India Backward Classes Union Social, led by P.C. Patanjali, Former VC |
| 61. | | | Members of the Media Fraternity (Editors) |
| 62. | | | Meeting with the Heads of Security Agencies |
| 63. | | | Meeting with Prof. Varun Sahani, VC, Jammu University |
| 64. | | | Meeting with Dr. B. Mishra, VC, Sher-e-Kashmir University of Agriculture Science and Technology, Jammu |
| 65. | | | Dr. I.A. Humal, VC, Baba Ghulam Shah Badshah University, Rajouri |
| 66. | | | Meeting with representatives of NGOs |
| 67. | | | Delegation of Students Union |
| 68. | | | Meeting with the members of Bar Association, led by Mr. Sunil Sethi |

| Sl. No. | Date(s) of Visit | Place(s) | Name of Delegation/Individual |
|---|---|---|---|
| 69. | | | Meeting with Mr. Satish Gupta, General Secretary, Jammu Chamber of Commerce and Industry and others |
| 70. | | | Delegation of Private Schools Management |
| 71. | | | Delegation of Backward Classes Welfare Organization led by Shri G.A. Kumar, Vice President |
| 72. | | | Delegation led by Mohd. Aslam Kohli, President, Jammu Migrants Front |
| 73. | | | Shri Bodh Raj Bhagat and others from J&K, SC & OBC Maha Sabha |
| 74. | | | Delegation from J&K Pradesh Congress Committee |
| 75. | | | Delegation of All J&K Gaddi & Sippi Tribes Welfare Association |
| 76. | | | Delegation of Pahari Cultural and Welfare Forum |
| 77. | | | Syed Mustakh Bukhari, VC, Advisory Board for Development of Pahari Speaking People, J&K State |
| 78. | | | Doctors Delegation led by Dr. Mehraj-ud-Din Bhat |
| 79. | | | Students Delegation |
| 80. | | | Mr. Nazir Gurezi, Member, J&K Legislative Assembly |
| 81. | | | Mr. Mufti Mohd. Bashiruddin |
| 82. | | | Jamait Ahlihadith J&K, led by Shri Showkat Ahmad Shah, President |
| 83. | | | All J&K Contested Candidates Forum, led by Shri Abdul Rashid Lone, Chairman |
| 84. | | | Industrialist's Association Khonmoh through Mr. Abid Ali, President |
| 85. | | | Delegation from J&K Political Migrants Front |

| Sl. No. | Date(s) of Visit | Place(s) | Name of Delegation/Individual |
|---|---|---|---|
| 86. | | | Retired Central Government Employees Welfare Committee, through Mr. A.Q. Rathore, Chairman |
| 87. | | | J&K Chopan Welfare Association, delegation led by Mr. Abdul Majid Chopan, General Secretary |
| 88. | | | J&K Physiotherapists Association through Dr. Vimal Singh Manhas, President |
| 89. | | | Delegation of Pakistan Occupied Kashmir, Migrant United Front-1947 |
| 90. | | | Delegation from the Chamber of Commerce and Industry led by President Y.V. Sharma |
| 91. | | | J&K People's Democratic Front, Shri Bhushan Gupta, General Secretary, |
| 92. | | | Delegation of the All India Backward Classess Union, led by Prof. Kali Dass |
| 93. | | | Delegation from Jammu State Morcha (P), led by Prof. Virender Gupta |
| 94. | | | J&K Council for Human Rights, Kashmir Chapter, Dr. Syed Najir Gilani, |
| 95. | | | J&K Paryavaran (Environment) Sansthan, Shri Madan Dogra |
| 96. | | | All J&K Youth Welfare Organization, led by President |
| 97. | | Rajouri-Poonch | Delegation led by President, Beopar Mandal, Rajouri |
| 98. | | | Delegation of the Gurdwara Prabandhak Committee, Rajouri |
| 99. | | | Mr. Shafqat Wani, President, J&K Muslim Youth Federation, Rajouri |
| 100. | | | Delegation of the J&K Peace Forum, Rajouri |
| 101. | | | Delegation of Students, Rajouri, led by Mr. Usman Gani |

| Sl. No. | Date(s) of Visit | Place(s) | Name of Delegation/Individual |
|---|---|---|---|
| 102. | | | Group led by Mr A.M. Mir, ED, J&K Voluntary Health Development Association |
| 103. | | | Captain (Retd.) Rattan Sharma, Distt. President, Sainik Cell, Rajouri |
| 104. | | | Mr Rajinder Gupta, Ex-President, Municipal Committee, Rajouri |
| 105. | | | Mr. Bharat Bhushan and Maqbool Qazi, President, Terrorists Affected People Front |
| 106. | | | Delegation of NGO, Sangharsh, led by Mr. Vikrant Sharma |
| 107. | | | Mr. A.K. Sawhney, President, Jammu Newspapers Guild |
| 108. | January 2011 | Srinagar, Udhampur, Jammu | Delegation of the Block Congress Committee, led by Mr. Vijay Kumar Manhas, President |
| 109. | | | Delegation of Islamic Relief and Research Trust, led by Mr. A.R. Hanjura, Advocate |
| 110. | | | Delegation of All Migrant Gramin Dak Sevak Families, led by Ms. Lalita Mattoo |
| 111. | | | Dr. Desh Ram and others, All Migrant Camps Coordination Committee, Mishriwala Camp |
| 112. | | | Delegation of the District Udhampur Development Forum, led by Mr. Rajinder Kumar, Advocate (President), |
| 113. | | | Vikram Singh Slathia and others on behalf of Lok Vikas Dal, NGO, Udhampur |
| 114. | | | Delegation of the Vichar Kranti Manch International |
| 115. | | | Delegation of the Associated Chambers of Commerce and Industry, Udhampur, led by S.S. Kalsotra |

| Sl. No. | Date(s) of Visit | Place(s) | Name of Delegation/Individual |
|---|---|---|---|
| 116. | | | Delegation of the J&K Ex-Service League, Udhampur, led by Mr. Balbir Singh Bhatyal, District President |
| 117. | | | Delegation of the Jagriti Old Age Home Udhampur |
| 118. | | | Delegation of the Amarnath Yatra Sangharsh Samiti |
| 119. | | | Delegation of Jammu Province People's Forum, led by Mr. Paviter Singh, Retd. Judge |
| 120. | | | District Congress Committee, Udhampur, represented by Mr. Anil Pachiala, Working President |
| 121. | | | Mr. Kishan Chander Bhagat, Member, J&K Legislative Assembly |
| 122. | | | Teachers from Jammu University, led by Mr. Dalip Singh Jaiswal |
| 123. | | | Delegation from Youth Democratic Front, Udhampur |
| 124. | | | Delegation of Kashmiri Pandit, Udhampur |
| 125. | | | Representatives of the Plywood Industries Workers Union, Pampore |
| 126. | | | Representatives of the J&K State Central Labour Union |
| 127. | | | Delegation of the J&K Khadi Grammudyog Federation, led by Mr. M.A. Qureshi, Secretary |
| 128. | | | Members of the Jammu State Morcha (Progressive), led by Roshan Lal Gupta, General Secretary |
| 129. | | | Dr. K.C. Sharma, Gujjar Haritage Society, Udhampur |
| 130. | | | Mr. Dina Nath Bhagat, District President, Udhampur |
| 131. | | | Delegation of the Associated Chamber |

| Sl. No. | Date(s) of Visit | Place(s) | Name of Delegation/Individual |
|---|---|---|---|
| | | | of Commerce & Industries, Udhampur, led by Mr. Ashok Kumar Sehgel, General Secretary |
| 132. | | | Shri Swatantra Dev Kotwal of Citizens Advisory Council, Udhampur |
| 133. | | | Office of Haz & Auqaf, Syed Shaukeen Shah |
| 134. | | | J&K National Panthers Party, Mr. Balwant Singh Mankotia |
| 135. | | | Organization of the Displaced Kashmiri Pandits, led by Mr. Ashwani Bhat |
| 136. | | | Chaudhury M. Iqbal Phambra, State Advisory Board for Development of Gujjars and Bakerwals, Udhampur |
| 137. | | | INC, delegation led by Shri K.C. Bhagat |
| 138. | | | NC Party delegation, led by Shri Rajesh Gupta |
| 139. | | | BSP led by State Secretary and District President, Shri Dhani Ram Atri |
| 140. | | | Members of the G&B State Advisory Board, led by Ch. Mohd. Shafi |
| 141. | | Delhi | Interactive Session with the students of Leh, Kargil and Ladakh at India International Centre |
| 142. | February 2011 | Srinagar, Sopore, Jammu | Mr. Rajiv Chunni along with other delegates from SOS International |
| 143. | | | Delegation of POK Displaced Persons Front led by Rachhpal Singh Chib |
| 144. | | | Mr. Pavitter Singh, and others delegates from Jammu Province People's Forum |
| 145. | | | M/s Fayyaz Ahmad Bhatt, Ram Singh Chauhan, Sheikh Ab. Rehman from Samajwadi Party |

| Sl. No. | Date(s) of Visit | Place(s) | Name of Delegation/Individual |
|---|---|---|---|
| 146. | | | Delegation from Nature-Mankind Friendly Global Movement, led by Mr. Babu Singh |
| 147. | | | Mr. Manish Gupta and other delegates from Early Times Newspaper |
| 148. | | | Delegation from Poonchi Brahman Maha Sabha, Jammu |
| 149. | | | Delegation of Jammu West Assembly Movement, led by Mr. Sunil Dimple |
| 150. | | | Mr. Subhash Chander, Individual on behalf of Gujjars and Bakerwals |
| 151. | | | Prof. Hari Om along with other delegates |
| 152. | | | Delegation from Khag District (Tehsil), Budgam |
| 153. | | | Delegation from the Kashmiri Pandit Amity Council, led by Sanjay Raina |
| 154. | | | Delegation from J&K Watan Parast Front, led by Mr. Khalid Tufail |
| 155. | | | Mr. Ghulam Mohammad Wani, Member RCM along with other delegates from National Union Postal Employees Group |
| 156. | | | Delegation from Valley Youth X-pressions led by M. Ashraf Khan |
| 157. | | | Delegation from Peace Mission India, through Mr Rajan Katru |
| 158. | | | Prof. Abdul Rashid Shawl and Gh. Nabi Qureshi, Individuals |
| 159. | | | Delegation of the Post and Telegraph Union led by Mr. Reshi Tantray |
| 160. | | | Delegation from Kapra Group headed by Mr. Muzaffar Bhat |
| 161. | | | Group of Media Persons from Dainik Bhaskar, Daily Excelsior, News-B, CNEB, etc |

| Sl. No. | Date(s) of Visit | Place(s) | Name of Delegation/Individual |
|---|---|---|---|
| 162. | | | Ms. Rifat Jan, Yashmeen, Roohi & Gulshan-Individuals |
| 163. | | | Dr. Sanaullah Kuchay from HMT Colony, HoD, Radiation Oncology-Individual |
| 164. | | | Delegation from Helpage Foundation-Ms. Nikhat Pandit and Mr. Iqbal |
| 165. | | | Delegation led by Shri G.M. Mir, Zonal President, PDP, Handwara |
| 166. | | Sopore | Interlocutors called on the parents of Arifa and Akhter in Sopore |
| 167. | | | Interlocutors called on the parent of Manzoor Ahmad Magray at Chowgam, Handwara |
| 168. | | | Ms. Fatima Tanveer |
| 169. | | | Mr. Nazar Farooq, Vice President, Muslim League |
| 170. | | | Mr. Abdul Qadir Dar, Pak released person (Individual) |
| 171. | | | Mr. Nazir Ahmad Sheikh, President of Khag, Ex-militants and others |
| 172. | | | Mr. Rao Ali, Journalist |
| 173. | | | Group of persons led by RTI Activist Mr. Muzaffar Bhat |
| 174. | | | Members of the Handicapped Association |
| 175. | | | Mr. Ghulam Hassan Dar, Individual |
| 176. | | | Mr. Jeelani Zabarwan, Writer-Individual |
| 177. | | | Group of Ex-Militants led by Mr. Nazir Ahmad Sheikh |
| 178. | | | Delegation of the Forum of Civil Liberties |
| 179. | | | Group of journalists led by Mohammad Tauseef, PPP |
| 180. | | | Group of people from Public Interest Litigation Forum, J&K High Court, led by Mr. G.M. Wani |

| Sl. No. | Date(s) of Visit | Place(s) | Name of Delegation/Individual |
|---|---|---|---|
| 181. | | | Meeting with Justice Bhashiruddin, Chairman, Human Rights Commission |
| 182. | | | Delegation of the J&K Waqf Board, led by Maulana Showkat |
| 183. | | | Mr. Mohammad Yashin Malik, Public Commission of Human Rights |
| 184. | | | Delegation of the LoC Traders, led by Mr. Asif Lone |
| 185. | | | Delegation of the Editors Association, led by Mr. Rashid Rahil |
| 186. | | | Ms. Shamima Firdous, Chairperson, Women's Commission |
| 187. | | | Delegation from the Watan Parast (NGO), led by Mr Khalid Tufail |
| 188. | March 2011 | Srinagar, Jammu | Conducted Women's Meeting in Srinagar inviting women from Jammu, Kashmir and Ladakh-members of J&K Government, legislator, political parties, civil society, opposition groups including Huriyat supporters and Minister of Social Welfare |
| 189. | April 2011 | Srinagar, Doda, Kishtwar, Jammu | Two-Day Interactive Conference with Intellectuals at SKICC |
| 190. | | | Group of MLAs led by Shri G.M. Saroori |
| 191. | | | Delegation of the Congress Party, led by Shri Haji Ghulam Hassan Mir |
| 192. | | | Delegation of the National Conference, led by Shri S.A. Kichloo |
| 193. | | | Delegation of the PDP, led by Syed Asgar Ali |
| 194. | | | Delegation of the BJP, led by Capt. Hukum Chand |
| 195. | | | Delegation of the Panthers Party, led by Mr. Anil Parihar |

| Sl. No. | Date(s) of Visit | Place(s) | Name of Delegation/Individual |
|---|---|---|---|
| 196. | | | Delegation of the BSP led by Capt. Dewan Chand |
| 197. | | | Delegation of the Sanatan Dharam Sabha, led by Shri R.K. Badyal |
| 198. | | | Delegation of Imams, led by Shri Farooq Ahmad, Imam, Jama Masjid, Kishtwar |
| 199. | | | Delegation of the Hill Development Council, led by Shri Noor Hussain Malik |
| 200. | | | Delegation of the SC Senior Citizen Retd. Employees Forum, led by Shri J.R. Aryan |
| 201. | | | Delegation of the Kishtwar Muslim Welfare Forum led by Shri Khursheed Ahmed Dev |
| 202. | | | People from NGO (Ashiana), led by Shri Sanjiv Parihar |
| 203. | | | Group of persons from J&K Yateem Foundation (NGO), led by Sheikh Abdul Hamid Kamal |
| 204. | | | Residence of Dachhan led by Haji Ghulam Hussain |
| 205. | | | Trade Association, Kishtwar, led by Shri Rakesh Gupta |
| 206. | | | Delegation of the Vishva Hindu Parishad, Kishtwar, led by Shri Rajinder Singh |
| 207. | | | Delegation of the Anjum-e-Islamia, Doda |
| 208. | | | Delegation of the All Party Action Committee for Chenab |
| 209. | | | Delegation of the PDP Block, Thatari |
| 210. | | | Delegation of the Chenab Valley Coalition Civil Society, Doda |
| 211. | | | Delegation of the Doda Welfare Society |

| Sl. No. | Date(s) of Visit | Place(s) | Name of Delegation/Individual |
|---|---|---|---|
| 212. | | | Delegation of the Bahujan Samaj Party, Doda |
| 213. | | | Delegation of the All India Backward Classes Union, Jammu |
| 214. | | | Delegation of the Kishtwari Socio-Culture Forum, Kishtwar |
| 215. | | | Group of persons from the Vishwa Shanti (NGO), Matta |
| 216. | | | Mr. Khursheed Ahmad, Advocate, Kishtwar |
| 217. | | | Delegation led by Mr. M.Y. Lone, Social Activist, Doda |
| 218. | | | Delegation of the All India Human Rights Association, Jammu |
| 219. | | | Delegation of the Dehati Forum, Doda |
| 220. | | | Group of people from Anjuman-e-Islamia, Bhaderwah |
| 221. | | | Group of persons from the United Muslim Council, Kishtwar |
| 222. | | | Delegation of the Bar Association, Jammu |
| 223. | | | All J&K Christian Minority Welfare Association, led by Shri Nasri Masih, Chairman |
| 224. | | | Mr. Surender Ambardar of Subah Foundation |
| 225. | | | Maulvi Abbas Ansari of Huriyat Conference |
| 226. | | | Interactive meeting with students (150) at SKICC |
| 227. | | | Group of Industrialist led by Mr Rishi |
| 228. | | | Delegation of the Akhil Bhartiya Gujjar Mahasabha led by President |
| 229. | | | Interactive meeting with the Lawyers at Jammu |
| 230. | | | Mr. Abdul Majid Wani, Member, J&K, Legislative Assembly, Doda |

| Sl. No. | Date(s) of Visit | Place(s) | Name of Delegation/Individual |
|---|---|---|---|
| 231. | | | Brainstorming meeting with National Security Advisory Board, New Delhi |
| 232. | May 2011 | Delhi | Interactive meeting with Journalists from J&K in Delhi at Jaisalmer House |
| 233. | | Srinagar, Jammu | Conference of the Peace Foundation at SKICC |
| 234. | | | Mr. Ghulam Hasan Dar, Ex-DFO |
| 235. | | | Mr. Yusuf Tarigami, CPM |
| 236. | | | Mr. Ashok Bhan and Mr. Abdul Salam Rather, Advocates |
| 237. | | | Interaction with Ms. Jodha Ficher, Civil Society |
| 238. | | | Meeting with Nizamuddin Bhat |
| 239. | | Pulwama | Delegation of Akhil Bhartiya Gujjar Maha Sabha, led by Mr. Poswal |
| 240. | | | Shri Ghulam Nabi Ratanpur, MP at Pulwama |
| 241. | | | Falahai Behboodi Committee, Pampore, led by Shri A.S. Majrooh, General Secretary |
| 242. | | | Saffron Youth Club led by Mohammad Ashraf Bhat |
| 243. | | | Youth Welfare Society; Pampore/ Tral/ Awantipora/ Kakapora/ Rajpora, led by Mohammad Shafi Shah |
| 244. | | | Civil Society Committee led by Mr. Mohan Singh |
| 245. | | | Hindu Welfare Society delegation, led by Mr. A.K. Rajpori |
| 246. | | | Delegation of KMD Association and other Transport Associations led by Ali Mohammad Zaffar |
| 247. | | | Delegation of Women Organization, led by Nahida Soz |
| 248. | | | Delegation of Social Welfare |

| Sl. No. | Date(s) of Visit | Place(s) | Name of Delegation/Individual |
|---|---|---|---|
| | | | Organization, led by Mr. Gamgeen Majid |
| 249. | | | Delegation of Industrialists Association of Khonmoh led by Mr. Shabir |
| 250. | | | Meeting with Social Organization (NG) led by Mr. Sanjay Tikkoo |
| 251. | | At Charar-e-Sharief | Delegation of RTI Activists led by Muzaffar Bhat |
| 252. | | | Delegation of Panches and Sarpanches, Charar-e-Sharief |
| 253. | | | Delegation of Students Union led by Mohammad Yasin |
| 254. | | | Delegation of NCP, PDP and Congress |
| 255. | | | Visit to Kashmiri Pandits Transit Housing, led by Mr. Moti Lal Bhat |
| 256. | | | Delegation of Student Community of Kashmir University at SKICC |
| 257. | | At Srinagar | Delegation of the Kashmir People Welfare Organization |
| 258. | | | Meeting with Director General Police |
| 259. | | | Delegation of the Saffron Growers Association led by Javaid Ahmad |
| 260. | | | Mr. G.M. Wani, Advocate, PIL, High Court |
| 261. | | | Meeting with the Chief Information Commissioner |
| 262. | June 2011 | Srinagar | Interaction with students of Kashmir University |
| | | | Interaction with students of SP College |
| | | | Interaction with students of Women's College |
| 263. | | | Interactive meeting with Sarpanches (10-Srinagar, 10-Badgam and 10-Ganderbal) |
| 264. | | | Visit to Vessu Kashmiri Pandits Transit Accommodation |

| Sl. No. | Date(s) of Visit | Place(s) | Name of Delegation/Individual |
|---|---|---|---|
| 265. | July 2011 | Srinagar, Anantnag, Kulgam, Kathua, Ramban, Riasi and Jammu | Interactive meeting with Panches and Sarpanches of Anantnag (42) |
| 266. | | | Interactive meeting with Panches and Sarpanches of Kulgam District (Total 46) |
| 267. | | | Delegation of Gujjars and Bakerwals of J&K |
| 268. | | | Delegation of the Kashmir Peoples Welfare Forum |
| 269. | | | Delegation of the Communist Party |
| 270. | | | Delegation of the Bahujan Samaj Party |
| 271. | | | Delegation of the Internationalist Democratic Party |
| 272. | | | Delegation of the Jammu State Morcha (P) |
| 273. | | | Delegation of the Ladakh Buddhist Association |
| 274. | | | Mr. Devinder Singh Bindu, NC Candidate, Kathua |
| 275. | | | Delegation of the West Pakistani Refugee Action Committee (1947) |
| 276. | | | Delegation of the Dogra Sanstha |
| 277. | | | Delegation of the Bar Association (Kulgam) led by Shri A.R. Mushtaq |
| 278. | | | Delegation of the People of Gool-Aranas, Ramban |
| 279. | | | Delegation of the Block Congress Committee, Reasi |
| 280. | | | Delegation of the Gurdwara Prabhandhak Committee, Kathua |
| 281. | | | Delegation of the Bhartiya Janata |

| Sl. No. | Date(s) of Visit | Place(s) | Name of Delegation/Individual |
|---|---|---|---|
| | | | Party, Kathua, led by Shri Ramesh Kumar, District President |
| 282. | | | Delegation of the National Panthers Party, Kathua, led by Shri Suraj Singh, Advocate |
| 283. | | | Delegation of the Peer Panjal Regional Forum led by Shri Liaqut Chowdhary |
| 284. | | | Shri Ajaz Ahmad Khan, Hon'ble Minister for Haj and Auqaf |
| 285. | | | Shri Ashok Kumar, MLA, Ranban |
| 286. | | | Shri Vikar Rasool, MLA, Banihal |
| 287. | | | Delegation of the RSS led by Shri Mohan Lal |
| 288. | | | Delegation of the PDP led by Abdul Ahad Wani, District President |
| 289. | | | Delegation of Senior Citizens led by Shri A.G. Manshoor |
| 290. | | | Delegation of Beoparmandal led by Mr. Ved Bhushan |
| 291. | | | Delegation of the SC/ST led by Hajji Mohd. Yaqoob |
| 292. | | | Delegation of the Hill Development Council led by Shri Arshad Malik |
| 293. | | | Delegation of NGOs led by Mohd. Arif Wani |
| 294. | | | Delegation of Journalists led by Shri R.K. Kichloo |
| 295. | | | Delegation led by Mirza Abdul Khurshid, Ex-Speaker and Minister, Rajya Sabha |
| 296. | | | Delegation of Al Huda Educational Trust, Rajouri, led by Amir Mohd. Shamsi |
| 297. | | | Delegation of the Ex-Municipal Councillors Association led by Mr. Rajinder Gupta |

| Sl. No. | Date(s) of Visit | Place(s) | Name of Delegation/Individual |
|---|---|---|---|
| 298. | | | Delegation of the District Rufugee People led by Mr Mohinder Prakash |
| 299. | | | National Forum for Peace for Human Rights led by Mr. Vivek Gupta |
| 300. | | | Delegation of the Pahari Cultural and Welfare Forum led by Mohd. Akram Khan |
| 301. | | | Delegation of the Terrorists Affected People Front led by Mr. Shafi Dar |
| 302. | | | Delegation from Sandarsh (NG) led by Mr. Suresh Kumar |

*ANNEXURE-III*

# Economic and Social Components of the New Compact: A Backgrounder*

## A Review of Socio-economic Progress

The people of Jammu and Kashmir have been denied peace and economic security, which their counterparts in the rest of the country enjoyed in the last two decades. The externally supported insurgency and militancy have not only jeopardized the functioning of democratic institutions but also disrupted normal life and eroded governance systems, including delivery of essential services to the intended beneficiaries. To overcome the economic hardships faced by the people, the Centre and the State Governments have over time taken various initiatives, the outcomes of which may be gauged from the improvement in indicators of development.

- In 2010-11, the Gross State Domestic Product (GSDP) at constant prices recorded a growth rate of 6.61 per cent, which was one of the highest in the recent years. Incidence of poverty, i.e. percentage of people below the defined poverty line, has also declined from 41 per cent in 1973-74 to 21 per cent in 2007-08, which demonstrates significant improvement in quality of life of the people. At least 98 per cent households in the State own a house, which is higher than the national average of 66 per cent or so.
- The overall literacy rate has risen to 68 per cent as per 2011 census, against 55 per cent in 2001. Literacy rate continues to be marginally higher in Jammu Division as compared to Kashmir Valley and Ladakh Division.
- However, an account of performance of school education, provided in the Report on Economic Survey 2010-11, presents a nuanced picture:

* *Source*: Interlocutors Report, 2012.

### Enrolment

The gross enrolment ratios at primary and middle levels are 79.13 per cent and 62 per cent respectively. The net enrolment ratio is 64 per cent and 47.07 per cent only.

### Quality of Education

As per NCERT Report 2003 on assessment of Class V student achievements, learning achievement in mathematics and in language in primary classes in J&K is 36.3 per cent and 49.6 per cent respectively as against the national average of 46.5 per cent in maths and 58.57 per cent in language.

Only 75 per cent of primary school teachers in the state are trained as against the national average of 89 per cent trained teachers.

- Access to secondary and post-secondary education in the State as well as Gross Enrolment Ratio (GER) is lower at every stage of education than the national average. For instance, the GER of higher education is only 10 per cent as against the national average of 12 per cent. For different reasons, quality of education is much to be desired as evident from lack of accreditation of programmes and institutions by any credible agency.
- The State economy suffers from simultaneous existence of shortage of professionally qualified staff and abundance of unemployable educated graduates. This indicates lack of preparedness of vocational and technical institutes to supply manpower required by the knowledge and technology intensive economy.
- The progress made for providing quality health care services also presents a picture of light and shade. While the life expectancy at birth for men and women is very close to national average of 65 and 68 years respectively, in 2010, the child sex-ratio at 859, in 2011, is one of the lowest in the country which calls for paying special attention to strengthen the welfare programmes on child and women development. In fact, mortality rate has substantially declined, though the State is far behind in realizing the target fixed for the current Eleventh Plan.
- Of late, there are a large number of reported cases of mental health disorders, victims of drug abuse and domestic violence, which are attributed to conflict-related trauma. In order to address

these problems, adequate infrastructure support, commensurate with requirements of the trauma and mental health care centres, to deal with all such cases would be required.

- An overall assessment of socio-economic indicators reveals that there is perceptible improvement in quality of life of people. This is despite the fact that the topography of the State and the political turmoil due to insurgency and militancy has adversely affected the development process. As a result of which the record of performance of the State in enhancing the quality of life through a credible peace process and engagement of people in various productive activities has been lower than the progress made by the majority of Indian states. An attempt is made below to outline the measures for expediting economic progress so as to arrest the growing alienation among people.

## Trends in Plan Expenditure and its Impact on Development

Jammu and Kashmir State is characterized by all kinds of diversities, which explain the plurality of political and economic aspirations of different regions and ethnic communities. Opportunities for reaping the benefits of development need to be equalized across various socio-economic groups and regions, which is however not possible without effective empowerment of people and restoration of normalcy in the State.

Intra-regional disparities in access to economic services induce a sense of neglect and resentment against the policies and programmes of the Government. It is imperative, therefore, to identify the sources of discontentment among different groups so as to initiate measures to redress them.

In the course of interaction with a large number of representatives from different regions and social categories, the group noted, among other things, that the people from Jammu and Ladakh have alleged discrimination in respect of both lack of political representation on all the elected bodies and inadequate allocation of funds, resulting in economic disparities across the regions. An attempt is made below to gain an insight into the allocation and utilization of funds as well as to assess the extent of socio-economic disparities in development across the regions. The pattern of expenditure during Eighth Plan (1992-97) through Eleventh Plan (2007-12) shows that of the total allocation of funds, 61 per cent was spent in the Kashmir region while the remaining 39 per cent was incurred in Jammu region. There are year to year fluctuations in the utilization of the total available funds. Of the ten completed Five Year Plans, at least in five plans, available funds to the extent of 10 to 25 per cent could not be utilized.

**Table 1:** Growth of Five-Year Plan Outlay and Actual Utilization of Resources with Priorities from 1950-51 to 2002-07

*(Rs. in crores)*

| *S. No.* | *Plan Period* | *Five year Plan Outlay* | *Actual Expenditure (% of outlay)* | *Priority Sectors* |
|---|---|---|---|---|
| I. | 1951-56 | 12.74 | 90.39 | Irrigation, Power, Transport, Communication |
| II. | 1956-61 | 38.92 | 76.49 | Agriculture, Irrigation, Transport, Communication and Social Services |
| III. | 1961-62 | 75.15 | 82.31 | Irrigation, Social Services and Agriculture |
| IV. | 1969-74 | 158.40 | 102.81 | Irrigation, Power, Social Service, Transport and Communication |
| V. | 1974-79 | 363.40 | 76.65 | Irrigation, Power and Social Service |
| VI. | 1980-85 | 900.00 | 102.02 | Social Service, Irrigation, Power and Agriculture |
| VII. | 1985-90 | 1400.00 | 116.90 | Social Service, Irrigation, Power and Agriculture |
| VIII. | 1992-97 | 4000.00 | 113.00 | Irrigation, Power and Social Service |
| IX. | 1997-02 | 10,000.00 | 75.43 | Social Service, Irrigation, Power, Agriculture, Rural Development |
| X. | 2002-07 | 14,500.00 | 101.03 | Social Service, Irrigation, Power, Agriculture, Rural Development |
| XI. | 2007-12 | 2583400.00 | — | Power, R&B, Education and Agriculture and Irrigation |

*Source*: Compiled from Second and Fourth Five Year Plans, J&K Economic Review 2006-07, Directorate of Economics and Statistics, Planning Department, J&K Government, Annual Plan 2008-09.

The Annual Plan allocation, as under, shows that budgetary provisions have been stepped up at the rate of 10 per cent per year. And the entire allocation of funds has not been utilized by the State for various reasons, including harsh climate in large part of the state during November to March due to which many activities slow down, lack of submission of utilization certificates by the state, delays in Central Government approvals of plan outlays, and release of funds in the last month of a financial year.

**Table 2:** Utilization of Funds under Eleventh Five-Year Plan (2007-12)

| *Year* | *Plan Outlays (in Crore)* | *Expenditure (In Crore)* | *Utilization percentage* |
|---|---|---|---|
| 2007-08 | 4000.00 | 3717.33 | 93 |
| 2008-09 | 4500.00 | 4067.31 | 90 |
| 2009-10 | 5500.00 | 5279.14 | 96 |
| 2010-11 | 6000.00 | 5572.00 | 93 |
| 2011-12 | 6600.00 | — | — |

*Source:* Compiled and computerized by the Group.

In addition, an allocation of over Rs. 32389 crore has been approved under Prime the Minister's Reconstruction Plan for accomplishing specific tasks of infrastructure development, including redressal of grievances of militancy-affected people. But the provision made on year to year basis is hardly utilized. Only one-third of the above allocation Rs. 10869 crore has been spent in the last six years. Of the total allocation of Rs. 1200 crore in 2010-11, for instance, less than fifty per cent was utilized.

It emerges from the foregoing that investment of resources for infrastructure development has not kept pace with the rise in prices, which may be interpreted to mean that investment in real terms has overtime declined in the State. The step up of merely ten per cent per year is not adequate enough to neutralize the erosion of resources due to inflationary pressure. Nor has the total allocation been fully utilized, let alone the realization of physical targets. It is not surprising, therefore, that economic opportunities for employment and income generation have shrunk. This has contributed to marginalization and alienation of the poor.

The impact of long-term public expenditure is reflected in overall development index, which is presented below to gain region-wise perspectives.

**Table 3:** Region Ranked According to their Aggregate Level of Development Index During 1980-81 and 2006-07

| *Region* | *1980-81* | | *2006-07* | | |
|---|---|---|---|---|---|
| | *Index of Aggregate Development (EDI)* | *Rank* | *Region* | *Index of Aggregate Development (EDI)* | *Rank* |
| Kashmir | 0.3481 | I | Kashmir | 0.4349 | I |
| Jammu | 0.3039 | II | Jammu | 0.4333 | II |
| Ladakh | 0.2432 | III | Ladakh | 0.3374 | III |

*Source*: Page 114 of the State Finance Commission Report, 2010.

On the basis of the above findings, the **State Finance Commission** has observed that:

> 5.96: The relative rate of improvement during the period under reference has been at a low pace in case of the Kashmir region and relatively faster in Jammu and Ladakh regions. There does not seem to he built-in discriminatory tendencies in development processes to bring about inequity in development levels between the regions.
>
> 5.97: While the Jammu region improved its development activities by 42.65 per cent between 1980-81 to 2006-07, the Kashmir region improved just by 25.22 per cent and Ladakh by 38.74 per cent in terms of Index values during the period under investigation. Therefore, the pace of development activities as mentioned above seem to be faster in the Jammu region in comparison to the Kashmir region and Ladakh during the period under reference. We can examine among the sectors the pace of development to know as which sectors have progressed well during 1980-81 to 2006-07 and which ones have grown at a slow pace of development.
>
> As per the index value of sectors, it is the social sector, agricultural sector and development sector which have grown fast thereby moving the regional aggregate development index of Jammu on higher side.

The relative positions of major districts are shown in the Table 4.

The purpose of this discussion is to demonstrate that : (i) due to differences in natural resource endowment of the different districts/region,

**Table 4:** Aggregate Development of Index Values of districts/regions for 1980-81 and 2006-07

| *District* | *1980-81* | | *District* | *2006-07* | |
|---|---|---|---|---|---|
| | *Index* | *Rank* | | *Index* | *Rank* |
| Srinagar | 0.3619 | 1 | Jammu | 0.4801 | 1 |
| Pulwama | 0.3403 | 2 | Srinagar | 0.4562 | 2 |
| Jammu | 0.3376 | 3 | Pulwama | 04471 | 3 |
| Anantnag | 0.3358 | 4 | Kathua | 0.4262 | 4 |
| Budgam | 0.3193 | 5 | Budgam | 0.4252 | 5 |
| Kathua | 0.3171 | 6 | Anantnag | 0.3946 | 6 |
| Kupwara | 0.2798 | 7 | Rajouri | 0.3934 | 7 |
| Baramulla | 0.2778 | 8 | Poonch | 0.3889 | 8 |
| Poonch | 0.2522 | 9 | Udhampur | 0.3747 | 9. |
| Udhampur | 0.2492 | 10 | Baramulla | 0.3555 | 10 |
| Kargil | 0.2491 | 11 | Kargil | 0.3438 | 11 |
| Rajouri | 0.2187 | 12 | Leh | 0.3411 | 12 |
| Leh | 0.2187 | 13 | Kupwara | 0.3346 | 13 |
| Doda | 0.2084 | 14 | Doda | 0.3218 | 14 |
| Kashmir Region | 0.3481(39.0) | I | Kashmir Region | 0.4349(36.07) | I |
| Jammu Region | 0.3039(34.0) | II | Jammu | 0.4333(35.94) | II |
| Ladakh | 0.2432(27.0) | III | Ladakh | 0.3374(27.99) | III |

*Source*: As above, Table 25 at 154-55.

the development indices may widely vary; (ii) the unit costs of economic services may differ across the regions due to the topography of the State and, therefore, absolute amount of income or expenditure may not reflect the quality of life or determine the alleged discrimination in government's allocation of funds for development; (iii) the pace of improvement in development index for all the district is almost uniform, due to which relative rankings have remained unchanged over the last 25 years or so; and (iv) indices of development for Jammu and Kashmir region are very close and are comparable, which disprove the alleged neglect or discrimination against the Jammu region as a whole.

There is moreover considerable inter-district disparity in income, literacy and other parameters of quality of life. Since allocation of plan expenditure and its efficient utilization are important indicators of development of districts, it is suggested that the districts which are categorized as backward on the basis of incidence of poverty, income and literacy, etc. should be provided adequate development support so as to enable them to raise the standard of living of people, at least to the average extent as obtaining in other districts.

*ANNEXURE-IV*

# List of Recommendations made in the Reports on the Visit of Interlocutors to the State

**First Visit: October 2010**

***Kashmir Related Recommendations***

1. Release all militancy-related prisoners who have not been charged with committing heinous crimes. Begin the process with stone throwers and well-known dissidents such as Shabir Shah, Asiya Andrabi, Mian Qayoom among others.
2. Take measures to provide job-oriented skills to young people released from jail.
3. Ensure that militants who have surrendered are rehabilitated.
4. Get the courts to expedite the case of under-trials involved in militant activities. Allow visiting rights, especially to women detenus.
5. Ensure speedy punishment of those accused of human rights violations. The mechanisms in place for this purpose, especially the State Human Rights Commission, must be strengthened without delay. Fraudulent complaints need to be publicly exposed.
6. Security forces must be given special training to respect the dignity of citizens. A ham-handed approach to the verification of ID cards and to frisking are tantamount to harassment. Similarly, while security interests are supreme they must be safeguarded in such a way that a curfew does not create hassles for day to day living which it does at present.

7. Peaceful protests must be allowed. The fear that they can degenerate into violence cannot be dismissed out of hand. Yet there is nothing to prevent the security forces from seeking the cooperation of senior members of the community to ensure that agents provocateurs do not breach the peace. Such cooperation has been tried out with great success in several riot-affected parts of the country.
8. The ostentatious presence of the security forces must be reduced to a minimum even while ensuring that they can be rushed to any spot to quell trouble at short notice.
9. Mass protests should be controlled in ways that do not lead to loss of life, grievous injury and damage to property. Special care must be taken to protect children, women and elderly.
10. It is urgent to establish recreational facilities, especially sports facilities, for the benefit of young people.
11. Expert advice needs to be sought to allow SMS services to function even while ensuring that these are not used to spread inflammatory rumours.
12. Government-controlled mass media must be used to highlight local cultures, highlight the achievements of Kashmiris in the country and abroad, drawn attention to the strides India has taken with the Muslim world and with the major powers.
13. Take effective steps to restore, preserve and promote Kashmir's cultural heritage. The Group was shown detailed projects concerning down town Srinagar and the Mughal Gardens along with several archaeological sites.
14. Arrange for Kashmiri youth to visit centres of educational, cultural and business excellence in the country together with film studios and tourist spots.
15. Announce more scholarships to Kashmiri students to pursue higher studies in well-known institutions in the country.
16. Strengthen the State's Human Rights Commission.
17. Implement all the provisions of the RTI Act to make governance as transparent and accountable as possible.
18. Increase monetary allocations to militancy-related widows and orphans. Take steps for rehabilitation of drug users and those suffering from psychiatric disorders.
19. Offer a slew of incentives to private sector enterprises to invest in Kashmir.

20. Seek a psychological closure of some 200 cases of disappeared persons, most of them from the 1990s.
21. Lift curbs on the media but also get them to observe a self-regulated code of conduct. Our Group had to cancel a couple of appointments because someone had dipped off the media to converge on the venues. The participants did not wish to be identified.
22. The Group was told that government advertisement in the local press is selective. It has been reduced in the cause of 'Greater Kashmir' and 'Rising Kashmir' but not in 'Kashmir Times' which is more pro-'movement' than the years. This practice, if true, needs to end.

***Recommendations Regarding Sikhs and non-Kashmiri Muslims***

1. Some 73,000 Sikhs are to be found in 126 villages located in 8 districts of Kashmir. Militancy has forced most of them to migrate to urban centres in the valley, leaving behind their agricultural land, orchards and homes. Their demands, which require urgent and sympathetic considerations are as follows : (a) issuance of state subject certificates; (b) granting of minority status; (c) compensation for the losses incurred by Sikhs in rural areas over the past two decades; (d) benefits on par with Kashmiri Pandits in terms of housing colonies, free education, rehabilitation measures and preferential employment. Currently, some 7000 educated Sikh youths are unemployed. They may be considered for jobs in Central Government institutions such as banks, insurance companies, airports and railways.
2. The main demand of the Muslim Pahadis, who form 22 per cent of the population of the State, is for securing ST status. Successive governments at the Centre, as well as the High Court, have supported the demand. But no action has been taken for more than twenty years. There are surely sound reasons why the demand has not been met. Our Group recommends some sort of a special status for the Pahadis who have always stood by India, using language and culture as criteria.
3. Muslim Gujjars and Bakerwals, who have also been stoutly pro-India, seek forest rights, enhanced development funds and representation in local and state-level political institutions and the bureaucracy. Our Group supports these demands.

***Recommendation regarding other Groups***

1. The Kashmiri Pandits living in cramped quarters in camps on the outskirts of Jammu want the monthly funds they receive to be raised substantially given the rising costs of living. Furthermore, they seek jobs, reserved from them in Kashmir, to be made available to them in Jammu itself. Our Group believes that both demands deserve sympathetic consideration. Our Group also backs the demand for the right to return and for representation in the Apex Committee for Rehabilitation. Likewise, we support the idea of a regular interaction programme between Kashmiri Pandits and Kashmiri Muslims.
2. The Shias, a dominant community in Kargil but who are also to be found in other regions of the state, want greater representation in the bureaucracy, better educational facilities, job opportunities and guarantees that their land is not usurped to provide space for, say, a police station. Our Group suggests that development projects and private sector units be set up in Shia-concentrated localities.
3. Migrants from PoK who have settled in Jammu from 1947-48 onwards also suffer from a feeling of neglect. Their entitlements are nowhere on par with those enjoyed by the Kashmiri Pandits. They also demand the issuance of state subject certificates and improvement in the living conditions in 39 camps where they have resided for decades. Our Group endorses these demands.

Finally, our Group fully supports the recommendations made by the Working Group on strengthening relations across the LoC. Opening up of new bus routes, increasing the frequency of bus services, simplifying travel procedures, encouraging cross-LoC trade and exchanges of cultural and academic groups deserve attention on a priority basis.

**Second Visit: November 2010**

1. Everyone wants a comprehensive and lasting political settlement to the issue of J&K state to be achieved sooner than later.
2. Most people agree that such a settlement will not be achievable without change on ground that would enable a dialogue with key stakeholders towards a lasting settlement.
3. Most people also agree that the long duration of the uncertainty

over the identity/status of J&K combined with its diversion in 1949 has added layers of complicity contributing factors to the conflict.

4. All agree that as a first step the way to address the problem is recognize the honour and dignity of all the concerned actors for peace.

**Third Visit: December 2010**

***Fear of Victimization must be Abated***

A majority of youth in the Valley suffer from fear of victimization by both the security forces/police and the separatist groups. They, therefore, refrain from coming out openly, lest they should be identified, to share their perspectives on the present turmoil and the prospects of defusing tensions in the State. Some people, mainly students, sought safer places to meet the Group so that they could not be seen and identified by police or separatists.

The traders and business community, who reluctantly respond to and yield to calls for *Hartals* or closure of shops, similarly suffer from a fear psychosis. Most people in the Valley stated that they are variously harassed by police as well as separatist groups. And, therefore, they are unable to effectively exercise freedom of expression and mobility in pursuit of social goals.

With a view to empowering the people to overcome their fear, the following confidence-building measures may be considered:

1. A closer working relationship between police and the elders from local community (Mohalla Committees) should be promoted by adopting such practices as may be acceptable to both the police and the community. This may require formation of joining groups of communities and police force for promoting understanding and cooperation for maintaining law and order in each locality. Peaceful existence of a cross-section of society should be entrusted to the community leaders and to MLAs.
2. In pursuance of the Government's commitment, under eight-point policy announcement for release of political prisoners, all the detainees under PSA without serious charges against them should be granted general amnesty and released at the earliest, preferably by end of January 2011. And, accordingly, a public

announcement should be made to demonstrate the Government's resolve to ensure justice to all. In cases of serious charges, the period under which people can be held under PSA should be limited to one week and after this due process of law should prevail.

3. Further, there are hundreds of FIRs against individuals on minor charges such as disturbing the peace, even for carrying out peaceful protests. These FIRs should be withdrawn. CM could announce the withdrawal of these FIRs as a continuance of his policy of allowing peaceful protest (at the same time a circular could be issued stating that police permission on route is required for all protests).
4. It appears that in some cases, police have also interrupted exams to arrest wanted stone pelters, apparently because this is the only time they surface from underground. While the police requirements are understandable, such actions further contribute to the fear psychosis and should be resorted to only for the rarest of the cases.
5. Under the overall supervision and guidance of the Mohalla Committee, comprising local community and police, as stated above, all the remaining bunkers, about 15, in residential areas of Srinagar should be removed in a phased manner by the end of January. GOI could also consider starting a survey of rural areas where security installations can be removed/redeployed out. These measures would surely promote mutual trust and confidence among the security forces and the local communities, which in effect would put in place a credible peace process.

### *Use of Non-Lethal Methods to Suppress Violent Activities*

The Group have had an opportunity of viewing a number of video clippings of encounters between security forces and stone pelters. During the interaction with the senior officials of security forces, it was noted that the forces did not use tear gas or water shells to disperse the mobs and to defuse tensions. Nor is there any evidence of scaring the mobs through the use of air firings, rubber bullets or resorting to firing below the waist. Had the forces used non-lethal methods of controlling violent activities, loss of lives of youth could have been avoided. The consequent backlash and loss of business opportunity could have also been controlled and averted.

1. We welcome the JK police's plan to issue an SOP regarding use of non-lethal methods of crowd control, and hope that they will ensure sufficient supplies of such materials are with them by this spring.
2. We also hope government is enquiring into the quality of manufacture of such materials, given that Tufail Mattoo was killed by an unexploded tear gas shell/canister. Has the manufacturer of the shell/canister been pulled up and asked to pay compensation?
3. In view of the above, security forces should be strictly advised to refrain from use of lethal weapons for controlling the stone-pelting mobs. No civilized society can afford to suppress people's resentment and stone-pelting through the direct use of bullets, without having made attempts to disperse the crowd through the use of other available means, as stated above unless, of course, there is a threat of lynching of security personnel or a threat of setting police vehicles, with people inside, on fire.
4. We are aware that security forces faced a serious threat in the months of unrest. There are, we believe, some 3000 injured security men in hospital. Better protective gear for them, along with ample supplies of non-lethal weapons, will also minimize the threat to them.

### *Re-deployment of Unemployable Youth*

During the interaction with a cross-section of people, an impression that the Group has formed is that most of the stone-pelters, including those have been recently killed, belong to educationally and economically backward families and that they are largely school drop-outs. Because of the limited economic opportunities in the Valley and lack of technical skills, the youth in the age group of 15 to 25 years or so are unemployable in the local job market. Economic and social constraints, including language barrier, hold them back from moving to the rest of the country, which offers huge employment opportunities. The youth is, therefore, frustrated and is easily exploited by politically active groups on the pretext of freedom movement.

The wages offered to the poor, Rs. 110 for 100 days in a year under the Rural Employment Scheme of MNREGA is much less than the market rate of Rs. 250 to Rs. 300 per day. Therefore, there is no worthwhile scheme in J&K under which the poor (unskilled) youth could be gainfully engaged in a constructive manner and on productive projects.

It is, therefore, urgent that:

1. All the aspirant job seekers, particularly the school/college drop-outs should be identified and be offered short-term vocational/ technical training the areas of their interest so that they could be easily employed on productive ventures.
2. Arrangements for their vocational education and training should be made outside the state of J&K, with a view to ensuring both employability in other Indian states and minimizing the chances of their being exploited by vested interests for illegal political activities.
3. The number of such unemployable youth may be less than one lakh. And, they can easily be taken care of in a phased manner at the least cost, since the cost of keeping them untrained and unemployed would be even much higher. Moreover, the proliferation of unproductive youth population could also be contained which in effect would minimize illegal activities of disgruntled elements.
4. Ways and means of establishing collaborative arrangements with the institutions of J&K and the organizations located in various cities should be explored on priority basis so that the youth's potential energy could be gainfully exploited and diverted to productive uses. Sooner it is done, the better. A comprehensive scheme should be designed and implemented expeditiously.
5. Though it may not be within the purview of the Group to explore the opportunities for re-deployment of youth through technical and vocational training, technical support and guidance could be provided, if thought, by the concerned government departments.

In view of the foregoing, the Group strongly feels that unemployed youth who respond to the calls for hartals, participate in violent activities and vitiate the atmosphere of peace, should be deployed on productive activities through adequate and relevant technical training schemes. The centre may provide both technical and financial support.

6. Apart from unemployed youth, there is also a wider problem of isolation that all young Kashmiris face, which has been exacerbated by the suspicious treatment they get in hostels and hotels when they visit the rest of the country. The Home Ministry

could consider issuing an advisory through police stations across the country, that Kashmiri youth should not be singled out for police reporting but should get the same treatment as other youth in the country.

7. Moreover, as an immediate measure, government could consider a massive field/study programme for university students this summer, under which they could go to universities/research institutions/professional organizations for a month/two month's study trip during their summer break. This could break the isolation problem in the short-term.

### *Ensuring Greater Transparency in Functioning of Government Departments*

The civil society organizations, which work for promotion and protection of social interests of different groups in J&K, have stated and asserted in their representations that there is rampant corruption or illegal manipulation in matters relating to recruitment process, award of contracts, allocation of resources across the regions/sub-regions, etc. They alleged that the benefits of huge central funding hardly percolate down to deserving poor people.

In the absence of adequate and relevant data and information, it is difficult to ascertain the truth. This also provides a fertile ground for floating rumours and promoting misinformation that suits vested interests.

In order to promote informed discussions and dialogue on issues of policy decision, and to encourage people's participation in democratic governance, it is imperative to ensure total transparency in functioning of various government departments.

1. All the government departments should, therefore, be advised to put in the public domain all the relevant details about recruitment process and public expenditure on socio-economic projects so as to enable the citizens to scrutinize the public action and thus contribute to a healthy dialogue process.
2. All the relevant details of government activities should be displayed on the respective websites of the departments. This exercise should be completed as per the provisions of the RTA Act within three months, preferably by the end of March 2011 so that the facts and figures are widely shared by all the stakeholders.

This would thus create a healthy condition for fruitful dialogue and discussion for both good governance as well as effective resolution of political conflicts.

***Promote Secular Values among youth, including University Students, who tend to view Kashmir issue from Communal Angle***

It is the youth of J&K who can shape the political future of the State. In contrast to the older generation, who has unquestionable faith in promoting harmonious co-existence of all the ethnic and religious communities, the younger generation perceive the problems of J&K from communal and regional perspectives. The youth, mainly the College students of the three regions—Jammu, Kashmir and Ladakh—widely differ in their approach to the resolution of Kashmir problem, owing mainly to regional and communal overtones. There is hardly any point of agreement among them on such vital issues as the state administration, funding mechanisms and political status of the different regions.

The youth should imbibe secular and democratic values of: living together with all the ethnic communities, having faith in brighter future of the country, and promoting unity and integrity of the country. In view of this, it is suggested that:

1. All the Universities/Colleges of the State should make concerted efforts to encourage interaction and mobility among students so as to enable them to exchange their views on different facets of life, share their concerns of mutual interests and promote understanding on federal set up and democratic policy of the country.
2. In particular, the institutions should organize on regular basis such events as cultural, games and sports activities so as to promote competitive spirit and to provide opportunities for greater interaction among them, which in effect would reduce all kinds of biases, divisive tendencies and communal divide among them;
3. The institutions of the state should, collectively and individually, make arrangements with our universities outside the state for encouraging mobility among students and teachers, which in turn, would not only widen their vision of India's development potential but also enhance standards of teaching and research in the State.

4. The Central and State Governments may advise the concerned departments to respond to the representations we have required to clarify their legal and policy dimensions. The representatives may be invited to meet the relevant officials.
5. On a continuous basis local and national media must be informed of government decision. So must those MPs who were part of the All-Parties delegation that visited the state.
6. We would like the government to ask a constitutional expert to examine four documents prepared respectively by the National Conference, the PDP, the break way faction of the NC (ANC) and Sajjad Lone. The objective would be to enumerate both the points of convergence and divergence. We have written to separatist leaders asking for their public positions on a political settlement. If and when we get their documents, we will be in a position to formulate the broad contours of a political settlement.

***Women in J&K***

1. Overall, most women talk about the impact of conflict on their lives—in particular, the toll taken by violence. This is an issue which has been neglected over the past two decades. Families who have lost their men have received little help other than a one-time compensation, in some cases as little as a lakh. In Rajouri, wemet a family of 7 widows whose husbands had all been killed in a single militant attack. They received Rs. 1 lakh each but after that no help in finding jobs or in employment for their children, who have not been able to benefit from the provision for jobs for militancy affected families because these pertain only to those living in the vicinity of the LoC.
2. This is an issue which requires attention but government agencies may not be the best to handle rehabilitation for widows and orphans. Available schemes need swift implementation and monitoring by respected NGOs, preferably local ones. Without this the chances remain high that many affected women will be left out of the loop.
3. Employment is another critical issue. This is a state in which women have traditionally worked, both in the fields and in the cities. The Rangarajan Committee could consider special provision for women's employment.

4. Women are also active in politics. The PDP and the much smaller ANC and Socialist Party are all three headed by women. If there Panchayat elections and if women candidates are fielded, they are likely to do well. Yet few of the mainstream parties have women's wings—though the Jammat-e-Islami and the hard-line separatists do (Dukhtaran-e-Millat). This is a gap our political parties need to look into as a matter of priority.
5. At a broader level, the role of women in peace-making—and especially in peace-building—is now recognized as contributing significantly to a meaningful peace process. Through women are active in various supportive ways in Jammu and Kashmir, they have not been sufficiently involved by government in "the healing touch". They could help with rehabilitation for widows and orphans and without monitoring women's employment.
6. In Leh, we were very impressed by the Mahila Congress delegation that came to meet us. Their principal concerns were employment for girls who are graduating from different courses, especially in pharmaceuticals and nursing. The demand for a Girl Scouts Brigade was universal and deserves implementation.
7. Finally, we propose to organize a women's meeting in Srinagar in late February, at which we hope to bring together women from all districts of J&K as well as from groups working with women, to discuss some of the issues listed above. The Srinagar meeting should the first of 4, to be followed by similar meetings in Jammu, Leh and Delhi (in Delhi we could take up the kind offer made by Gandhi Smriti and Darshan to help).

**Fourth Visit: January 2011**

***Certain Common Features Emerged from the Discussions on a Political Settlement***

1. The settlement must treat Jammu and Kashmir as a single unit. There should be no bifurcation or trifurcation of the State (on this subject, different voices are heard in Leh).
2. The special status of Jammu and Kashmir guaranteed by Article 370 must not be disturbed.
3. Efforts should be made to vest the state's constituent units with such powers that may be required to address the political, economic, social and cultural aspirations of the people.

4. Powers must be devolved to the constituent units in a multi-layered manner reaching down to the Panchayat level to allow for effective, democratic participation on development.
5. The exchange of people, goods and ideas across the LoC must be facilitated through hassle-free procedures.
6. The country's internal and external security concerns must be fully factored into the political settlement.

***Rights of Gaddi and Sipi Tribes: Implement Reservation Policy***

1. Enquire into the causes of non-implementation of the reservation policy for the said ST communities so as to avoid such lapses that tarnish the credibility and image of the Governments.
2. Extend the socio-economic benefits to these communities as per the relevant reservation policy.
3. Suitably compensate the said communities for the loss of benefits due to lapses on the part of the implementing agencies.

***Promote Khadi and Gramodyog Institutions and KVIC Schemes as in North-East States***

1. Given significant potential of Khadi and Village Industries for promoting employment and income generating activities, KVIC and the Ministry of Small and Medium Enterprises may be advised to design, develop and implement programmes for promotion of Khadi Institutions.
2. To consider establishment of a Wool Bank, location of KVIC's state office in Srinagar, inclusion of Kashmir embroidery in MDA programmes of KVIC and fiscal incentives on the pattern of North-East states.

***Rationalization of Subsidies and Fiscal Incentives for Industrial Development***

1. In order to avail subsidy, the industrial and business organizations have to employ at least 90 per cent of staff from the State of J&K itself whereas in certain disciplines and trades, professionally trained and technical proficient workers are not available locally. Hence, if they hire staff from outside the state, they are deprived of the benefits of industrial subsidy. Therefore,

the norm of recruitment of 90 per cent local staff should be relaxed in respect of requirements for technically and vocationally trained and skilled staff.

2. Commercial and industrial activities which have suffered during the turmoil/insurgency in the state should be provided with adequate incentives, like tax concessions and waiver of loans etc.

*Release of Salaries, Incentives*

1. Arrears of pay on account of enhanced salaries as per the recommendations of the Sixth Pay Commission to be released forthwith.
2. If necessary, the Centre may extend financial support at reasonable terms to the state to overcome the crisis.

**Fifth Visit: February 2011**

*Security — Related Recommendations*

1. To end the intimidation and harassment of citizens by the police, the para-military and the army.
2. To release the stone-pelters and political detainees not charged with serious offences.
3. To speed up the trail of militants languishing in jail for many years by setting up fast-track courts.
4. To curb the indiscriminate use of the PSA.
5. To bring to book those responsible for human rights violations.
6. To re-deploy the army to the borders and place severe limits on the use of special powers vested in them.
7. To ensure that passports for *Haj* pilgrimage are delivered on time.
8. To stop the discrimination of family members who happen to be related to militants.

*Points of Consensus towards Political Settlement*

1. Political settlement will emerge from a sustained, serious, sincere and inclusive process of dialogue with all stake-holders (including separatists), civil society, etc.

2. No political outfit, whether of the mainstream or the off-stream, could claim to be sole spokesman of the people of the Valley; let alone of the state as a whole.
3. Unity and territorial integrity will have to be preserved.
4. Special status of the state in the Indian Union.
5. Need to share legislative, executive, financial and administrative powers between the three regions, although political aspirations in the state are diverse and divergent.
6. Open as many routes as possible linking J&K with regions of the erstwhile princely state that has been under the *de facto* control of Pakistan.

### *Non-political Issues/Recommendations*

1. Establish a grievances Redressal Commission—a quasi-judicial body—for settling claims of war/insurgency affected persons;
2. Reform education policy for increasing its responsiveness to the challenges of development faced by the State.
3. Constitute an Expert Committee on State Finances with a view to identify measures for: (a) mobilization of resources from alternative resources, and (b) economy in expenditure on unproductive activities.
4. Review of poverty alleviation programmes.
5. Constitution of J&K Minority Commission.
6. Implementation of Supreme Court's decision on Reservation Policy for OBCs.

### *Confidence-Building Measures*

1. Rehabilitation of the arrested youth-vocation training etc.
2. Allowing visit of social workers for providing temporary education to detenus in jails.
3. Organization of cultural and sports events and educational visits for the youths.
4. Providing support to the local NGOs and civil society groups doing good work in the areas of education, social welfare, drug de-addiction, rehabilitation, poverty reduction, arts and culture, etc.

## Sixth Visit: March 2011

### *Recommendations suggested during the women's meet*

1. A special task force, comprising of eminent women from all the three regions, should be set up to address the problems of women victims of violence—widows, half-widows and orphans, including relief for parents of the disappeared persons.
2. Urgent requirement of setting up a trauma counseling centres.
3. Redeployment of troops out of residential areas and removal of security installation in residential areas.
4. Stopping indiscriminate use of PSA.
5. Addressing the problems of migrants women, especially the Kashmiri Pandits, may be through a respected NGO.
6. Special status for J&K, and along with that, internal devolution at the regional level, district and Panchayat levels is a must.
7. Political settlement could be in two stages : special status with India, to be followed by an agreement with Pakistan as and when it comes on board.
8. Women to be involved in the dialogue towards peace process.

## Seventh Visit: April 2011

### *Points of Agreement that Emerged*

1. The absolute imperative to maintain the unity and territorial integrity of J&K. Division along communal lines would spell havoc for the substantial minorities that are to be found in most districts.
2. The state must be vested with such powers as it needs under Article 370 of the Indian Constitution which must be identified through intensive consultations within and between the three regions of the state, including the separatists.
3. Pluralism of political, social and economic and cultural concerns, interests and aspirations of the people of the state must be recognized and addressed.
4. Open all roads connecting J&K to PoK to end the state's isolation.
5. Political autonomy of the state would be incomplete without a strong economic content.

6. Release of stone-pelters and militants, arrested under PSA and AFSPA, against whom there are no serious charges.
7. Dialogue process between India and Pakistan should continue.

**Eighth Visit: May 2011**

***Following main issues emerged from the Discussions with various Groups***

1. There has to be visible change on the ground regarding the presence and conduct of the police, para-military forces and the army.
2. The application of PSA and other related acts needs to be thoroughly reviewed.
3. Special needs to be paid to youth, especially regarding their employment.
4. It is important to engage with the separatists.
5. A political settlement must emerge from within the State itself.

**Ninth Visit: June 2011**

1. Payment of honorarium/salaries to Panches and Sarpanches.
2. Sarpanches and Panches demand transfer of administrative and financial powers, as under 73rd and 74th Amendments.
3. Study tours to selected Panchayats, for example, Himachal Pradesh, Goa and Rajasthan.
4. NREGA to give market rates.

**Tenth Visit: July 2011**

***During the Two-day Conference in Jammu on "Pluralism", the following Recommendations were evolved***

1. Bring together writers, poets, performing artists, painters, architects, heritage experts from all the three regions on the same platform in all major towns and cities both in the state and in the rest of the country.
2. Take steps to nurture all languages spoken in the State, especially through the state media.
3. Create institutions along the lines of Academies in Delhi and in the other states.

4. Promote cultural exchanges between J&K and the regions of the State under Pakistan's administration.
5. Allow exchange of newspapers, periodicals and books between the two sides (LoC).
6. Restore museums to their pristine glory and, especially, at least one art gallery in Srinagar to exhibit works by contemporary painters and sculptors.
7. Allow TV channels from Pakistan to be seen in J&K.
8. Allow people in the state to reach out to people on the other side on the telephone.

**Eleventh Visit: September 2011**

1. The Panches and Sarpanches emphasised on the need to strengthen Panchayati Raj in the State so that they can fulfil the promise they have made to the voters.
2. The powers they sought are the ones provided to their counterparts in other states under the 73rd and 74th Amendments. of the Indian Constitution. They also wanted remuneration to be provided to them along the lines provided to the other elected representatives of the people.
3. Sarpanches and Panches suggested to ameliorate the lot of people along the border areas and those living in remote, forested areas.
4. They proposed to improve governance at the local level and, in particular, highlighted the need for uniform criteria to provide employment opportunities for youth.
5. Specific issues concerning the welfare of people, including migrants, and development of the district should be looked into urgently.
6. As pointed out by MLAs, former MLAs and representatives of various political groups and civil society groups, Jammu region had suffered from discriminatory policies over several decades. This too needs to be looked into.
7. No political settlement in the State would be possible without placing the welfare of the people as main focus.
8. We have to set our sights firmly on the future—a future not burdened with the contentious baggage of history, the baggage of rival ideologies, political ambitions and narrowly-defined interests of this or the other stakeholder.

9. The political settlement issue should be addressed taking into account the diverse political, social, economic and cultural aspirations without disrupting the unity of the State and its special, constitutional status in the Indian Union.
10. A broad consensus to reach the solution, duly respecting people's entitlements, viz. direct stake in power at every level of governance, the level of state, the region and the sub-regions.

# Bibliography

Allen, S.W. and Leonard, J.W. (1966), *Conserving Natural Resources*, McGraw Hill, New York, p. 21.

Amnesty International (2007), Impunity for enforced disappearances in Asia Pacific Region must end. Public Statement. Index: ASA 01/ 007/2007 (Public) *News Service* No: 167).

Anon. Kashmir Muslims DEFY India Curfew. BBC online.

Arora, R.C. (1979), *Integrated Rural Development*, published by S. Chand & Co. Ltd., New Delhi, p. 261.

ASCE, (1972), *Ground Water Management, Manuals and Reports on Engg. Practice No. 40*, New York.

Barlowe, R. (1963), *Land Resource Economics*, Prentice Hall, Englewood Cliffs.

Barnett, Harold J. *et al.* (1967), *Scarcity and Growth, the Economics of Natural Resource Availability*, John Hopkins, Baltimore, p. 7.

Bazaz, P. N., (1978) *Democracy Through Intimidation and Terror. The Untold Story of Kashmir Politics*. pp. 220-223 Heritage Pub., New Delhi.

Bazaz, P. N. (2003), *The History of Struggle for Freedom in Kashmir*, (ed). pp.91-97, Gulshan Publications. Kashmir.

Bhat Waseem, (2009), "1931: Uprising degenerates into collaboration" pp. 36-39, *Conveyor* vol. I No.2, Bhat Pub. Srinagar.

Bhindouriya, B.P.S. and Dua, S.C. (1986), *Rural Development Strategy and Prospective*, Anmol Publication, Delhi, India, p. 53.

Biswas, A.K. (ed.) (1975), *Selected Works in Water Resources*, Inter. Water Assoc., Illinois.

Bowers, Paul (2004), "Kashmir (region, Indian subcontinent): The Kashmir Problem—Britannica Online Encyclopedia". "Kashmir." Research Paper 4/28, pp. 45-48, International Affairs and Defence, House of Commons Library, United Kingdom. ISSN 1368-8456.

Brasnett, N.V. (1953), *Planned Management of Forest*, Ruskin House Museum, London.

Brewin, C.R., Andrews, B., Valentine, J.D. Meta-analysis of risk factors for post-traumatic stress disorder in trauma-exposed adults. *J Clin Consult Psychol.* 2000; 68:748–766. doi: 10.1037/0022-006X.68.5.748.

Brown, K. (2002), Innovation for Conservation and Development, *The Geographical Journal*, Vol. 168(1), p.17.

Burton, I. and Kates, R.W. (Eds.), (1965), *Reading and Resource Management and Conservation*, Chicago University Press, Chicago.

Champion, H.G. and Seth, S.K. (1968), *Forest Type of India*, F.R.I., Dehradun, U.P.

Chandra Bipan (2000), *India after Independence 1947-2000*, pp. 320-322, Penguin Books, New Delhi.

Clark, Colin (1986), *Population Growth and Land Use*, the McMillan Co. Ltd., New York.

*Conveyor Magazine* Vol. 1 November 2009.

*Conveyor Magazine* Vol. 1. June 2009.

*Conveyor Magazine* Vol. 2 February 2010.

*Conveyor Magazine* Vol. 2. July 2009.

*Conveyor Magazine* Vol.1 January-February 2011.

Dakshinamurti, C. *et al.*, (1973), *Water Resource of India and their Utilization in Agriculture*, Water Technology Centre, Indian Agriculture Research Institute, Monograph No. 3, Delhi.

Dasman, R.F. (1976), *Environmental Conservation*, Wily, New York, pp. 220-40.

De Jong, K., Kam, S. van de, Ford, N., Hargreaves, S., Oosten, R., Cunningham, D., Boots, G., Andrault, E., Kleber, R.J. (2007), The Trauma of ongoing conflict and displacement in Chechnya; Quantitative assessment of living conditions, and psychosocial and general health status among war displaced in Chechnya and Ingushetia. *Confl Health.* 4:1-13.

Desai, Vasant (1991), *Forest Management in India—Issues and Problem*, Himalaya Publishing House, Bombay.

Diettrich, S.D. (1948), Florida's Human Resources, *Geographical View*, Vol. xxxviii, 2, p. 278.

*District Gazetteers of Mirzapur*, (1988), Government Press, Allahabad.

Dube, R.K. (2003), Population Growth of Sultanpur District, *Ind. J. of Landscape System and Ecological Studies*, Vol. LVI.

Duncan, C. (1962), Resource Utilization and the Conservation Concept, *Economic Geography*, Vol. XXXVIII, p. 119.

Finkelhor, D., Hotaling, G., Lewis, I.A., Smith, C. (1990) Sexual abuse in a national survey of adult men and women: Prevalence, characteristics, and risk factors. *Child Abuse and Neglect*; 14: 19–28. Doi: 10.1016/0145-2134(90)90077-7. [PubMed]

Forster, G. (2007), *A Journey from Bengal to England through the Northern Part of India and Kashmir,* (2007), pp. 34-69, 108-123, Kessinger Publishing, U.S.A.

Freeman, T.W. (1968), *Geography and Planning*, Hutchison University Library, London. pp. 74.

Ganguly, Rajat and Ian Macduff (2003) (Edit.), *Ethnic Conflict and Secessionism in South and Southeast Asia: Causes, Dynamics and Solutions,* pp. 105-107, Sage Pub., New Delhi.

Ganguly, *et al.* (eds.) (2003); *The Kashmir Question – Retrospect and Prospect*, London, Frankclass and Company.

Ganguly, Sumit (1999), *The Crisis in Kashmir: Potents of War, Hopes of Peace*, Cambridge: Cambridge University Press.

Ganguly, Sumit (2002); *Conflict Unending: India-Pakistan Tension since 1947*, Columbia University Press.

Garnier, J.B. (1976), *Geography of Population*, Longman Group Ltd., London, p. 3.

Ghosh, S. (1976), The Planning of Our Forest Resources, in *Yojana*, Planning Commission, XX/16, p. 10.

Herlihy, J., Scragg P., and Turner S. (2002), Discrepancies in Autobiographical Memories—Implications for the Assessment of asylum Seekers: Repeated Interviews Study. *Brit Med J.*; 324: 324–327. Doi: 10.1136/bmj.324.7333.324. [PubMed]

Household survey manual: diarrhoea and acute respiratory disease control. World Health Organization, Division of Control of Diarrhoea, Acute Respiratory Disease. Geneva; 1994. http://whqlibdoc.who.int/hq/1994/WHO_CDR_94_8.pdf.

*Imperial Gazetteer of India* (1908), volume 15. pp. 99-102. Oxford University Press, Oxford, London.

Jasjit Singh (1999). Kargil 1999: *Pakistan's Fourth War for Kashmir*. pp. 33-36, South Asia Books. New Delhi.

Jeelani, Mushtaq A. "Kashmir: A History Littered With Rigged Elections (by) Media Monitors Network" Article. Mediamonitors.net. http://www.mediamonitors.net/jeelani4.html. Retrieved 2-2-2010.

*Kashmir Media Service* (Data of various years).

Kaur, P. (1996), *Human Resource Development for Rural Development*, Anmol Publication, New Delhi.

Kerr, J.M. and Swarup, R. (1997), Natural Resource Policy Management Problems in India, in John M. Kerr *et al.*, *Natural Resource*

*Economics, Theory and Application in India*, Oxford and IBH Publishing Co. Pvt. Ltd., New Delhi.

Kleber, R.J., Brom, D. (2008), Theory, prevention and treatment. Lisse: Swets & Zeitlinger; 1992. Coping with trauma. de Jong K., Kam S. van de, Ford, N., Lokuge, K., Fromm, S., van Galen, R., Reilley, B., Kleber, R. *Conflict in the Indian Kashmir Valley II: psychosocial impact. Confl.* Health. 2:11. [PubMed]

Kohli, U. and Gautam, V. (1988), *Human Resource Development and Planning Process in India*, Vikas Publishing House Pvt. Ltd., Delhi.

Kumar, A. (1992), *Human Resource Development; An Inter Disicipilinary Approach* (set of 2 vols.), Anmol Pub., New Delhi.

Lawrence, Walter R. (2005), *The Valley of Kashmir*, pp. 304-307. Asian Educational Pub., New Delhi.

Lopes, Cardoso B., Bilukha, O.O., Gotway, Crawford C.A., Shaikh, I., Wolfe, M.I., Mitchell, I., Gerber, M.L., Anderson, M., (2004), Mental health, social functioning, and disability in postwar Afghanistan. *JAMA*.; 292:575–584. Doi: 10.1001/jama.292.5.575. [PubMed]

Margoob, A.M., Firdosi, M.M., Banal, R., Khan, A.Y., Malik, Y.A., Ahmad, S.A., Hussain, A., Majid, A., Wani, Z.A., Rather, Y.H., Muzamil, M., Khanday, S.A., Shah, M.S. (2006), *Community Prevalence of Trauma in South Asia – Experience from Kashmir*. Jammu Kashmir-Practitioner. 13.

Mehta, S.L. and Bandyopadhyay, A. (2004), Sustainable Agriculture Farming Systems and Natural Resources, in Sundaram, K.V. *et al.*, (ed.) *Natural Resources Management and Livelihood Security*, Concept Publishing Company, New Delhi.

Moonis Raza, A. Ahmad, A. Mohammad, (1978) "*The Valley of Kashmir*" Vol. I. The Land, pp. ix-xi, Vikas Pub. New Delhi.

Murthy, Y.K. (1977), Water Resources Development in India and its related Problems, *Hydrology Review*, Vol. 3, Nos. 1, 2; 23-39.

Pino, N.W., Meier, R.F. (1999), *Gender differences in rape reporting*. Sex Roles. 40: 979–990. Doi: 10.1023/A: 1018837524712.

Raina, S.K., M.A (Hindi & English) Ph D. Author of 15 books and winner of Several Academic Awards.

Raina, Shiben Krishen, formerly Fellow, Indian Institute of Advanced Study, Rashtrapati Nivas, Shimla.

Rasool, P.G., (2009), "*Jammu, Massacre: Let Truth Prevail*", pp. 26-31, Conveyor Vol. I No.5 Bhat Pub., Srinagar.

Robert, G. Wirsing, (2008). *Brown Journal of World Affairs.* The Kashmir Territorial Dispute: The Indus Runs Through It.

Shah, S.L. (1986), *Planning and Management of natural and human resources in mountains; a micro level approach*, Yatana Pub. New Delhi.

Sharma, S.K. (1992), *Development of Water Resources—An Integrated Approach and their Environmental Effects*, Pub. No. 113. Central Board of Irrigation and Power, New Delhi: 85-88.

Shekhawat, Seema. (2006). *Conflict and Displacement in Jammu and Kashmir: The Gender Dimension*. pp. 25-27 Saksham Books International, Jammu.

Shibli, Murtaza, (2009), "Kashmir: Islam, Identity and Insurgency", pp. 22-24, *Kashmir Affairs Journal*.

The Official Site of the Government of Jammu & Kashmir. http://jammukashmir.nic.in

Tolin, D.F., Foa, E.B. (2006), Sex Differences in Trauma and Posttraumatic Stress Disorder: A Quantitative Review of 25 Years of Research. *Psychological Bulletin*. 132: 959–992. doi: 10.1037/0033-2909.132.6.959. [PubMed]

*World report on violence and health*. World Health Organisation, Geneva; 2002. http://whqlibdoc.who.int/hq/2002/9241545615.pdf

# Index